DATE DUE

OCT 2 4 2001	
BRODART	Cat. No. 23-221

The Orchestration
of the Media

International Communication and Popular Culture

Series Editor John A. Lent, Temple University

Media Beyond Socialism: Theory and Practice in East-Central Europe, Slavko Splichal

The Orchestration of the Media: The Politics of Mass Communications in Communist Poland and the Aftermath, Tomasz Goban-Klas

FORTHCOMING

Asian Popular Culture, edited by John A. Lent

Human Rights and the Media: International Reporting as a Global Watchdog, Frederic Moritz

Radio Practices and Social Uses, Lucila Vargas

The Orchestration of the Media

The Politics of Mass Communications in Communist Poland and the Aftermath

Tomasz Goban-Klas

Westview Press

BOULDER • SAN FRANCISCO • OXFORD

International Communication and Popular Culture

Copyright © 1994 by Westview Press, Inc.

Published in 1994 in the United States of America by Westview Press, Inc., 5500 Central Avenue, Boulder, Colorado 80301-2877, and in the United Kingdom by Westview Press, 36 Lonsdale Road, Summertown, Oxford OX2 7EW

Library of Congress Cataloging-in-Publication Data
Goban-Klas, Tomasz
    The orchestration of the media : the politics of mass
communications in communist Poland and the aftermath / by Tomasz
Goban-Klas
        p.   cm. — (International communication and popular culture)
    Includes bibliographical references and index.
    ISBN 0-8133-1868-8
    1. Mass media—Social aspects—Poland—History—20th century.
2. Communism and mass media—Poland.   I. Title.   II. Series.
HN539.5.M3G6   1994
302.23'09438—dc20
                                                                                        93-15759
                                                                                        CIP

Printed and bound in the United States of America

The paper used in this publication meets the requirements
of the American National Standard for Permanence of Paper
for Printed Library Materials Z39.48-1984.

10   9   8   7   6   5   4   3   2   1

*To those courageous
Polish journalists, editors, and printers
who in various ways opposed the Communist party controllers,
safeguarding the freedom of thought
and fighting for the freedom of the press.*

Contents

Acknowledgments

Data for this book have been gathered for over two decades, which makes the roster of those who helped to collect them too long to reproduce. Certain institutions, however, assisted more than others. Among these were the libraries of the Johns Hopkins University at Bologna Center, the Institute for European Studies in Vienna, Hebrew University in Jerusalem, and the Research Institute at Radio Free Europe in Munich. I found most of the relevant English-language publications there. For Polish sources, I am particularly indebted to the documentation section of the Press Research Center in Cracow.

Professor George Gerbner, dean of the Annenberg School of Communications at the University of Pennsylvania, and Professor Alex Inkeles of Stanford University found the time to read introductory chapters and, on such an uncertain base, voiced firm encouragement for my completing this book. Professor Jane Curry, the best U.S. expert on Polish censorship and Polish journalism, added some important rectifications. Eventually, by the end of 1992, a grant from the Central European Research Scheme in Prague for the project "From Closed to Open Communication Systems" helped me to focus entirely on editing this book.

For personal acknowledgments, I especially single out students in the Stanford Program in Cracow in 1989, at the Institute for European Studies in Vienna in 1990-1992, at the University of Wisconsin at Stevens Point who were in the External Program at Cracow in the fall of 1992, and in the University of California Program Abroad in Budapest in the spring of 1992. Their interest, insightful remarks, perceptive questions, and even unfamiliarity with the region and issues were most inspiring.

Chris Weber from the University of Guelph devoted many hours to correcting errors in English in the typed manuscript. Lillian Sutton, my dear cousin from Los Angeles, found the time and persistence to read the manuscript, make corrections, and suggest amendments. Cheryl Carnahan, the copyeditor from Westview, polished my English and checked the typescript. I am truly grateful for their assistance.

On the most personal level, I acknowledge the warm support and prolonged patience of my wife Teresa and my daughter, Iwona, without which it would have been impossible to complete this book.

Tomasz Goban-Klas

PART ONE

In Context

From Stettin in the Baltic to Trieste in the Adriatic, an iron curtain has descended across the Continent. [All the capitals of Central and Eastern Europe] lie in the Soviet sphere of influence and all are subject to very high and increasing measures of control from Moscow.

—Winston Churchill, 1946

Changes in Eastern Europe and the Soviet Union have been as much the triumph of communications, as the failure of communism.

—James Eberle
Understanding the Revolutions in Eastern Europe

1

Media and the Rise and Fall of the Soviet Bloc: An Introduction

On November 9, 1989, bewildered television viewers witnessed the collapse of the Berlin Wall. Essentially, the wall was destroyed twice: physically by young East Germans using sledgehammers and symbolically by television crews covering the event. Thus, the physical barrier between the eastern and western parts of Berlin was broken, and the most visible and real symbol of the great East-West divide was also destroyed.

The Berlin Wall: Who Made It, What Destroyed It?

As it is well known, the wall was built by East Germany's regime in 1961 to halt escapes of its subjects to the West. However, although such a structure was a genuine East German idea, it was derived from the very essence of the system built by Joseph Stalin. Being maniacally suspicious of a free flow of people and ideas, he had imposed an almost total separation of the Soviet Union and the countries of Central and Eastern Europe from the rest of the world.[1]

Naturally, the tearing down of the Iron Curtain was met with enthusiastic approval in both the East and the West. Its destruction meant the true end of World War II and the termination of that war's political successor—the Cold War. However, one can and should wonder why the dominolike fall of Communist regimes in autumn of 1989 was so surprising for so many Western politicians and political scientists. This seemed an exemplary illustration of a dismaying weakness of the predictive potency of political science and political journalism. "East

3

Germany Will Survive," wrote the editor of the German weekly *Die Zeit* Theo Sommer, in *Newsweek*'s opinion column, precisely one month before the wall's fall.[2]

The reason for such political myopia lays, at least partially, in taking ideological declarations for reality. Orthodox Communists declared their system to be, in principle, unchangeable, as—although for opposite reasons—dogmatic anti-Communists did. Both sides became casualties of the simplified theory of totalitarianism which excluded any possibility of conflict within society, except power struggles at the top. This theory posited that East European societies were based solely on Marxist-Leninist ideology and on party and police control. Hence, it simply disregarded the fact that political doctrines and political practices always differ. Moreover, and contrary to common wisdom, communism was never a fixed system, even in the Stalinist era.[3] Yet, its transformations were hardly reflected in changes in ideological verbiage and in the basic political and economic structures. Therefore, although changing constantly, communism seemed stable and strong; in fact, it had become feeble and rotten.[4]

For Western observers, the determination of the leaders of Communist parties to cling to power seemed made of steel. Westerners' views were strengthened by the constant assertions of Communists that their systems would never change. In reality, when the allegedly captive nations of Eastern Europe showed their will for change and began to march, as did the East German youth in Leipzig in October or the young Czech students in Prague in November 1989, the regimes gave up easily and instantly collapsed. An allegory suggested itself: the walls of Jericho blown down by the sound of trumpets. The year 1989 was thus proclaimed *Annus mirabilis*, a year of miracles.[5]

However, there are no miracles in politics. A so-called miracle always has a definite social background and various, usually very distant, origins. The collapse of the Communist system was not a phenomenon of a deus ex machina type but was the result of a long, painstaking, and gradual process of transformations of the system through internal political and economic struggles leading to social compromises and mutual adaptations.[6] That evolution had been overlooked by external observers who analyzed separately the policy declarations of the leadership (which were more or less the same) and dissident movements (which were more or less impotent). Society and various interest groups were absent from that picture, and so was the media, both national and foreign.[7] In reality, the media was instrumental both in building the system and then destroying it. Some uncontrolled communications, long before the wall went down, transcended the Iron Curtain, bringing information about alternative ways of living. It should be noted that contrary to its name, the Iron Curtain was never idea-proof; it always had some rips. The process of enlarging them had begun in the aftermath of the death of Stalin. And, as is critical for my purposes here, the process began in Poland.

The final collapse of the Soviet system was marked by many small-scale revolts and peaceful revolutions. Enumerating these in reverse chronological order one has to point out Gorbachev's glasnost policy, the Polish self-limiting Solidarity revolution of 1980-1981, Pope John Paul II's visit to Poland in July 1979, the Prague Communist reform movement abruptly stopped by the Warsaw Pact invasion of Czechoslovakia in 1968, the bloody Budapest uprising of November 1956, and, initially, the intellectual ferment in Poland that culminated in the peaceful revolt in October 1956.[8] As a political system, communism apparently survived all of those attempts at change and reform from both above and below. In the process, however, it somehow adapted to those challenges and found ways to cope with them that were not limited to sheer force and oppression.[9] In the process of changing the nature of the system, the mass media, both official and illegal, national and foreign, played large and various roles. It raised expectations, then fueled frustrations. It spread official propaganda; it also provided alternative information. In the words of Z.A.B. Zeman: "The media supported the Communist regimes and helped to defeat them."[10] That power of the media was known to Walter Ulbricht, secretary general of the East German Communist Party and a builder of the Berlin Wall. When he successfully separated his kingdom from the West, he still bitterly complained: "The enemy of the people stands on the roof," meaning television antennas receiving the West German television.

Why Polish Mass Media?

The fall of communism has already generated many studies of its causes, diagnoses of the present situation, and predictions about the future. Very little, in contrast, has been written about the East European media and its role in fueling the changes that led to this fall. Only a handful of scholars have investigated how the press, radio, and television changed under communism and thereafter. Little is known about those who ran the media or what their professional ideologies were. Even the startling Polish innovations in media organization and programming are virtually unknown.

The Polish party-controlled press was the most active and the most subversive of all Eastern European media. Its influence dates from the early 1950s, the period of cultural "thaw." Although this influence was slowed by subsequent "frost" waves, it erupted in the explosion of

Solidarity and reemerged in the last years of the regime, in the late 1980s. Moreover, along with the party maverick media, there were various independent communications in Poland, which, since the late 1970s, had culminated in the flood of underground (samizdat) publication. Consequently, Poland's mass media has the most intriguing and the most breathtaking roller-coaster history of all the media in the East European countries, which did not end with the fall of communism.

The Polish mass-media evolution is interesting enough to deserve a special book. Poland's unpredictable transformation has not ceased to surprise even the most knowledgeable analysts. Furthermore, Poland had been on the international media agenda several times: as early as 1956, then in March 1968, during the 1979 papal visit, and again after the summer of 1980 and the emergence of the heretic trade union Solidarity. Such a history makes inquiry even more pertinent and intriguing for communications researchers and political scientists. That was already stated by Flora Lewis, an American journalist, in her perspicuous book about the Polish first peaceful revolt against Stalinist rule in the middle of the 1950s: "For a study of Poland has a dual interest—that of the captivating, unpredictable land that is Poland itself and that of the inner working of communism which only Poland has revealed."[11]

In quoting this, as a Polish mass communications scholar, I am not magnifying the importance of my topic and my country. Poland was only one of many Communist countries, neither a superpower nor a stronghold of communism. In fact, it was the least sovietized of those countries and so was its media, which was both typically Communist and uniquely Polish. At the very beginning, the Polish media system was utterly typical in the construction of a Communist media monolith. Then, it became atypical in terms of the ways in which the monolith was gradually crushed. This process took almost thirty-five years. Because it lasted so long, it confirms the value of the freedoms of expression and of the press. It also reveals much about natural human curiosity and courage, the longing for truth, and ways of opposing absolute power, as well as about ingenious ways of creating a network of independent communications.

My goal in this book is to portray the Polish mass media in its sociopolitical setting. Such a task cannot be done exclusively and adequately by outside observers, however perceptive they might be. A serious, in-depth analysis requires regular and prolonged access to official and unofficial, political and scientific material and resources, among others: access to the Communist party archives, to collections of censored articles, and to research findings; and access to content analyses of the media, audience ratings and polls, surveys on journalists' motivations and attitudes. Such resources have been available, partially at least, to

Western scholars.[12]. Nevertheless, an outsider would need years to locate relevant documents in the jungle of archives and collections, which still lack modern retrieval equipment.

Of all of the former Communist countries, Poland was also the most atypical in the field of mass-media research. Since 1956, vigorous, internationally respected research in social sciences—in particular sociology, public opinion, and, to a lesser extent, political science—had been developed. This formed a sound basis for the advancement of media studies, an area in which Poland has been the most productive of all East European countries, constantly accumulating data and findings.

From 1971 to 1987, I was research director of the main Polish mass-media center (Ośrodek Badań Prasoznawczych) in Cracow. Accordingly, I was an insider in the Polish mass media. The position assured me of access to documents of various types and orientation and allowed me to attend party meetings on the tasks of the press, to listen to discussions at informal caucuses of journalists, and, most important, to organize empirical research on the mass media and journalism. I had to write copiously on the mass media for Polish journals, both scholarly and general. However, some findings could not be published then because of censorship, and any comprehensive appraisal of the party's communications policy was simply out of the question.

The idea to write this book came to me in February 1989, when, as an expert, I was attending the Polish roundtable negotiations. That forum for debate between Solidarity and the government was a breakthrough in the process of a radical change in the Polish political and mass-media system. When the party reluctantly but voluntarily agreed to give up its monopoly on political power and on the mass media, both the basic tenets of the Leninist creed, it became obvious that its rule in Poland would some day end. I felt it was high time to describe that final chapter in Poland's Communist history. But that event, despite its importance, should be seen in a much wider context. Therefore, this book deals with the entire postwar period, not only with the final collapse of the political system.

Overview

In general, in this study I have three fundamental purposes. First, and most important, I provide a coherent and comprehensive description of the entire process of the setting up and then eroding of the monolithic media system in Poland. Second, I investigate the professions, institutions, and individuals supporting, opposing, or reforming the existing media system in various historical periods. And third, I identify today's dilemmas in shaping the new media system in Poland.

The recent history of the mass media in Poland, in contrast to that of the other East European states, is so tangled and complicated that the most challenging problem was how to compress so many interesting and revealing data into a book of reasonable size and clear structure. The most natural solution was to divide the evolution of the media policy into distinct chronological phases, reflecting the changes in general Communist policy against the background of the internal dynamics of the society and the media.

Part 1 deals with a theoretical and political consideration of the entire study. In it I place the Polish mass media in a broader context. First in a theoretical context, then in a political one—of the Soviet doctrines and practices of the media control that were imposed on the Polish press after the Communists seized power. Finally, Chapter 4 deals with the Polish tradition of journalism and media uses by the nation under foreign occupation.

The chapters of Part 2 make up the body of the book. Exploiting the comparison of the media to an orchestra, a parable favored by Soviet media controllers and also used in the early 1980s by Konstantin Chernenko, I employ musical terminology in the chapter titles. This emphasizes the changes in pace, dynamics, and synchronization of the mass media at different intervals of Polish history, from 1944 to 1989.[13]

Part 3, "Beyond Solidarity: Media by Request," exposes issues that emerged after the popular rejection of the system in elections in June 1989. All three chapters address the present-day (1994) dilemmas and difficulties the post-Communist media faces on the road toward independence and pluralism and examine lessons that can be drawn from the past. The initial optimism that it would be enough to condemn and reject the model of totalitarian control in order to build free, independent, and robust media has been withering away, not only in Poland but in all of Central and Eastern Europe. The new, emerging media in the region has been influenced as much by the immediate past as the Communist media was by the traditions and style of pre-Communist journalism. Both influences in the region were not liberal in principle. Therefore, for the benefit of discussion of the nature of the emerging media system in the region, one needs to see the Communist past as one of the factors deciding, sometimes *à rebours*, today's thinking about the media.

The book is addressed to both specialists in Communist systems and to a wider audience. For the former, I have included many Polish reference sources in notes. To allow corroboration of my analyses, I refer in the notes to the Communist party documents that were published or that are kept in the state archives. For a wider audience, I have written in a more popular style. To encourage non-Polish speakers to consult the sources and relevant literature, whenever possible I refer to English books and articles. The quotations have been taken, when possible, preferably from volumes providing English-language translations of Polish documents.

This book is not intended as an encyclopedia of all of the worthwhile information pertaining to this subject. Rather, significant and essential characteristics of the media policy were outlined and shaped into a perspicuous sketch of the whole. It should therefore be useful for students of political science, journalism, mass communications, East European studies, and perhaps for Western consultants involved in various forms of assistance or joint ventures in media, education, banking, and business. For the latter, the concluding chapters, with an updated review of the present media landscape and an analysis of the post-Communist media policy, might be of special interest.

In general, there are some lessons to be learned from the Polish experience with communism and postcommunism. One of the most important was already formulated in words of Flora Lewis who, writing as early as in 1958 in a book entitled *A Case History of Hope. The Story of Poland's Peaceful Revolutions*, almost prophetically stated:

> The most important meaning of Poland's experience, and so, I hope, the most important meaning of this book, is that there does seem to be a way for the subject of the Communist states to improve their lot and to restore friendly relations with the West without cataclysmic violence.[14]

This book is also about hope for the whole of mankind as it shows that with so many constraints, deterrents, and penalties for people seeking sovereignty and emancipation, there is a road to freedom without bloodshed.

Notes

1. Under totalitarian rule, only three elements preserve some independence from the state control: the family, memory, and cultural tradition. It is little wonder that tyrants attempt to overpower even them.

Nothing can better illustrate Stalin's policy of crushing all forms of free flow of people and ideas than the campaign against the Ukrainians in the early 1930s. After Moscow's control was imposed on the Ukraine, the only means to sustain the independence and strength of its culture were the *kobzars*, local bards, who wandered through the country singing their ballads and reciting the ancient legends. In the words of the famous Russian composer Dimitri Shostakovich, they were "a living museum, the country's living history: all its songs, all its music and poetry" who sustained the national identity of the Ukrainian people. Stalin could not tolerate this. On his orders, several hundreds of bards were invited to a meeting where, instead of receiving recognition, they were arrested and then, as Shostakovich reports in his *Testimony*, "almost all these pathetic blind men were shot" (related to and edited by Solomon Volkov; New York: Harper & Row, 1979, p. 165).

2. "East Germany is not on the verge of collapse, and it will be around for a while yet," in *Newsweek*, October 9, 1989. Sommer was not unique in his political myopia. Jeanne Kirkpatrick stated categorically, "the Soviet Union is not going to withdraw from Europe," in an interview after the fall of the Berlin Wall, quoted in Alan Pater and Jason Pater, eds., *What They Said* (Palm Springs: Monitor Books, 1990), p. 284. To her credit, however, later she admitted her failure by writing a book *The Withering Away of the Totalitarian State . . . And Other Surprises* (Washington, D.C.: AEI Press, 1990).

3. A note on terminology is necessary. The word *Communists* has been used in the West to indiscriminately describe East European countries, the Soviet Union, and the members and leaders of the Communist parties. It was, however, rarely used in Poland. The preferred term in the 1940s was *people's democracy*; later, especially in the late 1950s and the 1960s, *socialism* and, ultimately *real, existing socialism*, or *advanced socialism* were favored.

At present, in all East European countries the terms *Communist* and *post-Communist* became fashionable. They are commonly used but with no explanation about what they mean. Of course, one could see a rejection of former ideological camouflage and praise the current linguistic usage as calling a spade a spade. In fact, this is not the case. For more objective observers of the East European scene nowadays there are no Communists in Poland, as there were only a few in the past. Obviously, there were numerous party activists, or militants, but they were usually called the party, or the PZPR, members (the Polish Communist party christened itself PZPR, the Polish United Workers' Party).

In Poland true believers in Communist ideology were even rarer than devoted party members. General secretaries of the PZPR, that is Władysław Gomułka, Bolesław Bierut, perhaps to a certain extent Edward Gierek and Wojciech Jaruzelski were certainly Communists, as were some writers and party ideologists in the Stalinist era. But here the list ends. The rest of the 3 million party members were simply opportunists, careerists, and talented people who wanted to participate in public life. They used their party card as a kind of driving license for managerial positions. Also, most intellectuals paid lip service to the party, declaring that they "were standing on the socialist ground," restricting themselves from harsh and open criticism of the system, but continuing with independent thinking.

Yet, despite the inadequacies of the terms, *communism* and *Communist*, in a book written for English readers I have had to use these ambiguous and sometimes misleading words.

4. In 1952, when the Polish Nobel Prize-winner Czesław Miłosz wrote *The Captive Mind* (New York: Alfred Knopf, 1953), the triumph of communism in Eastern Europe seemed to him inescapable. The intellectual there could either collaborate or escape, either to the West or to an "internal emigration," which meant withdrawing from public life.

Fortunately, Miłosz's diagnosis and therapy proved false. In October 1956 Hungarians tried to free their country from the yoke of Soviet oppression. And, beginning in 1954-1955, Polish intellectuals commenced to reform the system from within. See, for instance, Peter Raina, *Political Opposition in Poland: 1954-1977* (London: Poets and Painters Press, 1978).

5. An enthusiastic editorial in *Newsweek* on January 1, 1990, noted "the remarkable year that transformed the world and nudged the course of history," explaining that "there have not been many years like it—1848, perhaps, or 1914—in the last two centuries."

6. Different forms of opposition appeared in the process of relieving the Soviet bloc of the totalitarian nature of Stalinist ideology. Soon after Stalin's death, various forms of "reform" thinking, promoting changes from the inside, were the only ones the system could tolerate. The revisionists referred to certain liberal trends of the Marxist doctrine. They demanded democratic changes, however, without fundamental transformation of the power structure. This strategy proved ineffective, which was evident by the end of the 1960s. Thus, since the mid-1970s, East European intellectuals had opted rather for a program of indirect opposition, described by Vaclav Havel as "living in truth" (also the title of a book; New York: Faber and Faber, 1987). Adam Michnik called it the "new evolutionism" (*Letters from Prison and Other Essays* [Berkeley: University of California Press], 1985, pp. 135-148).

It was smart to subvert the semitotalitarian political system simply by claiming rights declared in Communist constitutions. Eventually, when the occasion arose, intellectuals instantly joined striking workers, helping to initiate the Polish Solidarity movement in 1980-1981. This tactic proved to be the most successful in the long run because it was supported by those for whom the regime claimed legitimacy: the working class.

7. "Media" used as a singular subject is a contemporary American usage, although that etymologically it should be plural.

8. Of course, both the Budapest uprising and the 1956 Polish October could not have occurred without events of much greater importance, which took place in the headquarters of communism, the Soviet Union. In February 1956, Nikita S. Khrushchev denounced the crimes of Stalin and condemned the "cult of personality." This apparently secret, but nevertheless official, condemnation, had far-reaching repercussions among the Communist regimes in satellite countries. See more in Chapter 7. More about the impact of Gorbachev glasnost policy in Tomasz Goban-Klas and Pal Kölsto, "Eastern European Mass Media: The Soviet Role," in Odd Arne Westad, Sven Holtsmark, and Iver B. Neumann, ed., *The Soviet Union and Eastern Europe: 1945-1989* (New York: St. Martin Press, 1994), pp. 110-136.

9. From the late 1950s, ideology was no longer a motivating or a binding force in Communist societies, even for the ruling elites. It is interesting that Stalin's "ideological" testament, *Economical Problems of Socialism*, already reflected that very motive: danger for the system from the decline of ideology. "What to do with these comrades [those who joined the party for privileges or purely pragmatic reasons]? How to educate them in the spirit of Marxism-Leninism?" Stalin rhetorically asked. In response, he pointed to the important role of education and propaganda. *Ekonomicheskie problemy sotsializma v SSSR* (Moscow: Gospolizdat, 1952), p. 21.

10. Z.A.B. Zeman, *The Making and Breaking of Communist Europe* (Cambridge: Blackwell, 1991), p. 311.

11. Flora Lewis, *A Case History of Hope. The Story of Poland's Peaceful Revolutions* (New York: Doubleday, 1958), p. xii.

12. David Mason wrote a book on *Public Opinion and Political Change in Poland: 1980-1982* (Cambridge: Cambridge University Press, 1985), based on Polish research, surveys, and public opinion polls. Jane L. Curry used similar data in her study *Poland's Journalists: Professionalism and Politics* (Cambridge: Cambridge University Press, 1990). She pointed out that for Western researchers, Poland was an environment where discussion and action were more open and visible than in other more stable and controlled Communist states. That was even true in the late 1950s. "It is possible in Poland," wrote Flora Lewis in 1958, "as nowhere else to learn what takes place behind the usually massive, soundproofed walls of a Communist regime" (*A Case History of Hope*, p. xiii). As a result, Poland has been described in the Western literature much better than any other Eastern European country. Thanks to accumulated research, both Polish and Western, its media forms a good starting point and a sound basis for in-depth analysis of political communication within the region.

13. That comparison, interestingly, was first formulated by Joseph Goebbels, the Nazi master of propaganda.

14. Lewis, *A Case History of Hope*, p. xii.

2

Theoretical Context: Three Perspectives on Media Systems

The mass-media system in postwar Poland was modeled after the Soviet Communist system and as such should first be analyzed from the perspective of its specific approach to communication in general. In other words, it should be put into the framework of the concept of a closed society.

Closed Versus Open Media Systems

To begin with, an allegory of "open" and "closed" society, introduced by Karl Popper,[1] might be useful to describe the two opposite models of the structure and organization of a communication system, and more important, that of their philosophical justification. A bipolar vision of open and closed systems is, naturally, a gross simplification. No system can be totally isolated or totally open. In real life, the distinction is always blurred. In any real open system there could be certain "closed" subsystems, such as, for instance, orders, sects, or gangs.

Nevertheless, this dichotomy can be useful in discerning between two approaches to the political organization of communication in society. The first seeks a maximum (in practice, an optimum) of openness, whereas the second seeks a maximum of closedness/isolation and secrecy.[2] An open, or liberal, system has a complex, internal, horizontal structure of lines of communication and a dense network of connections in and out of its external environment. In systems of this kind, messages may flow freely in all directions, vertically as well as horizontally. Corresponding media doctrine stresses the value of freedom of expression and the profits of openness.[3] A closed system has a much simpler communication structure. Not only do vertical lines of communication dominate, but the information that flows is differentiated. From above come plans, orders, regulations, and propaganda. From the masses might come complaints, suggestions, and information about corruption; however, positive support for the leadership is expected above all. Both external and internal communication lines are strictly controlled and regulated. The corresponding doctrine demands responsibility and stresses dangers of unrestricted communication and expression. Such a system was perfectly visualized in a typical spatial organization of Communist party conventions in the form of a pyramid with the leaders on top and the followers at the base.

The open communication system is a relatively new social invention. Throughout the ages, a tendency to control, to censor, and to ban overshadowed a tendency to tolerate, to approve, and to permit. It was naturally expressed in the authoritarian doctrine of the press.[4] This doctrine was abandoned in Western Europe in the nineteenth century and in the United States even earlier, whereas in Eastern Europe and in Russia it formed a background for the new Soviet media doctrine.[5] Still, the communication system in tsarist Russia was partially similar to its Western counterpart, as it was based on private ownership of the media and some pluralism of the media contents and orientation. The Soviet media system that replaced it was very different. It was developed as an utterly simplified, painstakingly controlled, and, in principle, wholly planned structure.[6] Unlike the authoritarian system, which was developed as a reflexive extension of authoritarian rule, this totalitarian variation was a deliberate scheme. As such it had founding fathers—Lenin and, after him, Stalin.

Lenin began with a utopian vision of a superdemocratic Communist society, promising absolute freedom for all, except Capitalists. However, immediately after the October Revolution, he pursued a different policy, which mixed revolutionary mass democracy with party dictatorship, banned "hostile" publication, and ended in 1922 with the realpolitik of censorship.[7] Stalin went one step further. Aiming to create an entirely programmed society, he gradually imposed total autocracy. His political construction was based on the assumption of maximum control and segmentation of society. All communications were regulated according to the ideal of a closed society. Such a system was a logical consequence of the doctrine of monopolization of power by the party, verbally justified by the interests of the working class and by the public welfare.

In plain, traditional authoritarianism, examples of which abound in history, individual thoughts matter little. Authoritarianism tends mainly to eliminate overt defiant behavior, seditious libel, and open rebellion.[8] In totalitarianism, the simple suppression of seditious utterances is not enough. It seeks total subordination—at the least, the universal acceptance of its ideology. It tries to impose its ideas on all of its subjects and imprint those ideas on their minds without reservations.[9] Hence, totalitarianism not only supports, with the help of meticulous censorship, the ignorance of the population, as authoritarianism does, but, above all, it constantly provides supportive pseudo-information as the main output of the ideological mass media. From such an observation results the thesis of Zbigniew Brzeziński that "Communist power is based, above all, on thought control. Communist leaders realize that force alone cannot impose and sustain social cohesion."[10] Although this statement exaggerates the real hold of the authorities on the population (no effective political power could be based on thought control because thoughts are subjective phenomena), it rightly stressed the importance of factors other than sheer force in sustaining Communist power. In that sense, unverifiable, even untrue information had a real influence—it showed people how to play their public roles of good citizens. If they had not followed hints, the police would have brought them back into line.[11]

Since information is a main instrument of social control, political power belongs to those who control information, to the programming unit. Monopolistic power requires a monopoly on information—to control all knowledge (collected in universities, archives, libraries, etc.) and the institutions that retrieve and analyze information (research institutes), process it (bureaucratic apparatus), and distribute it (media). The monopolization of information, communication, and decisionmaking is not accidental; on the contrary, it is a part of any form of totalitarianism.[12]

Monopolization of information was, therefore, not a secondary feature of the Communist system.[13] It had to create pseudoinformation, partial information, and disinformation. As Edgar Morin wrote, "Its basic need to hide its true nature is its true nature."[14] The world of ideology and propaganda was an integral and essential part of the Soviet world. The normative messages, which could not be considered true by any kind of empirical verification, were vital for the system and very effective for its functioning.[15] They provided the "pattern" of what could and should be said or expressed in public. In such a system, there was control on more than overtly political information. All words and images were controlled, that is, the entire public discourse. At the least, there was a declared tendency to control everything.

The Communists displayed their terminology, their criteria, ideology, and logic as a unique and true picture of the world. For that reason they presented the guiding ideology, Marxism-Leninism, as a science, the only true and universal science. This was, obviously, a major abuse of the concept of science. By definition, no science can pretend to be true, universal, and one. However, only such a pretension gave the party and the state a monopoly on knowledge and science, that is, on the truth.

The Communist information-propaganda apparatus developed along the structures of the party apparatus. It designed what should be known and said at any given moment, censoring and schooling creative writers, spreading fear and ignorance among audiences, teaching the only correct answers in a particular situation. Truth was not absolute; it depended on party interpretation. Stanisław Barańczak observed: "In totalitarian thinking, there is no objective truth and no objective reality: only those facts and objects exists which are allowed to exist by the ruling power."[16] Censorship, camouflage, and fabrication worked together in creating the image of reality that Alain Besançon once wittily called "surreality." The idea of camouflage is epitomized by the most hypocritical of Stalin's sayings: "Life has become better, Comrades; life has become more joyful."[17] He announced this in 1935, in the middle of his cruel purges, two years before launching the most extensive murder and mass-terror campaign ever known. Nobody dared to contradict this.

The Stalinist ideological media output created the most complete "constructed reality"—to use a term from symbolic interactionism—in the history of the mass media. This constructed reality was not fixed; on the contrary, it was flexible, changing according to the changes in the party line. Such a system could not last forever. Totalitarianism is identical to the ideological-political organization of a society. In practice, it results in suppression of a civil society—the elimination of any kind of societal pluralism. It is simply contrary to human nature.

Therefore, the seeds of resistance in Soviet bloc countries were always present, although as long as Stalin lived they were totally suppressed publicly and thus were invisible. Nevertheless, it would be wrong to ignore them, especially when describing the history of imposing and sustaining a system of maximal communication control.

Many moves made by the Communists were dictated by resistance to their policies; many independent actions were taken to fight such control, and as a result many latent compromises were made. In Poland, among other concessions, some independence was allowed in the social sciences and ties with Western culture were permitted because of the October 1956 unrest. The workers' revolt on the Baltic coast in 1970 resulted in the first serious opening to the West; the Solidarity revolution was followed by a significant increase in freedom in the official press and a factual recognition of the right of the political opposition to exist. Two waves of strikes in 1988 led to roundtable talks, with eventually disastrous compromises for the Communists on elections and on the access of the opposition to the mass media. Therefore, a new, more specific perspective on the analysis of the media in the Soviet-type societies should be introduced if the changes in the media policies are to be understood and explained.

Civil Society Against Total Control

The changes in the political system were closely connected to the readiness of different groups to protest and to demand their rights. On the theoretical level, that perspective was elaborated by Polish philosopher Leszek Nowak in his theory that communism consisted of a triple monopoly, on the means of coercion (politics), production (economy), and indoctrination (media).[18] It was not only a triple-rule system but had a corresponding triple-lords class structure as well.

The initial phase of the system was purely totalitarian, in which much of the terror was directed against the rulers (Stalinist purges of Communist party cadres). This was replaced by a second phase, a kind of mutual adaptation between the rulers and the ruled. Nowak saw the internal dynamics of the system, which cannot contain the internal contradictions:

> In the Stalinist system, the rulers prove unable to extricate themselves from the system of self-repression. Salvation comes, thanks to the increasing ability of the masses of citizens to resist. Social life gradually passes from the official relations of the "citizen-ruler-citizen" type to a revival of the autonomy of the "citizen-citizen" type and in this way civil society is gradually recovered.[19]

Therefore, to understand communism as a changing political and media system, one must use the perspective of the civil society.[20] This idea emerged as a reinterpretation of the relationship between the state and society.[21] On a political level, the doctrine was formulated by Eastern European dissidents in the 1970s, when strict Communist (or rather Stalinist) rule eased but the system remained totalitarian in structure. It did not allow any spontaneous, autonomous activity on the public level. Not having the means for effective control, the regime still considered any tendency toward such activity illegal.[22]

Most law-abiding citizens paid lip service to ideological party demands. However, a few of the most determined and nonconformist intellectuals found the courage to oppose the regime in public. They challenged the artificial and inefficient system of state control by undertaking different independent activities, which simply means they tried "to live in truth." They stressed the need to restore civil society in Eastern Europe, characterized by legality, human rights, and freedoms and the revival of the public sphere and public opinion. In such a perspective the totalitarian state was counterpoised against society, or, rather, against a sphere composed above all of associations and publics, acting as an independent social entity.[23]

This viewpoint was amended by Elemer Hankiss, a Hungarian sociologist, who saw the dichotomy of the "first society," i.e., officially approved social life, and the "second society," i.e., factual behavior, often illegal.[24] The second society comprised a series of subsystems—the second economy, the second public, the second culture, the second polity, and the second, or independent (from the state) communications. This last element was a particularly significant component of both civil and "second" society.

These independent communications should not be limited to their best-known manifestations, as, for instance, illegal printing, or samizdat.[25] They included such actions as listening to foreign radio stations, which were officially called hostile stations, exchanging books from private library collections or printed publications smuggled in from abroad, or conversing in small circles of friends. The aim was safeguarding such values as truthfulness, honesty, and reliability. The ultimate goal was the change of the inhuman system by the way of bloodless revolution. "One word of truth outweighs the world," declares an old Russian proverb. Both party media controllers and dissident intellectuals believed in the wisdom of this proverb. The party oversensitivity with meticulous control of all public spheres, including all communications, words, and images, assigned unproportional significance to any independent, autonomous media, or literary output, and to uncensored words and pictures. Never in the history of humanity were creative writers, artists, journalists so carefully observed, sometimes nursed, sometimes prosecuted; if obedient, there were "kept in the velvet prison,"[26] if not, they were "sent to Gulag."[27] Apparently innocuous words, if otherwise interpreted by media controllers, acquired new meaning and political significance. To a certain extent, the same can be said about alternative media, like foreign radio stations or underground publications. Therefore, paradoxically, censorship and official media dependency on the Communist party added value to all messages and media people.

Even an absence from the media scene could increase someone's popularity—as in the case of a writer whose book was banned, but word about it spread among the reading public and it was broadcast over Western radio stations. Media people were powerful by definition, as the authorities consistently verified. But were they inclined to use their power independently? And if they did, for what reasons and to serve what kind of interests?

The Journalism Profession: In Whose Service?

The third perspective of this study refers, therefore, to the professional ideology, interests, and power relationships among the major groups involved in the mass communication process, perhaps the most important of which, besides the Communist media controllers, was journalists—from editors-in-chief and columnists to rank-and-file newspeople.

The importance of professionalism in preserving at least some independence of the official mass media was stressed by Jane L. Curry in her thoughtful study *Poland's Journalists: Professionalism and Politics.*[28] She found traditional Western theories of socialization, of interest group behavior, or of changes in Communist societies of little use to explain Polish journalists' behavior in 1980-1981 and in earlier periods of political crises.[29] She referred to the theory of professionalization to explain why, as early as late 1954, young journalists were more loyal to each other, thus departing from the major tenet of Leninist journalism.[30]

In fact, the point was not overlooked by George Mond, a vice-president of the Association of Polish Journalists, who in 1958 concluded that "since 1956, the writers and journalists [of Poland, Hungary, and Czechoslovakia] have become an intermediary body between the party and the people, a pressure group which exercises its influence as well on the party as on public opinion."[31] The issue was also indicated by Frank Kaplan in his comprehensive report on the revolt of the Czechoslovak journalists in 1963-1968, when he described the press activism in the party reform movement.[32] He rejected the outmoded monolith concept that did not see interest groups or professional associations as actors in the process of change in a one-party system.

The story of communication policy in Eastern Europe is, therefore, the story not only of successful party control but also of its sluggish withering away.[33] The deeper and broader view of the history of the Communist media must consider not only the built-in tendency of the system to closedness and the political monopolistic control of the mass media but also the factors acting against such a doctrine and practice. The Communist policy had various types of deviators, adversaries, and open enemies, also in the ranks of the Communist party and its media personnel.

The internal deviators from the Communist media system were those people who worked for the system because of the lack of choice but who did not share the aspirations of the political regime.[34] Whenever the opportunity emerged, they tried to change the contents of the message to be responsive to the needs of society and not to the needs of the rulers.[35] Only a few of such people were stubborn and courageous enough to oppose the system overtly, but their attitudes and performance modified the general output of the media.

Stefan Bratkowski was one of these professionals. He was a thoughtful, skillful, and respected journalist and was a party member until 1981. As a professional, he continually issued calls to improve the media, but not merely to better serve the party. It is little wonder that after many unsuccessful attempts to reform Polish journalism since October 1956, in 1980 he became an open opponent of Leninist doctrine and practice. Thus, he joined the open enemies of the media system—those journalists and writers who rejected the system of censorship and developed their own independent media and information networks. That, however, could only have happened in the conditions of relative tolerance of the late 1970s.

Only in the final phase of Communist rule could the declared enemies of the system begin to work openly, and they did so in ever greater numbers. Naturally, in the fully totalitarian phase of the Communist system, the early 1950s, there could have been no independent professionals. Any dissenters, external enemies, or internal reformists were physically eliminated or, at least, silenced. After the mid-1950s, when the semi-totalitarian era began, internal reformists had the opportunity to engage in cautious and timid actions. The move from full-blooded totalitarianism to semitotalitarianism, as reflected in the media, is the main subject of this book. This could also be called the process of closing, then piercing, and eventually raising the Iron Curtain.

Notes

1. See Karl Popper, *The Open Society and Its Enemies* (London: Routledge, 1980). The study was first published in 1945.

2. Osmo A. Wiio advanced a similar approach in his chapter "The Mass Media Role in the Western World," in Anju G. Chaudhary and John Martin, eds., *Comparative Media Systems* (New York: Longman, 1983), pp. 85-94. He stressed that the "openness" of a mass communication system can be measured in many ways. In a Communist system, constraints on the message system may be governmental (censorship), ideological (party), or any other kind of restriction that limits the selection of messages.

3. This is the so-called libertarian theory of the press, first described by Frederick S. Siebert, Theodore Peterson, and Wilbur Schramm in *Four Theories of the Press* (Urbana: University of Illinois Press, 1956).

4. The authoritarian doctrine of the press was characterized in ibid. Its roots go as far back as Plato's political philosophy, which according to Popper contained a belief that "there must be a censorship of all intellectual activities of the ruling class, and a continual propaganda aiming at molding and unifying their minds. All innovation in education, legislation, and religion must be prevented or suppressed." Popper, *The Open Society*, p. 87.

5. Edward Kennan, a Harvard historian, regards "ne-glasnost" (lack of openness) as part of the very essence of traditional political culture. See E. Kennan, "Muscovite Political Folkways," *Russian Review* 45, 1986, p. 119.

6. Alex Inkeles, *Public Opinion in Soviet Russia: A Study in Mass Persuasion* (Cambridge: Oxford University Press, 1950), p. 143.

7. Hence, his rule might be called "utopia in power," or an actual attempt to build a perfect society. See Michael Geller and Alexandr Nekrich, *Utopia in Power: The History of the Soviet Union from 1917 to the Present* (London: Hutchinson, 1982).

8. I allude here to the famous phrase of the last Polish king of the Jagiellonian Dynasty, Sigismund Augustus, "I am not the king of your conscience," which reflects the state tolerance of different religions.

9. It is important to note that in a totalitarian system, power is exercised not by the state alone but by the party-state.

10. Zbigniew Brzeziński, "Foreword," in Madeleine Korbel Albright, *Poland: The Role of the Press in Political Change* (Washington, D.C.: Praeger, 1983), p. v.

11. The link among censorship, secret police, and the law in the Soviet Union was always very intimate. Censorship eliminated certain information from mass dissemination and the secret police from private conversation; the law—armed with paragraphs of the Penal Code warning against "anti-Soviet propaganda"—shipped nonconformists to the Gulag.

12. Edgar Morin, *O naturze Związku Radzieckiego* [De la Nature de l'U.R.S.S, On the Nature of the USSR] (Polish translation from French) (Warszawa: Volumen, 1990), p. 43.

13. Why did communism, initially a doctrine of participatory democracy that opted for the emancipation of mankind, end up as a totalitarian doctrine and, more important, a totalitarian system? The answer is that the road to totalitarianism was deadly logical. From its very beginning, communism was a secular religion that offered answers and solutions to all problems, thus containing a kernel of totalitarianism. The Communist utopia was so far from reality and from the nature of ordinary human beings that the regime had to use sheer force to maintain the pretense of fulfilling its promises.

14. Morin, *O naturze*, p. 45.

15. A simple propaganda slogan of the 1970s shows this a-empirical character of Communist messages: "The Youth always with the party." The omission of the verb *is* was not accidental; it made empirical falsification of the slogan impossible. In fact, the slogan read "The Youth should always be with the party" and as a normative statement was neither true nor false.

16. Stanisław Barańczak, *Breathing Under Water and Other East European Essays* (Cambridge: Harvard University Press, 1990), p. 12.

17. The citation was taken from Roy Medvediev, *Let History Judge; The Origins and Consequences of Stalinism*, trans. George Shriver (Oxford: Oxford University Press, 1989), p. 352.

18. Leszek Nowak, *Power and Civil Society: Toward a Dynamic Theory of Real Socialism* (Westport: Greenwood Press, 1991).

19. Leszek Nowak, "'The Post-Communist Society?' An Attempt at a Theoretical Analysis," in Dietrich Herzog, August Pradetto, and Helmut Wagner, eds., *Revolution und Reconstruction* (Berlin: Freie Universität Berlin, 1991), p. 64.

20. Zbigniew Pelczynski, "Solidarity and the Re-Birth of Civil Society in Poland," in John H. Keane, ed., *Civil Society and the State: New European Perspectives* (London: Verso, 1988). William Echikson observed that Americans often find the concept of civil society difficult to grasp because their country has always had a multitude of voluntary, independent organizations and local governments.

In Communist Eastern Europe, the opposite was true. See *Lighting the Night: Revolutions in Eastern Europe* (London: Sidgwick and Jackson, 1990), p. 156.

21. The concept of "civil society" was expressed by Hobbes, Locke, Hegel, de Tocqueville, and Marx. However, the latter used that concept as a derogatory term, an equivalent of Hobbes's war of all against all. Civil society subjugated everything to commercial interests, greed, and profit. Certainly, it was not a model for civic virtues. Marx's viewpoint was challenged by an eminent Italian Marxist, Antonio Gramsci. According to him, civil society was not a gathering of alienated, profit-driven individuals, but a complex system of social activities and institutions. It included trade unions and voluntary associations, all not controlled by the state. See D. Forgacs, ed., *A Gramsci Reader: Selected Writings, 1916-1935* (London: Lawrence and Wishard, 1988), p. 420.

In the 1960s, the Polish party revisionists, including Julian Hochfeld, Adam Schaff, and Jerzy Wiatr, were studying Gramsci's writings in a hope to heal the split between the party, the state, the society, and the individual. Perhaps, the idea of civil society somehow trickled down to the "dissent" movements in the 1970s, because some of the eminent dissidents were disillusioned Marxist revisionists. More about the use of this idea by the opposition in Jacques Rupnik, "Dissent in Poland: 1968-78," in Rudolf Tökes, ed., *Opposition in Eastern Europe* (London: Macmillan, 1979), Chapter 6.

22. Although Adam Michnik, an eminent Polish dissident, described the "tolerant" Communist policy since the late 1970s as "totalitarianism with a few teeth knocked out," it was still a policy of fear—not necessarily a fear of death, torture, or even jail, but of losing a job, position, and privileges, like getting a passport or state bonuses and grants. *Letters from Prison and Other Essays* (Translated by M. Latynski, Berkeley: University of California Press, 1985), p. 137.

23. See Andrew Arato, "Civil Society in the Emerging Democracies: Poland and Hungary," Margaret Latus Nugent, ed., *From Leninism to Freedom: The Challenges of Democratization* (Boulder: Westview, 1992), pp. 127-152.

24. Elemer Hankiss, "The `Second Society': Is there a Second Special Paradigm Working in Contemporary Hungary?" (Budapest, 1986, typescript). A detailed discussion of Hankiss's dichotomy can be found in H. Gordon Skilling, *Samizdat and an Independent Society in Central and Eastern Europe* (London: Macmillan, 1989), pp. 160-171.

25. In the Soviet Union this independent form of printing reappeared in the late 1950s because of the urge to overcome governmental control of the Gutenberg-type presses.

26. The expression of a Hungarian dissident, Miklos Haraszti (*The Velvet Prison* [New York: Universe Books, 1987]).

27. This was the plight of artists under Stalin's rule. There are too many examples to mention; Mandelstam may be the best known. Later, the situation changed. Artists were expelled, like Solzhenitsyn, to the West, or, like academician Sakharov, they had to live outside Moscow. But the threat of even more severe punishment was always present and was occasionally carried out.

28. Jane Leftwich Curry, *Poland's Journalists: Professionalism and Politics* (Cambridge: Cambridge University Press, 1990).

29. Ibid., p. 3.

30. Ibid., p. 41.

31. George Mond and R. Richter, "Writers and Journalists: A Pressure Group in East European Politics," *Journalism Quarterly* 43 (Spring 1966), p. 95.

32. Frank L. Kaplan, *Winter into Spring: The Czechoslovak Press and the Reform Movement, 1963-1968* (New York: Columbia University Press, 1977).

33. After the elimination of open opposition from the media in the late 1940s, the Communists left only journalists who competed for a better expression of the party line. No one had the courage to voice objections openly. But only nine months after Stalin's death, when even small opportunities appeared, the young, allegedly indoctrinated journalists began to revolt. Harsh pressures of reality and the regime's demands induced desires for autonomy. Moreover, Marxist idealistic values learned in universities helped them to resist policy pressures.

34. As the system was penetrating all spheres of life, only sabotage or open rebellion could be counted as an activity not supporting the regime. Everything else was, in one way or another, "building socialism." However, because of the efficiency of the secret police, both sabotage and open rebellion were eliminated. This made the situation dramatic.

Adam Michnik, debating the *correct* behavior of the people in countries ruled by Stalin, quoted a writer who gave the Shakespearean answer: "They should die." "Maggots and Angels," in *Letters from Prison*, p. 184. This is a rather theoretical solution for a normal human being; thus, less heroic ways to cope with the situation were found. The most frequent of these was the attempt to adapt to the system and to use cautious means to try to change it whenever possible.

35. Echikson gives an example of a Rumanian newscaster, George Marinescu, who for two decades praised the greatest of despots, Nicolae Ceauscescu. As soon as demonstrators took over the television studio in Bucharest in December 1989, he went on air and offered mea culpa: "I lied. I was commanded to lie." Later he became the chief anchorman for Free Romania Television. "I was not a hero," he said afterward. "I had to feed my family and there was no other television station for which I could work." *Lighting the Night*, p. 7.

3

Political Context:
The Changing Doctrines
of the Soviet Media

The Communists always regarded the press as merely a propagandist arm and an indispensable adjunct to the party, never as a collector and distributor of independent information. Long before the Bolshevik Revolution, Lenin elaborated the doctrine of a party press, demanding that a newspaper would be a "collective propagandist, a collective agitator, and a collective organizer."[1] In the latter role the illegal press was to serve—in his words—as a scaffold that allowed party sympathizers to communicate and, by engaging them in illegal activity, to gradually transform fellow-travelers into members of a well-disciplined, centralized party.

The Making of a New Type of Journalism

From party journalists, Lenin demanded above all a party spirit (loyalty to the party line with full dedication to its cause). At a time when the Bolsheviks were operating illegally (in the so-called underground) such discipline seemed a logical requirement for safeguarding their political identity. Lenin did not perceive it as a conflict of interest or a contradiction of the principle of freedom. He argued that as long as journalists were free to leave party organs, to keep their moral integrity, they might choose publications with different political persuasions.

Being a Machiavellian tactician, Lenin fully used the "bourgeois" freedom of the press that Russian journalism enjoyed after the 1905 revolution.[2] However, in the months following the 1917 February Revolution, which abolished censorship, he regularly and fiercely attacked Kerensky's democratic government. His writings on the press were at best ambiguous, at worst hypocritical.[3] Proclaiming communism to be superdemocratic, Lenin boasted that only its victory would bring absolute and previously unheard-of freedom of the press for workers and working classes.

However, immediately after the Bolshevik coup in October the same year, he changed his stand and disavowed all former promises of freedom of the press.[4] The Decree on the Press, signed by him, imposed a ban on the "bourgeois" press and, despite mild terminology, de facto abolished freedom of the press in general in Soviet Russia.[5] It announced: "Subject to closure shall be only those organs of the press that (1) urge open resistance or defiance to the Workers' and Peasants' Government; (2) sow discord by distorting facts and obvious slander; (3) call upon people to commit patently criminal acts."[6]

To lessen its gloomy significance, the preamble pledged that "when the new order is consolidated, it [the press] will be granted a full freedom within the limits of its responsibility before the courts, in conformity with the broadest and most progressive press laws."[7] Despite this, such a departure from Lenin's former policy pronouncements shocked even some Bolsheviks.[8] But instead of backing down, Lenin went further, imposing by a second decree a state monopoly on advertising so that the press immediately became dependent on Soviet power.[9]

The third decree curtailing freedom of the press was more harsh and direct. Enacted on January 28, 1918, it set up special press tribunals throughout the country. These had three members, usually orthodox Bolsheviks who considered any criticism of the regime to be a counterrevolutionary activity. The tribunals had the power, without right of appeal, to close down any paper guilty of such offenses as publishing "all untrue or distorted statements about public life" and to fine or imprison those responsible for its publication.[10] They could also send accused publishers, editors, authors, and printers into the jails of the much feared Cheka-security police.

All of these measures were thoroughly carried out. Thus, by July 1918, the last papers of the bourgeoisie parties had been closed down.[11] The press of the anarchists opposing the Bolshevik regime, such as the Maximalists,[12] survived until 1921. The press of the leftist Socialist Revolutionaries survived a few months longer.[13] It was obvious that the nonparty press must be eliminated to allow the domination of the new Communist press. The Bolshevik tradition of close control of its party's press, a practice familiar to all political parties, became a norm for the entire Soviet press, changing the party press into the state press and vice versa. This was indeed a unique press system. Not only independent journalism was eliminated. Lenin imposed the monopolistic control over all book production, explaining that "literature is a powerful weapon, and its control should be in the hands of government. Leadership in literature is necessary, but it should be in the hands of the State Publisher—this is one of its tasks."[14] Following Lenin's suggestion, a single and monopolistic state book publisher, Gosizdat (Government Printing Office), was established in 1919. It eliminated any private publishing until 1921—up to the end of war communism (policy of the rationing basic foods and commodities by the state) and the beginning of the New Economic Policy (NEP).

Obviously, it can be claimed that the civil war and famine in Russia partly justified such a dictatorial system.[15] The third article of the 1917 Decree on the Press, promising that the decree "shall operate temporarily," could sustain such an illusion.[16] But after the Civil War, when it finally seemed that the stability of the regime would allow for the revocation of the decree, an opposite move was taken. On June 8, 1922, the Council of People's Commissars announced the formation of a Main Press Committee, whose purpose was to "unify all existing forms of censorship in Russia."[17] Two months later, the Main Literature and Art Administration (*Glavnoe Upravlenie Po Delam Literatury i Isskusstva* [*Glavlit*]) was established as the main Soviet censorship agency.

According to its founding decree, the duties of *Glavlit* included "prior examination of all literary work, periodical and non-periodical publications, maps, etc., intended for publication and distribution." In addition, *Glavlit* was to "issue all official authorizations for printed works of any kind, prepare lists of banned books, and work out provisions governing printing establishments, libraries, and the book trade."[18]

Censorship in Soviet Russia was, therefore, reborn in 1922, during Lenin's lifetime and with his full approval.[19] Initially, *Glavlit*'s role was not important, but under Stalin's rule, by a series of decrees, it assumed a new position. The decree of 1931 changed its charter and structure so much that it became almost a new organization.[20] Using Lenin's allegory of imperialism as the highest stage of capitalism, one may call *Glavlit* the highest stage of censorship. Indeed, *Glavlit* was much worse than the infamous tsarist censorship, being a kind of bookish companion to the Soviet concentration camps, the *Gulag*.

The censorship issue should not overshadow the other, more important form of press control which was exercised by the party through positive recommendations and guidelines. Lenin wanted much more than neutrality, and he did not limit himself to the elimination of anti-Bolshevik press or content. In his articles of 1918-1919, he elaborated guidelines for the Bolshevik press, both general and detailed. Later these were named the doctrine of "the press of a new type." Lenin called for a Soviet press that would concentrate on the "economic education" of the masses, creating a new economic order and eschewing the evils of capitalist media (advertising and sensationalism). Lenin especially valued the letters to the editor as a feedback channel. Since his time, the Soviet press has cultivated a network of peasant-worker correspondents (*Rabselkors, rabochiye i sel'skiye korrespondenty*). They were called official instruments for party glasnost.[21]

Mark Hopkins stressed that in Lenin's view the press had a double role as both a government agency and a medium of communication.[22] These functions did not clash. Their common purpose was to influence people's consciousness and bring it close to the ideal according to the political and ideological norms and values of Communist society. The press, according to Lenin, had to be goal-oriented. All facts and opinions would be published considering their relevance to the building of a Communist society. Lenin's guidelines, therefore, showed what Bolshevik journalists should and should not write. Therefore, they made the journalist de facto a party functionary and the press the party mouthpiece.

The NEP, announced in January 1922, compelled all newspapers to be economically sound, which resulted in the disappearance of many Bolshevik newspapers.[23] Even worse for die-hard Bolsheviks, to win readers, the survivors had to use more human-interest stories, news, and entertainment. In addition, the output of the newly established private commercial presses was growing much faster than that of the party and the state. This, in turn, was perceived as a danger to the Soviet-Russian culture and as a betrayal of lofty journalistic principles. It is little wonder that the Third Congress of Soviet journalists, held in 1922, reasserted the importance of party guidance of the press. The members of the Bolshevik party were obliged to subscribe to at least one party newspaper to sustain falling readership levels. All nonparty publications had to be monitored and surpassed in quality by party organs.[24] Therefore, by using the pretext of defending national culture and Russian identity, the professional association helped in stricter control of the profession.

In the early 1920s, as more people became literate, the number and circulation of Bolshevik publications slowly increased. By the mid-1920s, there were newspapers in many different ethnic languages but all with the same official message.[25] As the political system became stronger, the press shifted its emphasis. From 1917-1921, it was devoted chiefly to the legitimization of the regime, whereas from 1922 until 1926, the focus became mobilizing the masses through upgrading the cultural and economic education of the populace.[26]

To sum up, the Soviet doctrine of journalism, based on Lenin's writings and practice of journalism, and later elaborated by party ideologists, stressed such principles as partymindedness (*partiinost*), high ideological content (*vysokaya ideinost*), truthfulness (*pravdivost*), national/popular character (*narodnost'*), mass character (*massovost'*), and criticism and self-criticism (*kritika* and *samokritika*).[27]

The way to combine partymindedness with truthfulness was explained or, rather, interpreted by the meaning assigned to the word *truth* (in Russian, *pravda*).[28] The truth was conceived as something more than simple facts, as their deeper meaning. Of course, the party knew the truth, and, therefore, only it could provide correct interpretation and selection of facts. Such Alice in Wonderland usage of words and facts, in which meanings were changed according to the wishes of the leadership, became a dominant feature of the next tide of the Soviet media doctrine, the Stalinist era.

Stalin's Longest-Range Weapon

On the surface, Stalinism presented itself as an exceptionally humanitarian and democratic regime, under which all citizens' freedoms were guaranteed by the USSR Constitution of 1936. In respect to the press, article 125 read:

> The citizens of the USSR are guaranteed by law: (a) freedom of press; (b) freedom of assembly, including the holding of mass meetings; (c) freedom of street processions and demonstrations. These civil rights are ensured by placing at the disposal of the working people and their organizations printing presses, stocks of paper, public buildings and streets, communications facilities and other material resources for the exercise of these rights.[29]

However, these guarantees were circumscribed by a clause specifying that such freedoms could be used only "in conformity with the interests of the working people, and in order to strengthen the socialist system."[30] In Stalin's words that idea was expressed beautifully:

> All that we have gone through in the last years has shown how, having destroyed the freedom of the press and all other bourgeois freedoms, the working class under the party's leadership has enacted such freedoms for the creative activity of the masses of workers and peasants that the world had not seen before.[31]

On the doctrine level, the classical Stalinist model operated with a simplistic and rigid set of ideas. In fact, it did not change Lenin's model; it only added the custom of self-criticism, the almost medieval practice of public confession of sins and errors. Such a routine served to break

mental opposition to Communist rule and ideology, but Stalin preferred
to justify it in political terms:

> So as to move forward and improve relations between the people and the
> leaders, we should keep the valve of self-criticism open. We should give the
> Soviet people an opportunity to criticize their leaders for their mistakes so
> that the leaders do not put on airs and the masses do not distance them-
> selves from their leaders.[32]

The linking of the leadership with the masses through different
channels was called the "transmission belt" system, in which the role of
the press was to be one element. Such an idea seemed to build a basis for
a genuine public relations model of the press in which the media was to
serve as an intermediary and a public forum. In reality, the transmission
belt concept was a cover-up for a system of one-man rule.[33]

When Stalin phased out the NEP in 1929, the short period of Soviet
press revival immediately ended. His media system was part of a larger
political system. Thus, it was based on open and hidden terror. Its
ideology was based on the concept of "ever-increasing ideological class
struggle" on both an international and a domestic level. This ideology
had a clear bearing on the Soviet communication system.[34] The model
of scrupulous control over the press was, therefore, well adapted to the
structure and strategy of the party and to his personal glorification. It is
little wonder that his model worked well under combined party, *Glavlit*,
and secret police, the *NKVD* (Narodnii Komissariat Vnutriennich Diel)
control.[35]

Stalin's political terminology was that of the military; thus, he called
the press "his longest-range weapon." As such it had to be treated like
a dangerous weapon. It was to be handled with care by the most trusted
and well-trained personnel, who would use appropriate verbal
ideological munitions, and to be directed against the enemies of socialism
and Stalin. By the same token, totalitarianism does not tolerate any form
of professionalism, as it cannot stand any form of independence.[36] The
agitprop departments were the main providers of ideas and facts. To
make the monopoly unescapable, *Glavlit* supervised all literary
production and all means of public communication. In the 1930s, *Pravda*
became more than the country's leading newspaper; it acquired a
supervisory role over all other newspapers and media. During the Great
Purge, he turned the paper into its private weapon or, more accurately,
into an ideological gendarme.[37] The paper was run directly from Stalin's
private office by Stalin's private secretary. Thus, the dictator could easily
control all media, which had to follow *Pravda*'s line.

An important feature of Stalin's policy was what Boris Pasternak called "the inhuman power of lie." No word about the 1929-1933 famine was allowed to appear in the press, although the number of deaths from this famine, which was caused by Stalin's policy of total collectivization of agriculture, "was higher than the total deaths for all countries in World War I."[38] However, despite Communist efforts, dreams about freedom of the press persisted.[39] In Stalinist Russia the voices for such freedom were silenced but never forgotten.

Khrushchev's Thaw, Brezhnev's Freeze, Gorbachev's Glasnost

Signs of change in the Soviet media system appeared in the press soon after Stalin's death in March 1953. A new, somewhat more liberal cultural policy was commenced, aptly called "the Thaw" by Ilya Ehrenburg, prominent Soviet writer. The breakthrough was Khrushchev's secret speech to the Twentieth Congress of the Communist Party of the Soviet Union in February 1956.[40] Afterward, Khrushchev granted and even encouraged media criticism of his political opponents if they were associated with Stalinism. This created the impression of liberalization of, or a thaw in, the media without changing the basic structures of party control.[41]

After Khrushchev's removal in 1964, stricter censorship was imposed and many creative talents were forced to emigrate, among them Alexander Solzhenitsyn. The Brezhnev leadership limited the growing openness of society and maintained the isolation of society as long as possible. However, in the 1960s the Soviet leadership could not restrict dissent as easily as it had in Stalin's time. Because of some political relaxation, new claims were made. Samizdat, a traditional Russian response to the excessive restriction of the freedom of expression, reappeared. One of the main demands of the newly born human rights movement in the Soviet Union was for glasnost within the Soviet system. Calls for openness sometimes appeared even in literary weeklies and scholarly works.[42] However, the ultraconservative agitprop apparatchik, Konstantin Chernenko, who became secretary-general of the Communist party in 1983, tried to reverse the current demanding more ideological vigilance, but it was obviously too late.

In 1985, Mikhail Gorbachev, new secretary-general of the Soviet Communist party, immediately announced that glasnost (derived from the word voice, *golos*, and translatable as publicity, openness, candor, even accessibility) would be the new information policy. Although glasnost is usually thought to be a Gorbachev invention, in fact it was not. This idea had a long tradition within both Russia and the Soviet Union.[43] The grass-roots glasnost movement in the 1960s proved this beyond any doubt. The term was used by Yuri Andropov in his campaign against corruption and mismanagement.[44] "The party and government would do better," he told the Central Committee in 1983, "if there were regular accountability of leading officials before the population."[45]

For Gorbachev glasnost was not an aim in itself. As George Gerbner commented, "It was, rather, a weapon for exposing and discrediting the past and the `old guard'."[46] However, it was more than that. Gorbachev also had conceived of it in a truly Leninist way, as a tool for the mobilization of the masses. "The better people are informed," he argued, "the more consciously they will act, the more actively they will support the party, its plans, and its programmatic goals."[47] His emphasis was less on the right to know and even less on the freedom of the press than on the utility to the regime of an informed and involved citizenry. Either way he was pointing to a more unfettered and realistic system of political communication.[48] In this he was in opposition to the traditional Soviet concept of the role of the press.[49]

Gorbachev, in contrast to the Russian legacy of secrecy and denials, demanded more openness and "calling things by their proper names."[50] The major post-Chernobyl' developments were the strident attacks by the journalists on official suppression of information and debate. After the Chernobyl' disaster, Gorbachev warned: "After all, publicly significant information could not be the privilege of only a narrow circle of the elect, or of the ordained among us."[51] To that *Izvestiia* added: "We all need to learn more about living in conditions of publicity and openness."[52]

The Twenty-Second Congress of the CPSU, in February-March 1987, opened a new stage in the glasnost campaign. It was marked by the criticism of what were once sacred principles of communism, like Stalin's role in the victory over Germany or—most sacred things of all—the ruling role of the party. The scope and depth of criticism were gradually enlarged. Despite occasional drawbacks, the glasnost policy led to the renouncement of total party control over journalism and the media, and to other liberal moves.[53] Nevertheless, glasnost had no legal foundation until the "Law on the Press and Other Mass Information Media," which was signed by Gorbachev on June 12, 1990. The law limited censorship to state security matters, and gave editorial staff considerable autonomy. Not everybody was happy with such a radical breakthrough with Russian tradition. The law was printed by the government paper *Izvestiia*, and the headline on the front page announced: "Prashchai Censura" [Goodbye, Censorship]; however, the law and the fact were not even mentioned during this time by the party newspaper *Pravda*.[54] Even the death of *Glavlit* was like its life: confidential and silent.

Gorbachev allowed all of the sacrosanct principles of Leninist-Stalinist media policy, especially the principle of partymindedness, wither away. Or, in other words, he tried to square the circle—reform the unreformable system. In reality, he made a full circle from that system, unintentionally breaking it first in Eastern Europe, then in the Soviet Union.

For this study it is particularly important that Gorbachev's information policy had a deep influence on Eastern European nations and on Communist leaders. The former felt encouraged to demand more freedom; the latter lost their self-confidence. As Gerbner put it, "The spirit of glasnost, the new [media] law, instant imagery, and the new technologies made complete control of communications no longer possible."[55] These influences were felt particularly strongly by two key elements of the Communist power structure—the intelligentsia (contrary to the orthodox Marxist view, I consider them, not the workers, to be the vanguard of change), and the core group of party nomenklatura. Both grew frustrated by being quasi-imprisoned because of being shielded from the West and its progress.[56] The situation matured to a revolution, but not to a traditional, bloody one.[57] The mood was for gradual and peaceful rejection of the corrupt, weakened system.

Notes

1. In "What Is to Be Done," written in 1902 as a plan for Communist revolution (Lenin, *Collected Works*, vol. 1 [Moscow: Progress Publishers, 1967]), p. 233.

2. Charles A. Ruud, *Fighting Words: Imperial Censorship and the Russian Press, 1804-1906* (Toronto: University of Toronto Press, 1982), p. 3.

3. Just before the October Revolution, Lenin advocated the nationalization of printing presses and newsprint "so as to allocate these resources to all parties in proportion to their popular strength." On September 28, 1917, he pledged: "State power in the shape of the Soviets takes *all* the printing presses and *all* newsprint and distributes them *equitably*. The state should come first—in the interests of the majority of the people. The big parties should come second—say, those that have polled one or two hundred thousand votes in both capitals. The smaller parties should come third, and then any group of citizens, which has a certain number of members or has collected a certain number of signatures. In this way, the revolutionary-democratic preparation for the elections to the Constituent Assembly would be fully guaranteed." *Lenin About the Press* (Prague: International Organization of Journalists, 1972), p. 188 (emphasis in original).

4. Michael Geller and Alexander Nekrich commented: "It is significant that the first decree of the Council of People's Commissars was a decree on the press putting censorship into effect and outlawing magazines and newspapers guilty of a critical attitude towards the new government." Vladimir Bonch-Bruevich, a close collaborator of Lenin, admits that "for some, even some of the Old Bolsheviks, it was hard to accept the fact that our old program from before the Revolution has called for "freedom of the press," but after the seizure of power this freedom was immediately abolished." Bonch-Bruevich formulated the "new demands of October" this way: "During a revolution there should be only a

revolutionary press and no other," *Utopia in Power: The History of the Soviet Union from 1917 to the Present* (London: Hutchinson, 1986), p. 62.

5. The decree was drafted by A. Lunacharskii, almost certainly with Lenin's encouragement and approval. See Richard Pipes, *The Russian Revolution* (New York: Alfred Knopf, 1990), p. 521.

6. *Lenin About the Press*, pp. 205-206.

7. Ibid., p. 205.

8. Not all Bolshevik organizations were against freedom of the press. It was necessary at the time to explain that sudden move against the freedom of expression. On the next day the editorial in *Pravda* justified the decree on the grounds that "the bourgeois press is one of the strongest weapons in the hands of the bourgeoisie." In Moscow the Bolshevik-controlled Military Revolutionary Committee went so far as to overrule it, declaring that the press once again could enjoy full freedom of expression because the Revolution was over. Among the intelligentsia the outrage was universal. On November 26, 1917, the Union of Writers issued a one-time newspaper, *Gazeta-Protest*, in which Russia's leading writers and artists expressed anger at this attempt to stifle freedom of expression. See Pipes, *The Russian Revolution*, p. 522.

More on the internal Bolshevik opposition to the muzzling of the press can be found in Victor Serge's book, *Year One of the Russian Revolution* (translated from French by P. Sedgwick [1930], London: Allen Lane of Penguin Press, 1972).

9. In the words of Victor Serge, Lenin responded to his opponents: "Let us set up a commission to inquire into the dependence of the bourgeois newspapers upon the banks. We would like to know what sort of freedom it is. Isn't it the freedom to buy up tons of paper and hire hordes of scribes? No more talk of this freedom of the press which is a slave of capital!" Victor Serge, *Year One*, p. 102.

10. Leonard Schapiro, *The Origin of the Communist Autocracy. First Phase: 1917-1922* (Cambridge: Harvard University Press, 1955), p. 191.

11. The story of the liquidation of the Menshevik party press is very illustrative of the Bolsheviks' tactics. The central Menshevik organ, *Rabochaya gazeta*, had been closed down on December 1, 1917, by the Military Revolutionary Committee. However, it reappeared the next day as *Novy luch*, which survived until May 1918. On June 11, 1918, the Mensheviks, a fraction of the Russian social-democratic movement, were expelled from the Central Executive Committee along with the Socialist Revolutionaries. Until mid-1918 an extensive Menshevik Party press was in existence, including *Vpereod* (closed in May), *Novaya zarya*, *Partynyya izvestiya*, *Rabochiy internatsional*, *Professional'ny soyuz*, *Rabochiy mir*, and so on. A few Menshevik periodicals appeared sporadically up until the spring of 1919, most, if not all, in the territories occupied by the White Armies. The Moscow Printers' Union, which remained predominately Menshevik until its forcible dispersal, published a journal (*Gazieta piechatnikov*) until 1919. Otherwise the Mensheviks had to rely on illegally handprinted newssheets which they succeeded, with considerable skill, in distributing. See ibid., pp. 192, 195, 196.

12. The Maximalist (anarchist) party was allowed to publish a weekly paper, *Maximalist*. The last surviving anarchist periodicals, such as *Vol'naya Zhizn'* and *Universal*, were closed down after the March 1921 Kronstadt rising. See additional discussion in ibid., pp. 182, 187.

13. The Communists succeeded in splitting the Socialist Revolutionaries party. For nine days, from March 20 to March 28, 1919, the newly legalized faction was allowed to publish *Delo Naroda*, one of the social revolutionary organs that had been closed down in January 1918. The short period of a free press was brought to an ultimate end by the too-insistent demands of *Delo Naroda* for free elections. Ibid., p. 186.

14. Peter Kenez, *The Birth of the Propaganda State: Soviet Methods of Mass Mobilization, 1917-1929* (Cambridge: Cambridge University Press, 1985), p. 100.

15. Even Maxim Gorky, a famous Russian-Soviet writer whose outspoken criticism of the Communists' behavior had led to the closing of his paper, *Novaya Zhizn*, in July 1918, was by December 3, 1918 (Civil War period) appealing in the pages of *Pravda*: "Follow us in the struggle against the old order—to freedom and to a beautiful life." Schapiro, *The Origin*, p. 197.

16. *Lenin About the Press*, p. 206.

17. Geller, *Utopia in Power*, p. 191.

18. *Izvestiia*, August 14, 1922. Quoted ibid., p. 192.

19. In Russia, censorship of theological publications was introduced under Peter the Great's reign; it became a general system in 1803. In the nineteenth century censorship had twelve separate agencies: general, ecclesiastical, educational, military, literary, press, postal, etc. There was even a supreme secret committee charged with censoring the work of censors. The worst censorship occurred during the reign of Nicholas I; it was liberalized after 1864, and almost disappeared between 1905-1914. Charles A. Ruud gives an excellent description of evolution of censorship in Russia in the nineteenth century; *Fighting Words*.

20. There are several good descriptions of *Glavlit*, its development, and rules of operation. See Robert Conquest, ed., *The Politics of Ideas in the USSR* (New York: Praeger, 1967), especially "The System of Restriction," pp. 43-49. Martin Dewhirst and Robert Farell, eds., *The Soviet Censorship* (Metuchen: The Scarecrow Press, 1973) containing an introduction "The System of Formal Censorship" by probably the leading scholar of Glavlit, L. Finkelstein (pp. 50-67). Merle Fainsfod wrote an excellent essay "Censorship in the USSR—A Documented Record," *Problems of Communism*, March-April 1956, pp. 12-19.

21. In 1922, the Rabselkors got their official title and were given an official job: to control private trading and corruption crimes that could best be checked by individuals familiar with their localities; to provide readers with news about their own regions; and to inform the central authorities about dissatisfaction in the countryside.

22. Mark Hopkins, *Mass Media in the Soviet Union* (New York: Pegasus, 1970).

23. Of the 802 papers in existence in January 1922, only 313 remained by July, this number increased to 423 by December 1922. Roger W. Pethybridge, "The Significance of Communications in 1917," *Soviet Studies* 1, 1967, p. 201.

24. In August 1922, the agitprop section of the Twelfth Party Conference set up a commission to provide state subsidies for the politically reliable press, because private journals continued to grow by offering sensational, gutter literature. The state press was guaranteed a financial base and less dependency on readers. The NEP period, therefore, brought mixed effects on the press. On the one hand, it helped to revive the private, sensationalist papers. On the other, it created a

network of workers and peasant correspondents and increased party surveillance over the press. The press was thus at a crossroads—between marketization and politicization. Ibid., p. 201.

25. The Bolshevik media model was both monopolistic and messianic. In July 1918, the Soviet government took over, and it monopolized the embryonic radio facilities. In 1922, longing for a world revolution, the most powerful radio station in the world, Comintern (Communist International), was built in Moscow and began to broadcast multilingual transmissions. Later, by the eve of World War II, the USSR was operating an extensive network of radio stations that preached the ideology of communism.

26. Low circulation and poor distribution of leading literary journals provide clear evidence of the elitist character of the press. *Molodaya gvardiya*, one of the most popular journals of this type, had a circulation of only nine thousand in 1922, and this had dropped to between five thousand and six thousand an issue by 1928. See Robert W. Pethybridge, "Railways and Press Communication in Soviet Russia in the Early NEP Period," *Soviet Studies* 2, 1986, p. 200.

27. *Partiinost*: partymindedness; party spirit; placing party interests above all else. *Narodnost*: nationality; national character; peopleness; the orientation of art and literature to mass needs and perceptions. Roy D. Laird and Betty A. Laird, *A Soviet Lexicon* (Lexington, MA: Lexington Books, 1988), pp. 78, 85.

28. The Russian language has two words that have essentially the same meaning as the English word truth: *pravda* and *isstina*. *Pravda* has a more fundamental, ideological meaning than does *isstina*.

29. Quote from John L. Martin, "Goals and Roles of the Media Systems," in Anju Chaudhary and John L. Martin, eds., *Comparative Mass Media Systems* (New York: Longman, 1984), p. 26.

30. It is worth noting that the latest version of the Soviet Constitution, amended as late as August 1, 1991, under Gorbachev's rule, did not alter this article. The change was minimal; thus, almost the same constitutional provisions covered the totally different media practice: "In accordance with the interest of the people and *in order to strengthen and develop the socialist system*, citizens of the USSR are guaranteed freedom of speech, of the press, of the assembly, meetings, street processions, and demonstrations." *Soviet Politics: Struggling with Change*, translated by Gordon B. Smith (London: Macmillan, 1992), p. 356 (emphasis added).

31. Adam B. Ulam, *Stalin: The Man and His Era* (London: I.B. Tauris, 1983), p. 374.

32. Joseph Stalin, *Sochinenniya* vol. 7 (Moscow: Polizdat, 1952), pp. 31-32.

33. In analyzing Stalin's doctrine of the media, David W. Benn succinctly stressed, not without irony, that of all the Soviet leaders it was Stalin who insisted most strongly that the masses must learn from their own experience. In the same context, Stalin was even prepared to recognize the possible rift between the party and the masses. *Persuasion & Soviet Politics* (Oxford: Blackwell, 1989), p. 62.

Stalin, although at the time the only Communist leader who was not yet a *vozhd* (the supreme leader) opted strongly for the legitimacy of Communist rule through effective propaganda. In his typical style he posed a rhetorical question: "Is it possible to impose party leadership upon the class by force? No, it is not.

In any case, such leadership cannot be of any lengthy duration," he said in January 1926. Stalin, *Sochinenniya*, vol. 8 (Moscow: Polizdat, 1953), p. 43.

A statement of this kind was totally at odds with Stalin's record of coercion and terror and with other things which he said. The most important point here, however, is not that Stalin was insincere, but that "he put forward a (not entirely unrealistic) concept of the role of the persuasion and public opinion which continued to be proclaimed during the Stalin era but which was not followed in practice." See Benn, *Persuasion*, pp. 62-63.

34. An excellent analysis is be found in Thomas Remington, *The Truth of Authority: Ideology and Communication in the Soviet Union* (Pittsburgh: University of Pittsburgh Press, 1988).

35. Nadezhda Mandelstam stressed in her memoirs that in the 1930s, because of the lack of external information, even the most educated people became so saturated with Stalinist propaganda that they simply could not imagine anything other than the Soviet way of life. She gave an example of the woman who was certain that in capitalist countries people starve to death, and that education for all is possible only under socialism; she also recalled a discussion of whether in Paris or London a residence permit is required. The indoctrination program was so effective that the senior guard who was convoying the Mandelstams on their way to exile in 1934 told them to fear nothing, because in the Soviet Union people were shot only for spying and sabotage. In the bourgeois countries, he went on, it was quite a different matter: There you could be strung up in no time for writing something they did not like.

"To some degree or another we all, of course, believed what was dinned into us. The young people—whether students, soldiers, writers or guards—were particularly credulous," concludes Mandelstam, *Hope Against Hope* (London: Penguin Books, 1975), p. 59.

36. Osip Mandelstam, who Joseph Brodsky feels was the greatest Russian twentieth-century poet, was doomed just because he was such a great poet. "The iron broom [Stalinist terror] that was walking across Russia could have missed him if he were merely a political poet—but he was more than that. That is why the iron broom, whose purpose was the spiritual castration of the entire populace, couldn't have missed him." Joseph Brodsky, *Less Than One: Selected Essays* (London: Penguin Books, 1987), pp. 136-137.

37. The best description of *Pravda*'s role can be found in Angus Roxburgh, *Pravda: Inside the Soviet News Machine* (London: Victor Gollanch, 1987).

38. Robert Conquest, *Harvest of Sorrow: Soviet Collectivization and the Terror-famine* (New York: Oxford University Press, 1986), p. 213.

39. In the first revolt against Communist rule, the Kronstadt uprising, which occurred on February, 28, 1921, the crew of the battleship *Petropavlosk* passed a resolution that became the charter for the revolt. Significantly, the main demands of the resolution were "freedom of speech and press for workers, peasants, and for the Anarchists, and the left socialists parties; freedom of meetings." Throughout the country similar demands were voiced; at a protest meeting Moscow workers also demanded "freedom of meeting and of the press." Schapiro, *The Origin*, p. 301.

40. For more on Khrushchev's speech, see Chapter 7 in the present volume.

41. Khrushchev explained his motives in a different way. During the press conference for foreign journalists he said: "I have been asked frequently why I decided to give such a speech to the Twentieth Congress in 1956, condemning Stalin's errors and distortions. It was my duty to say the truth about the past, without taking into account personal costs and personal risks. Already Lenin taught us that a party which is not afraid of telling the truth would not die." Quote from a close adviser of N.S. Khrushchev, Fiodor Burlackyi, "Khrushchev," *Literaturnayia Gazeta*, February 24, 1988, p. 3.

42. Yasen N. Zassurskii, ed., *Zhurnalistika v Politcheskoy Strukture Obschestva* (Moscow: Polizdat, 1974), pp. 81-82.

43. In the late 1820s, an academician George Parrot, a counselor to Tsar Nicholas I (1825-1855), advocated glasnost as the means to improve central policy decisionmaking. Also, Grand Duke Konstantin Nikolayevich, son of the tsar, cleverly used glasnost during a debate on the reform of naval military regulations. The concept of glasnost reappeared during the last decade of Tsar Nicholas's reign. It was supported by a group of reformers, so-called enlightened bureaucrats, within the central government as an idea to bring about a more open and candid exchange of opinions about much-needed social and economical reforms (*pereobrazowanie*).

The idea emerged again under the reign of the next tsar, Alexander the Second (1855-1881), following the thinking of Michael Speranski, one of his preceptors and an adviser to his father. It was called *organizovannaiya glasnost* (organized glasnost) or *iskusstvennaya glasnost* (artificially induced debate). Some liberals even tried to extend glasnost to include free political debate in order to strengthen the reform but not the revolutionary movement. See W. Bruce Lincoln, *Nicholas I: Emperor and Autocrat of All Russians* (Polish translation, Warszawa: PIW, 1988); and W. Bruce Lincoln, *In the Vanguard of Reform* (DeKalb: Northern Illinois University Press, 1983). Also see Natalie Gross, "*Glasnost'*: Roots and Practice," *Problems of Communism*, November-December 1987, pp. 69-70; and Pal Kölsto, *An Appeal to the People: Glasnost'—Aims and Means* (Oslo: Institutt for Forvarsstudier, 1988), pp. 10-11.

Gorbachev was not the first Soviet leader to use the word and the concept. The term can be found occasionally in the works of Lenin. Even more frequently Lenin proposed the practice of glasnost as a form of controlling the Soviet bureaucrats and party cadres.

44. "Boris Yeltsin: Moscow's Champion of Glasnost'," *Radio Liberty Research Report*, 1987.

45. *Pravda*, June 16, 1983, p. 1.

46. George Gerbner, "Instant History: The Case of the Moscow Coup," *Political Communication* 10, 1993, p. 198.

47. *Pravda*, March 15, 1985, p. 1.

48. Thomas J. Colton, *The Dilemma of Reform in the Soviet Union* (Washington, D.C.: Council on Foreign Relations, 1986).

49. In a classic orthodox formulation of the Communist press doctrine, Victor Afansyev, editor-in-chief of *Pravda* in the 1980s, expressed the goals of the paper in the following words: "We inform masses of the decisions of the party and government, propagandize these decisions, mobilize the Soviet people to carry

them out, accumulate and mold public opinion, and concentrate people's efforts on solving precisely those tasks which are the most important and most necessary for the country and for the party." Roxburgh, *Pravda*, p. 52.

50. *Pravda*, February 26, 1986, p. 1.

51. *Pravda*, June 26, 1986, p. 1.

52. *Izvestiia*, June 26, 1986, p. 3..

53. Censorship in the USSR was abolished in August 1990.

54. See Vladimir Wozniuk, "Soviet Censorship's `True Colors': A Chameleon Adapting to Glasnost," in Ilan Peleg, ed., *Patterns of Censorship Around the World* (Boulder: Westview, 1993), p. 40.

55. Gerbner, "Instant history," p. 203.

56. I owe this observation to Dr. Gerhard Wettig, a well-known German researcher on the impact of international broadcasting.

57. This was clearly shown during the time of the failed coup of August 1991. The Moscow coupsters were more accustomed to controlling the media than to manipulating them. Five years of glasnost made Soviet journalists more confident, more brave, and more professionally oriented. They did not give up easily.

4

Historical Context:
The Legacy of the Polish Past

In spite of the Communists' declaration that they were building a completely new media system, Poland's past experiences profoundly influenced the development of journalism and mass communications long after 1944. Dominant among these legacies were a patriotic and political commitment on the part of journalists and a history of media dependence on the state and the Roman Catholic church; both traditions go back to the very beginnings of the Polish press.

Looking for the Roots

Among East European countries, Poland has the longest history of journalism. The first Polish newspaper, *Merkuriusz Polski*, was set up in Cracow in 1661.[1] Its editor, the king's secretary, Hieronim Pinocci, gave it the character of a royal publication. Despite prominent protectors, the paper was closed down after a few issues. The next Polish periodical, *Nowiny Polskie* (Polish News), appeared in 1729.[2] The king's privilege gave the publisher a monopoly on printing newspapers and the paper lasted until 1790. After that, the press became fragmented and political papers emerged. The short period of a free and lively press was possible because the political system was in disarray and the central authority could not exercise effective control over all manifestations of public life.[3]

Unfortunately, the internal weakness of Poland in that period was exploited by rulers of the neighboring countries. By the end of the eighteenth century Poland's territory was partitioned by Frederick the Great of Prussia, Catherine the Great of Russia, and Maria Theresia of Austria. For the next 130 years, the Poles were subjects of the German, Austrian, and Russian autocratic governments.

Although Poland had disappeared from the political map of Europe, Polish patriotism survived. The main aim of the intelligentsia was to sustain national identity and keep spirits high. Journalists, when they could, tried to be leaders in national culture and language. Patriotic writers used metaphors, allusions, and so-called Aesopian language to smuggle banned information or opinion past the censors. The idea of intellectuals as preservers of the national consciousness continued to be crucial to the journalists' self-image even in the Communist era.[4]

The legal and political conditions for publishing books and newspapers differed in each partition. However, everywhere the basic rule was that any publication had to be presented to the censors of occupying powers. Foreign censorship was rigid and severe, although vague in principle and very narrow-minded in application.[5] The policy and practice of control of the press were not fixed and stable during that long period of foreign rule. They grew tighter or became more liberal, in accordance with the changes in the political situation in each of Poland's occupying countries. In general, during the whole period, it was the most severe in the part of Poland taken by Russia. Occasionally, as after the unsuccessful Polish uprising in 1863, censorship in Russian Poland was tightened, while in Russia it was liberalized.[6]

Foreign censorship pushed Poles to find ways to avoid alien control. One method was to bypass censorship by printing forbidden books abroad. A popular practice in Russian Poland, especially after the November uprising in 1831, was smuggling in patriotic books and pamphlets, initially from France and later from the Austrian partition where censorship had been eased.[7]

Modern Poland was reborn in 1918. However, after more than a century under semicolonial rule, most peasants were still illiterate, the society was poor, and the economy was in deep crisis. The country then was multiethnic and multinational; Jews, Ukrainians, Byelorussians, and Lithuanians formed large minorities.[8] On the technological level, printing presses and paper plants were old and worn out. These and other factors strongly influenced the style of journalism and the reach of the press. The predominant form of the newspaper was the "journal d'opinion," or advocacy paper, not one of information.

Despite difficulties, the press had been developing rapidly. Minorities published numerous ethnic and foreign-language newspapers and magazines, although their average circulations were not impressive. The press in interwar Poland represented all shades of public opinion. Most cultural and religious organizations, professional associations, and ethnic minorities had their own periodicals. Some journals were sponsored and subsidized by the government, but most were published by independent sources and oppositional political parties. Dailies were usually published as organs of a political party or a similar type of political association. They were strongly partisan in orientation, serving more as trumpets for political orientations than as an information service. Polish journalists were, therefore, not in a position to adopt the principle of separating news from opinion.

A popular commercial press was also developing rapidly. Some papers were overtly sensationalist. "Put blood on the first page," was the usual cry of managing editors when they wanted crimes, murders, and rapes to be exposed. Such newspapers were nicknamed "red papers" (*czerwoniakowe*), not for their political orientation (they were strongly anti-Communist) but because of the red color of their shocking headlines.[9]

Living Underground

There is no darker chapter in Polish history than that of World War II. On September 1, 1939, Nazi troops invaded Poland's western border. A few weeks later, the Soviets marched into eastern Poland, and once again the territory and the nation were divided between the Germans and the Russians. More than 6 million Polish citizens, predominantly Jews, perished in the Nazi concentration camps. Million others were send by the Soviets to the Siberian gulags.

Both occupants immediately banned all Polish papers and liquidated radio networks. In the territories incorporated into the Third Reich, the Nazis imposed a Goebbels type of media system designated to serve their administration needs. Polish radio was replaced by a network of loudspeakers in main public places, which broadcast police information, regulations, and political propaganda. Moreover, several newspapers were published in German. A German press chain, *Zeitungsverlag Krakau-Warschau GmbH* replaced the two Polish publishing houses in the region called *General Governement*. The *Ostdeutscher Zeitung* and the *Katowizer Zeitung* were published in Poznań and Katowice, respectively.

In addition to German-language papers, a dozen newspapers were published in Polish. Among them was the *Goniec Krakowski* (Cracow Courier), with a circulation of about sixty thousand. The Nazis also published propaganda papers in Ukrainian and even published two newspapers for the Jews: *Gazeta Żydowska* (Jewish Gazette) in Polish and *Geto Zeitung* in Yiddish.

The Nazi-supported papers were commonly called "reptile" papers; they were occasionally read but rarely believed.[10] Rather, they let the readers understand meanings "between the lines," so they could draw some information from the lies and half-truths of the German propaganda. Skills that had been gained during Poland's more than one hundred years of Russian, Prussian, and Austrian partitions were put to use again.

The Poles also did not give up their own press. A large and varied group of underground publications, perhaps the largest in any occupied country, appeared during the war. Despite cruel punishments imposed for any form of participation in the publishing of underground papers, some were published with surprising regularity, as weeklies or even dailies.[11] There were other underground publications. For example, in the Warsaw Ghetto the Jews had published their own illegal press.[12]

Most underground papers appeared weekly or bimonthly and were printed on flat machines, although occasionally linotypes were used. Historians registered about 1,500 titles of underground periodicals.[13] In their information service, these papers were limited to news heard over Allied radio stations. Polish authors provided editorials, essays, and humor.[14]

Although the possession of a radio receiver was considered illegal and was punishable by the death penalty, many courageous citizens dared to keep receivers or even to build them. Foreign broadcasts were the sole source of regular and reliable information.[15] The most popular and reputable station was the BBC service in Polish. Listeners usually reported to others what they heard, so the reach of those broadcasts was extensive. The habit of listening to foreign broadcasts appeared and became fixed social behavior during World War II.

The Soviet occupation penetrated society much more than the Nazi occupation. In the territories under Soviet rule, no underground papers could be published regularly. Nevertheless, other sources of news such as using grapevines, listening to foreign broadcasts, and learning from the official propaganda were used—even more so in the years after the war when the Soviets took control of the entire country.

This brief review of the plight of Polish journalism and the media uses reveals at least six components of the Polish press tradition that are relevant to the analysis of the media in Communist Poland: (1) the dependence of the press on political rather than commercial interests; (2) the commitment of the journalist to the cause; (3) the mixing of news and opinions in all journalistic genres; (4) the tradition of engaging in the publishing and reading of the underground, illegal press; (5) the skill of the audience, especially of the intelligentsia, in deciphering hidden meanings and a tendency of journalists to use Aesop's parables, or allusions, to convey their own opinions and to smuggle information, despite censorship; and (6) the dependence on foreign sources of information, particularly foreign radio stations. To this list should be added the state monopoly of radio broadcasting.[16] The institution of repressive (i.e., postpublication) censorship also existed in interwar Poland; as a means of control of the press it operated after the authoritarian coup in 1926.[17]

All of these traditions had formed the background for both official and alternative media systems in postwar Poland and have influenced the development of the free press well after the fall of the Communist system.

Notes

1. Cracow, a former capital of Poland, was the cradle of the Polish printing industry.

2. In the same year the newspaper was renamed *Kurier Polski z Uprzywilejowanymi Wiadomościami z Cudzych Krajów* (Polish Courier with Privileged News from Alien Countries).

3. It was a rule that the newspaper could flourish in areas where authority was weak, such as in seventeenth-century Germany.

4. Jane L. Curry, translator and editor, *The Black Book on Polish Censorship* (New York: Vintage Books, 1984), p. 36.

5. The absolutist regimes that controlled the Polish lands naturally interfered with the development of the press. In the first half of the nineteenth century, virtually no publications existed in Galicia or Prussian Poland. There was only an official and colorless press in the Dutchy of Warsaw, which was controlled by Russia. In 1818 the first uncensored political daily, the *Gazeta Codzienna Narodowa i Obca* (Daily National and Foreign Gazette) appeared, but it quickly succumbed when censorship was introduced in 1819. Editors operated under constant pressures including arrests and heavy fines. Only a few strictly conformist papers proliferated. See Piotr Wandycz, *The Land of Partitioned Poland: 1795-1918* (Seattle: University of Washington Press, 1974), p. 97.

6. The most severe censorship occurred under the reign of Nicholas I. In his time censorship in Russia, as Norman Davies put it, "assumed the proportion of a major industry." *God's Playground: A History of Poland* (Oxford: Clarendon Press, 1981), vol. 2, p. 98. Russian censorship in Poland was particularly harsh regarding manifestations of Polish history; hence, any references to "Golden Freedom," Elections, or the Constitution were crossed out. The king of Poland had to be referred to as the grand duke of Poland, so as not to offend the status of the tsar. Ibid., pp. 98-99.

7. It is interesting that Jewish traders helped to smuggle in banned Polish classics from abroad.

8. In 1937, a total of 2,792 periodicals were published in Poland: Of these, 2,355 were printed in Polish, 130 in Yiddish and Hebrew, 125 in Ukrainian, 105 in German, 9 in Russian, 8 in Byelorussian, and 60 in other languages. There were also 184 daily papers, of which 47 were in Warsaw, with a total circulation close to 2 million copies daily. Four of the dailies, printed in Polish, were Jewish. Oscar Halecki, ed., *Poland* (New York and London: Praeger and Stevens & Sons, 1957), p. 129. Warsaw at that time was the biggest publisher in Europe of the books in Hebrew. Marian Fuks, *Prasa żydowska w Polsce: 1823-1939* [The Jewish Press in Poland: 1823-1939] (Warszawa: PWN, 1979).

9. In the United States, such journalism was called "yellow" because of the yellow color of headlines.

10. Ewa Celińska, *Szkice z dziejów prasy pod okupacją niemiecką (1939-1949)* [Essays on the Press Under the Nazi Occupation] (Warszawa: PWN, 1979).

11. People caught printing were executed or, in rare and best cases, sent to a concentration camp.

12. Joseph Kremish, "On the Underground Press in the Warsaw Ghetto," *Gazette* 1, 1962, pp. 1-21.

13. During the war the number of such illegal publications increased each year. In 1939 there were about fifty such papers, in 1940 over two hundred, in 1941 more than three hundred, in 1942 about four hundred, in 1943 about five hundred, and in 1944 over six hundred. These papers formed the largest such collection in Europe. Halecki, *Poland*, p. 130.

14. Ibid., p. 130

15. A department of the Home army had a special section for recording foreign broadcasts. It worked as an underground press agency, sending its bulletins to the underground papers.

16. This dependency had obvious consequences. The Polish state-run radio had to base its news bulletins on the information provided by the state press agency, the Polish Telegraph Agency. In addition, a special agreement with the Association of Publishers of Newspapers and Magazines forced the radio news bulletins to broadcast information items whose "dissemination is in the interest of the state." Thus, there is no tradition of the radio as an autonomous medium. M.J. Kwiatkowski, *Tu Polskie Radio Warszawa* [This Is Polish Radio–Warszawa] (Warszawa: PIW, 1980), p. 292.

17. From time to time, seizures of papers that did not follow the rules and suggestions of the state censoring agencies kept the publishers in line.

PART TWO

The Media Orchestra

Our whole system of ideological work must act like a well-tempered orchestra, where every instrument has its voice and plays its parts, and harmony is achieved by skillful conducting.

—Konstantin Chernenko, General Secretary of the CPSU, June 15, 1983

In that process of change the loss of Communist monopoly over mass communications is the key to the breakdown of Communist totalitarianism.

—Zbigniew Brzeziński, *The Grand Failure*

5

Prelude: Arranging and Tuning Up
July 1944 to December 1948

In its essentials, the political history of postwar Poland is extremely simple. It tells how the USSR handed power to its chosen protégés, and how it has kept them in place till 1989. In detail, however, it was extremely complicated.
—Norman Davies, *God's Playground*

The story of the mass media in any country cannot be separated from its political history. Usually, the media reflects a dominant ideology and follows political changes; occasionally, it heralds or even provokes incoming political developments. Consequently, it should be analyzed within a framework of political and social processes as well as a framework of its own dynamics.

General Pattern of Communist Takeover

In the aftermath of World War II, the Polish media had little autonomy or independence; to the contrary, in many ways it was auxiliary to and dependent on the powers-to-be. Thus, the media could not develop its own style and diversity; rather, it mirrored the political scene. From the beginning it was a result of a deliberate policy by the newly established, Moscow-selected government. Dana A. Schmidt, in an examination of *The Anatomy of a Satellite*, depicted the Communist policy in plain words:

Immediately upon seizing power in a country, the Communists do four things: they abolish all opposing political parties and establish a one-party dictatorship; they create a secret police; they establish a ministry of propaganda to tell people what they should know and how they should think; and, finally, they surround the whole system with an Iron Curtain.

It is moot to ask which comes first. They are interdependent; take one away
and the entire structure is threatened. They are the four walls of the
Communist house.[1]

Schmidt has accurately captured the essence of the Communist takeover and, important for this study, the effect of isolation from the West
and the monopoly had on propaganda. However, the imposition of the
Soviet model on the countries of Eastern and Central Europe was much
more complicated and prolonged; it was not one simple and brutal police
action.

Hugh Seton-Watson was closer to the truth when he discerned three
main phases in the Communist seizure of power.[2] In the first stage there
was some form of genuine coalition: Several political parties competed for
power. However, only parties committed to the platform called the
National Front were allowed to take part in public life. The Communists
initially took three key ministries: defense, the interior, and telecommunications. Although seriously inhibited by Red Army censorship, freedom
of the press and of association were still partially observed.

In the next stage, a simulated political coalition was imposed. Non-
Communists were still involved in government, but they became
subordinate to the Communist party (PPR). Peasant parties, which were
still permitted to exist, were driven into opposition. This phase ended
after the Communist International (Comintern) meeting in September
1947. In the third and final phase, after 1948, the establishment of a
Soviet-type monolithic regime was achieved and it became so firmly
rooted that it stayed in place for the next forty years, well outliving its
founders.

The history of building the media system in Poland reflects these
political phases fairly closely, although not completely. In addition to its
primarily political dimension, the media served as an instrument and
carrier of culture and entertainment; it also reflected, at least to a certain
extent, changes in the intellectual and spiritual life of the nation. As a
result, the modes of its operation changed much more frequently than
did its political configuration. In fact, with the exception of the postwar
period of 1944-1948 and the Solidarity interval of 1980-1981, political life
in Poland was monotonous, broken only by occasional crises. Social and
cultural life was much more spirited and had its own dynamics, which
was reflected even in the official mass media. The media was, therefore,
more mercurial. In various ways it shaped public opinion, sometimes
raising expectations, sometimes fueling frustrations; in both cases, it
created the climate for political change.

Thus, there were more distinct phases in the history of the postwar
mass media than there were changes in the political system. In this

chapter, I describe its beginnings—the preliminary phase in the making of a Communist media system. Of these three main stages in the making of the new political system, the most important was the initial takeover of all key levers of the state apparatus—the army, the security police, and telecommunications. Telecommunication services then became either military or governmental. The army exercised military censorship in combat zones, the police did the same in rear zones, and they cooperated in keeping the same propaganda line.

Initial Political Situation: 1944-1945

In July 1944, the Soviet army, reinforced by Polish divisions, entered the Polish ethnic territories. With these forces came a new government, the Polish Committee of National Liberation (PKWN).[3] On July 21, the PKWN announced a manifesto, which sounded very liberal and democratic:

> [The government] declares hereby solemnly that all democratic freedoms will be reinstated for all citizens irrespective of race, religion, nationality; those freedoms to be: freedom of free associations in political and professional fields, freedom of press and information, freedom of conscience.[4]

However, in case the Poles wanted make these wishes reality, the proviso of the manifesto contained a clear, though not well-defined, restriction: "these freedoms cannot serve the enemies of democracy." Who were those enemies? Who had the right to designate them? These questions were left unanswered, although in practice the job was done by the security apparatus.

At that time the Communists supported the idea of a national front, because they were still weak and had to show some tolerance for emerging political parties and their freedom of expression.[5] The manifesto, therefore, was purely propaganda move made in very special circumstances: in the midst of an ongoing war against Nazi Germany, the presence of the Soviet army on Polish territory, and the hostility of the population toward Communist rule.[6] The new authorities never kept their promises. The non-Communist deputy prime minister, Stanisław Mikołajczyk, chairman of the opposition Polish Peasant party (PSL), wrote in his memoirs about breaking the manifesto declaration:

> I thought bitterly of the manifesto issued by the Communists on July 21, 1944, in Lublin, and of our earlier Moscow Agreement that had said the same. In the matter of press, it had not only guaranteed the Polish Peasant

Party freedom from censorship, but it had also promised a just proportion of newsprint and full rights to mechanical equipment and distribution agencies. As matters turned out, the Polish Peasant Party's publications were held up for months while we sought equipment which Communist papers were getting.[7]

Mikołajczyk had many concrete reasons for complaining about the duplicity of his coalition partners:

We had enough requests for subscriptions for a daily print of 500,000 copies of *Gazeta Ludowa*, but we were never given newsprint for more than 70,000. Hundreds of copies of our paper were sabotaged by Communists in the distributing plants and services. Newsstand keepers and bookstores which sold our paper and periodicals were threatened with confiscatory taxes. Individual subscribers were warned that if they did not cancel subscriptions they would be fired from their jobs. When we formed our own distributing service, its directors, employees and their families were terrorized, its news-boys were publicly whipped.[8]

On December 31, 1944, the PKWN changed its name to Provisional Government of the Polish People's Republic, but as such it was recognized only by the Soviet Union.[9] Following the Yalta Agreement of the Allies in February 1945, a new Polish government emerged in July of that year. It was an outcome of a political compromise between the legal Polish government-in-exile (London) and Lublin's Communist government.[10] Although named the coalition government, it was in fact dominated by the Communists: of twenty-five members, sixteen came from the Lublin government, including the prime minister and the president.[11] The first deputy prime minister, Stanisław Mikołajczyk, was designated from the London government. However, much of the real power belonged to Władysław Gomułka, nominally only second deputy prime minister but also, and far more important, general-secretary of the PPR.[12] Jakub Berman, a Jewish expatriate from the Soviet Union, was charged with matters of ideology and, significantly, also internal security. As the main supervisor of the Polish media, he kept that position for more than ten years, earning much justified hatred among both the party cadres and liberal intelligentsia.

The provisional government lasted until January 1947, when the first postwar election was won overwhelmingly by Communists. The elections were an apparent fraud; however, their outcome allowed the PPR to immediately eliminate its declared and alleged enemies which, in addition to the PSL, included some other minor democratic parties. To maintain a share of power, the opportunist fractions of banned parties created the United Peasant Alliance (ZSL), the pro-Communist peasant party, and the Democratic Alliance (SD), the small-business and middle-class party. Officially called "allied" parties, in fact minor partners under the vigilant tutelage of a big brother, those parties survived the entire Communist period.

Even after the fixed election victory, the PPR still had to share its power with the Polish Socialist party (PPS). The Socialist PPS was stronger than the Communist PPR, had a longer tradition, and enjoyed much more popular support. However, under the Communist sun there was no place for two. The Socialists had to be eliminated. The final step was taken in December 1948 when the PPS was forced to merge with the PPR, together forming the Polish United Workers' party (PZPR), which endured until January 1990. The era of licensed pluralism ended, and the straight Soviet-type monolithic system became a model for Poland. Its imposition formed the next chapter in the media history.

Preconditions of the Development of the Press

The war had cost Poland the loss of one-fifth of its population and the destruction of over one-third of its national wealth. The pool of skilled media personnel was decimated. One-fourth of the printers and about one-third of the most experienced journalists had been killed. Many survivors, afraid of political repression, escaped to the West or went into hiding. Many others could not or did not want to work for the new rulers.[13]

On a technical level, the situation was tragic. After the Warsaw uprising of 1944, all printing plants in the capital were in ruins. The civil telecommunication network simply did not exist. In all of Poland more than 70 percent of the paper mills and about 50 percent of the printing plants had been destroyed. To make matters worse, the Soviet army dismantled as much of the remaining industry as it could (in the former German territories) and shipped it back to the USSR. In 1945, paper mills could produce merely one-fifth of their prewar output.[14]

In pursuing its socialist policy of widespread industrial nationalization, the government took over the previously state-owned printing plants. In addition, in the former German territories it appropriated all factories whose owners had escaped or were temporarily absent. By summer 1945, the state had become the country's biggest publisher. It possessed approximately three hundred printing houses, whereas all other organizations and private persons combined owned only about one hundred.[15] Despite various technical and political difficulties, all printing mills and publishing houses that had not been completely destroyed were immediately put to work again.

By December 1944, all newsprint had been appropriated by the state,[16] secretly to limit the circulation of the Catholic newspapers. After November 15, 1945, it became illegal to trade newsprint on a private basis. Distribution was arranged solely by the Ministry of Propaganda and Information.

As early as June 1945, a bill limiting private ownership in the printing industry was introduced. It was then clear that at the first opportunity the printing industry would be expropriated by the state. This eventually occurred on January 3, 1946, when a decree nationalized all printing plants and all paper mills as well. The monopoly on the production and use of newsprint was, therefore, already established in 1946. If this were not enough, the 1948 decree centralized the allocation of newsprint and printing paper. However, the distribution of newspapers and magazines was still organized by publishers until 1949, when a decree imposed a state monopoly on this activity, too. Newspapers could still be published by various political and social organizations, but their diversity was decreasing rapidly.

Reconstructing the Press

Despite the PKWN manifesto's promises of freedom of the press, all printed works were put under military censorship and, after 1946, under state censorship. The Communist government immediately moved to control news agencies, radio stations, and press distribution, ostensibly because of postwar shortages. Gradually, it used that control to make survival exceedingly difficult for papers that did not support the Communists.[17] Local Communist party branches occasionally went further. They issued guidelines and instructions influencing new papers' contents through the party-appointed editors-in-chief and they recruited, or at least approved, journalists who staffed the media. Wiktor Woroszylski, later the editor of the *enragé* weekly *Nowa Kultura*, vividly described his reception into the party in 1945:

> The secretary of the district committee, signed my application, asking: "Where do you want to go? The Youth [organization], the U.B. [secret police], or Political Education?" I would surely have picked the U.B. if, a few days later, a fourth possibility had not presented itself. *Głos Ludu* [Voice of the People—then the Communist party paper] published my first rhymed bit of invective, pathetic and badly formed, titled *Before Berlin*. After which I was taken on as a reporter for the local edition.[18]

From the beginning, the supply of foreign news to the press depended upon the state enterprise, the Polish Press Agency (PAP), which was instituted in the spring of 1944 under the name Polpress. The major political parties set up their own agencies, such as the Socialist Press Agency and the Workers' Press Agency (Communist). They, however, provided news only to papers of their parties. Following the pattern of the merging of Communist and socialist parties, their information services were integrated in December 1948 into the Workers' Agency (AR).

By 1946, the underground press of the Home army and of the political opposition, which was so well developed in 1944, was wiped out, although a few London government papers persisted.[19] In addition to the main official organ, *Rzeczpospolita Polska* (Republic of Poland), there were some unofficial papers, such as *Naród w Walce* (Nation in the Fight), *Echa Leśne* (Forests' Echoes), and *Monitor Białostocki*. These, too, soon disappeared.

The history of the postwar Communist press begins with military papers, the only papers that could be published legally under war conditions. The two Polish army newspapers, founded in 1943, *Zwyciężymy* (We Win) and *Orzeł Biały* (White Eagle), were published by "printing plants on wheels" and followed soldiers on their way to Berlin. Some others were printed in the USSR in Polish: *Wolna Polska* (Free Poland), *Wolność* (Freedom), and *Nowe Życie* (New Life). However, their faulty Polish language and apparent Soviet bias (despite lofty titles) repelled the readership. Even Polish Communist authorities complained about their heavy propaganda, which contradicted the more subtle approach of local journalism.[20]

The first newspaper of the new pro-Communist government was *Rzeczpospolita* (Republic), launched two days after the PKWN manifesto in July 1944. Interestingly, it was Stalin who demanded its creation: "It is necessary," he said to Polish emigrés in Moscow, "that an official paper of the Polish government be launched as soon as possible."[21] Therefore, Stalin became a godfather not only of the Polish Communist regime but of its press as well.

The newly born Polish press became basically a political press, directly and openly connected with the organizations that instituted and financed it. Thus, the balance of power in the PKWN determined the political structure of the press system. In September 1944, the first Communist party paper, *Trybuna Wolności* (Tribune of Freedom), was issued as a continuation of the party underground publication. Beginning in November 1944, the daily *Głos Ludu* (People's Voice) strengthened the Communist nationwide propaganda. The Polish Socialist party launched its first paper, *Barykada Wolności* (Barricade of Freedom), that same month. Two months later *Robotnik* (Worker), a continuation of the prewar popular socialist daily, was launched. The People's Alliance, a peasant leftist party, began to publish *Zielony Sztandar* (Green Banner) the same year. The press of the PSL, particularly its most important daily, *Dziennik Ludowy* (People's Daily), was the most popular and widely read of the newspapers. Because the daily was openly critical of the Communist system, it was harassed in ruthless and unlawful ways.[22]

Party newspapers, either Socialist or Communist—except the PSL press—had very low circulations, partially because of difficulties in distribution but mainly because of their feeble appeal among the Polish audience.[23] More diverse and entertaining types of journalism were much more preferred. Therefore, occasionally journalists took the initiative to publish their own newspapers, which is how *Życie Warszawy*, the daily still popular to this day, was born. It was soon seized by the *Czytelnik* (Reader) newspaper chain and was then turned over to the RSW (Workers' Publishing Cooperative, owned by the Communist party).

The newly founded Ministry of Information and Propaganda developed a vast network of publications, mainly bulletins, information handouts, and local newspapers. Their press runs averaged from one hundred to a few thousand copies.[24] Until 1947, more than fifty titles of bulletins publicizing land reform were issued by the ministry. Later, all governmental papers were taken over by the *Czytelnik* chain.

Following the policy of obtaining cooperation from the Poles, the authorities allowed a few local Catholic papers and periodicals to be published. In February 1945, in Katowice a local Catholic weekly, *Gość Niedzielny* (Sunday Visitor), reappeared. In Częstochowa the weekly *Niedziela* (Sunday) and in Poznań *Głos Katolicki* (Catholic Voice) were permitted to be published. By the end of 1945, the national Catholic press also secured authorization to be distributed because of the policy of national conciliation, as the government realized it could not simultaneously fight so-called reactionary forces (anti-Communist political parties) and the church. In Cracow *Tygodnik Powszechny* (Universal Weekly) appeared, which began as a church paper but was soon transferred to lay Catholics who were cooperating with the hierarchy of the Roman Catholic church. In Warsaw, a weekly, *Dziś i Jutro* (Today and Tomorrow), and a daily, *Słowo Powszechne* (Universal Word), were launched. These Warsaw papers, however, had very short life spans and were soon closed down by the Communist authorities.

A policy of cooptation into the process of rebuilding of the country was adopted toward the Jews. Although very few survived the Holocaust, a certain number came from the Soviet Union, mainly from Polish territories seized in 1939 by the USSR. The majority were Communist in orientation. Relatively favorable conditions for the reemergence of Jewish organizations were created, which also facilitated the reappearance of the Jewish press.[25] After 1945, those Polish Jews who were only Yiddish-speaking organized various Jewish organizations (among them clubs for older people and for the youth), libraries, schools, associations, the Historical Institute, and the Jewish State Theater—the only one of its kind in Europe. They collaborated closely with the "Joint" (the American-Jewish Joint Distribution Committee). There was a Yiddish daily newspaper, *Folkshtime* (People's Voice), with a Polish-language supplement, *Nasz Głos* (Our Voice); a literary monthly, *Yiddishe Shrifn*; and a publishing house, Yiddish Buch.[26] In a special booklet on the 1968 March events, the Institute of Jewish Affairs, in association with the World Jewish Congress, stated: "In all fairness it must be said that these varied Jewish activities in Poland were possible until recently [i.e., until March 1968] because the authorities were generally sympathetically inclined toward [the Jews]."[27]

Other nationalities, like Ukrainians or Germans, were less fortunate and were not permitted to have their own presses. Nonetheless, the Ukrainian minority published illegally.

Adjusting Journalism

The postwar newspapers proudly called themselves a "new press," or a "press of a new type," not because they were edited by a new brand of journalists but because they voluntarily endorsed, except for the Catholic and peasant party press, a new style of journalism. This journalism wholeheartedly rejected the idea of commercial or independent newspapers. Such sentiment was openly and strongly worded by an editorial in the governmental daily, *Rzeczpospolita*:

> Our press is different and would be different from the prewar press: it would not cover the sensational court trials, print popular romances or easy articles catering to the lowest instincts. We belong to a new generation which considers seeding campaigns, picking up potatoes, blueprints of agriculture machines, a nursery, or a new school much more important than the trial of Gorgoniowa [famous juridical case of the 1930s] or the murder of the wives of Henry VIII.[28]

This proclamation heralded a new style of "socialist" journalism. Instead of objective reporting, it sought to mobilize the masses for "building a new, better society." Such an approach deliberately referred to a long tradition of social and political commitments of journalists.[29] The main aims of news and commentaries were to mobilize citizens for the reconstruction of the country from war ruins and to gain support for the Polish army still fighting the German troops or the Nazi resistance. It strove to infuse the Polish intelligentsia with the new political system, propagating land reform and nationalization of big industry and eventually inducing some sympathy toward the Soviet Union, as the strategic ally and "liberator" of Poland from Nazi occupation.

A very important element in the propaganda of the day was movies, particularly newsreels. They played the same role as television news did in the 1970s. They showed the national audience visual proof of the success of "building socialism" in the Soviet Union and other "friendly countries" and illustrated the achievements of Poland's "postwar reconstruction." Seeing is believing; hence, their impact was stronger than that of the press, especially on less-educated people. Moreover, movies, like radio, were easier to control than was the press, because from the very beginning of the Communist rule, they were managed by nominated officials of the government.

The History of the Ministry of Information and Propaganda

Prior to 1945, Poland had no tradition of state propaganda in an institutionalized form. The first Ministry of Information was established in 1918 and was promptly dissolved. In the interwar period of 1918-1939, the governmental communication policy was a corollary of the interplay of political forces, rather than a uniform policy of the state.[30] After 1926, the authoritarian government reintroduced "repressive censorship," control of the press by the state organs after publication. At the time, this control was exercised at the central and local levels by the branches of the general state administration, not by a specialized censorship agency. Moreover, prewar censorship was open and legal; decisions could be argued in court, and in printed publications censored items might be left blank, testifying to a censor's intervention.

With the outbreak of World War II, the Polish government immediately instituted the Ministry of Information and Propaganda, but this operated for just a few days. After Poland's defeat, its activity was continued by the information section of the government-in-exile in London, which, among others, supervised the Polish radio and the Polish Telegraph Agency and published a daily paper, *Dziennik Polski* (Polish Daily). In Nazi-occupied Poland, the London government set up the underground "Delegature." Its Department of Information and Propaganda published a newspaper, *Rzeczpospolita* and some other periodicals. The main resistance organization in the country, the Home army (AK), had an extensive propaganda network, of which a special section prepared transcripts of the broadcasts of the allied radio stations for use by the underground press.

Impressed by the successes of the London-directed underground information network, the Polish Communists in Moscow decided to handle propaganda in postwar Poland not through the party organization but under the guise of a Polish state institution. Therefore, the PKWN set up its own Department of Information and Propaganda in August 1944.[31] Significantly, its first director was Jerzy Baumritter, former editor-in-chief of *Na Zachód* (Go West), a military paper of the Third Division of the Polish Communist army.[32] At that time those given responsible posts in the media were selected according to the "Communist-combatant" merits—active participation in the Communist underground, participation in the emigré political organization in the Soviet Union ("Polish Patriots"), or military service in the Polish army (formed in 1943 in the Soviet Union).[33]

The charter of the Department of Information and Propaganda defined its tasks very broadly. These included the guidance of the daily and periodical press and of news agencies, radio stations, movies, and propaganda publications in Poland and abroad.[34] The charter also contained the ruling that gave state bodies, recognized political parties, trade unions, and other legal social organizations and associations the exclusive right to publish. Publishing by private citizens and by parties opposing the policy of the PKWN was strictly forbidden.[35] Of the seven divisions of the department, the press section controlled the state-owned publishing house, *Rzeczpospolita*, and its press. By the decree of December 31, 1944, the department was upgraded to the Ministry of Information and Propaganda. As such it was charged with allocating newsprint and managing all means of mass information.[36]

Initially, the organs of state propaganda had the legal status of branches of local administration, but in fact they operated as plenipotentiaries of the central bodies—the Ministry of Information and Propaganda, the Ministry of Public Security, and the Customs Office. Thus, control over propaganda was highly centralized. The political control over both ministries was exercised by a Communist Politburo member, Jakub Berman who also supervised the main office of the control of the press (censorship), all other propaganda institutions, and, not coincidentally, the Ministry of Public Security.

Within the structure of the Ministry of Information, the most important unit was the Department of Information and Propaganda. It had several sections, one of which, the political information section, compiled information from branches of the government and distributed it to the press. The press section controlled all publishing houses, collaborating closely with censorship offices at the Ministry of Public Security. It also issued permissions to publish newspapers, decided about their circulation and frequency, and evaluated the contents for accordance with the political platform of leftist parties.[37] The technical section administered production of the press and allocated newsprint to publishing houses.

Although staffed mainly by prewar socialists, the Ministry of

Information and Propaganda was in fact controlled by the Communists. Naturally it exercised pressures on the press in a fairly overt manner, In the battle over the 1947 elections, it closed down or restricted circulation of most non-Communist papers. It also allowed a few prewar editors and journalists to be members of the journalist union; therefore, they could not stay in the "closed shop" profession. Simultaneously, vast resources were poured into the Communist press, so that it ultimately overshadowed any oppositional press that had survived all other attacks.

In June 1945, the technical section dealing with newsprint became an autonomous governmental department, the Central Office of the Management of the Paper.[38] That same month, the Main Administrative Board of the Printing Industry took over control of all printing presses and paper mills.[39] This illustrated the importance of meticulous control of all printing resources to the new political system.

Setting Up Censorship

Up to the end of war operations in May 1945, censoring was performed mainly by the Soviet and Polish military authorities. They simply banned everything regarded as fascist, reactionary, or right-wing. Although these were very nebulous and obscure notions at the time, they served to eliminate any Western and emigré publications and influences.

In addition, the civil press control board began to function as early as August 1944, keeping an eye on the contents of local newspapers.[40] Censorship guidance and recommendations were issued by the Department of Information and Propaganda, by the vice-premier, Jakub Berman, and by the minister of public security. They could be revealed only to the most trusted members of the editorial boards of party papers. The overt directive was the implementation of the spirit of the PKWN manifesto.[41] The first paper to be banned using this directive was a provincial daily, *Gazeta Otwocka*, which was accused of having a connection with the Polish national resistance movement.[42]

The decree of September 1944, changing the charter of the Department of Information and Propaganda, empowered it with "supervision of the press and censorship."[43] The surveillance extended even to governmental publications, such as *Monitor Rządowy* (Governmental Monitor) and legislative regulations and decrees.[44]

The temporary decree of the Ministry of Public Security, on January 19, 1945, established a new censorship agency within the ministry, called the Main Office of Control of the Press, Publications, and Public Performances (GUKPPiW). This office obtained the exclusive right to issue permissions to publish newspapers and to censor their contents. It also kept a register of publishers and of all printing machines.

Significantly, the information about the establishment of censorship was censored itself, and, only because of an editor's omission, the news appeared in only one local paper.[45] Nothing can better illustrate the true nature of censorship as its discretionary operation.

The decision to take over the main office of the press control sent a clear sign of mistrust from the Ministry of Public Security, which regarded the personnel of the Ministry of Information and Propaganda, despite their leftist orientation, as too unreliable for a such delicate task as maintaining political supervision of journalism. This led to a period of short but fierce struggle for control of the media.

However, the attachment of censorship to the Ministry of Public Security placed it in a bad light. The oppositional PSL protested loudly, mainly because it had no representatives in the agency.[46] In autumn of 1945, the government sought to redress the situation by placing censorship beyond the structure of both institutions. The real aim of the reorganization of censorship was to blur the ties between control of the press and the secret services.[47] On November 15, 1945, GUKPPiW was taken out of the Ministry of Public Security and nominally placed under the tutelage of the presidium of the Council of Ministers. Of course, the ministry kept the reigns. The winner was, naturally, the Ministry of Public Security; the Ministry of Information and Propaganda was dissolved in 1947.

To secure legal basis for censorship, the Communists advanced the distinction between so-called "pure," or "absolute," freedom of the press, guaranteed by the "bourgeois constitutions," and "limited" but real freedom of the press which bans the freedom of expression for "enemies of the people, reactionaries, and the Nazis."[48] The PSL and the Roman Catholic church supported this distinction to a certain extent; however, each defined it differently. The political opposition approved only the ban on attacks on vital interests of the Polish state. The church favored the ban on criticism of religious beliefs. Both were against formal censorship. To no avail.

The final stage in setting up censorship was achieved on July 5, 1946, when, despite the vocal resistance of the PSL,[49] a decree approved the existence of censorship under the Main Office of Control of the Press, Publications, and Public Performances.[50] The decree, although called "temporary," had a very long life—it endured until October 1981. Censorship itself, regulated by a new special law, lasted nine years longer, until June 1990.

The decree establishing GUKPPiW stipulated in article 2 that the office had the task of supervising all kinds of works executed by means of the printing press, among others, in order to prevent (a) subversive activities against the Polish state, (b) disclosure of state secrets, (c) infringement of the international relations of the Polish state, (d) violation of law and decency, (e) misleading public opinion by spreading untrue news.[51] From today's perspective, the most ridiculous was the point about the spreading of untrue news. It made censors the guardians of official truth, the clerks of the imaginary Orwellian "Ministry of Truth."[52]

Censorship executed control of the press in four stages, called by its agents introductory control, actual control, "postpublication" review, and secondary analysis. This practice was maintained until the end of this institution. Introductory control referred to the duty of a publisher to reveal the contents of a publication to censors before printing. Actual control checked the first printout to see if the initial demands were met. The postpublication review compared the printed and distributed material with the approved and stamped copy. In the last stage, the special division of the main office prepared weekly, monthly, and yearly analyses of censors' interventions, compiling statistics on "deviating" papers and editors, and reviewing censored items. It also pointed out "unjustified" interventions—those done by overzealous censors, and, what was worse, censors' "omissions," that is, items that should have been censored. Eventually, sweeping analyses of how the press followed the guidelines of the propaganda policy served as the material for discussion and for the instruction of personnel.

Justified by the necessity of safeguarding military secrets, control over the press was very rigid. For example, the Cracow censorship branch stopped printing the communiqué of the Polish Airlines about new local flights, arguing that because everyone who used the line already knew the timetable, there was no need to print such information. This decision was, however, criticized later by the censorship supervising board as an "unjustified and damaging intervention" that merely "made us look silly."[53]

Censors never had trouble finding excuses for rejecting requests for permission to publish new periodicals. The most frequent reasons given were an applicant's alleged ties to prewar rightists or nationalistic (fascist) political parties and collaboration with the London government or the Home army. The periodicals tied to the Christian Democratic party, as, for example, *Odra*, could be charged with "being not enough democratic" or "expressing negative attitudes toward the press which follow the line of the PPR." Similar charges were fabricated against prosocialist papers.[54] Even legally operating parties, such as the PSL, had long waits to obtain authorization for their publications.[55]

The decree so broadly defined the duties and scope of the censoring organ that it could easily operate within a variety of political circumstances, both at the height of Stalinism in the early 1950s and during the Solidarity period in the early 1980s. This was possible because censors could both censor and disregard whatever they (or, rather, the authorities) wanted.

Despite its extensiveness, the 1946 decree on censorship had been amended several times, always increasing the degree of censorship allowed. Even wedding invitations, business cards, and rubber stamps did not escape the office's control. In 1949, the main office began to oversee the importation of books and periodicals from abroad (called a "communication debit"). Later, it extended censoring to radio and television.

The most censored topic, banned almost until the end of Communist rule, was any reference to the murder of Polish war prisoners in Katyń Forest in 1940. When 4,321 corpses were accidentally discovered by German troops in 1943, the Soviets claimed that the Poles were killed by the Nazis in the winter of 1941. The claim was easily refuted by an autopsy and by the fact that all of the corpses had summer uniforms. Although Soviet guilt could have been established beyond any doubt, the commission selected by the Soviets also had no doubts—the Nazis were to blame.

Stalin used the case as a pretext to break relations with the Polish government in London, which demanded an independent investigation. Significantly, during the Nüremberg trial of Nazi leaders, nobody accused them of this odious crime. Polish attorneys were simply excluded from the trial. Although almost everybody in Poland knew the truth, Communist propaganda insisted that the murders were done by Germans. However, to make the coverup more secure, censors did not allow the publication of any allusion, even anniversary obituaries, to the names and the place or the date of death, because these would have made it obvious who committed the crimes.[56]

This example illustrates clearly how censorship worked for one side only, protecting the regime from any criticism. Despite its charter demanding a ban on "false information," censorship was not a guardian of the truth. Vagueness of the provisions of the decree allowed censorship to regulate the structure of the press system and its contents in a fully optional way.[57]

In the late 1940s, censorship was especially harsh with the Peasant party press.[58] It became obvious that the Catholic press would be the next victim.[59] But in this stage of the Communist takeover, the so-called "peaceful, democratic revolution," a masquerade was necessary; therefore, censors not only tolerated some independent papers but even demanded avoidance of using in print phrases like "Communist Poland," or even "socialism," when describing the political Polish system. Preferred terms were *people*, *democracy*, and *nation*. Of course, censors were very lenient toward Communist propaganda. Despite the censors' vigilance, they sometimes overlooked such "slips of the tongue" as found in a slogan in a May 1, 1946, issue of a Communist newspaper: "We struggle to have but one government and one party!"[60] It was true; however, it should not have been seen in public and the censor was reprimanded.

In addition to censorship control, a special decree of June 13, 1946, qualified certain offenses as particularly dangerous in this time of national reconstruction. Authors who wrote texts that were considered harmful to state interests or as escalating social tensions were to be severely punished. Needless to say, the courts always rendered verdicts that pleased the Communist authorities.

Building the Socialist Press Chain *Czytelnik*

The first major new publishing institution was the publishing cooperative *Czytelnik* (Reader). It was founded in September 1944 as the progovernmental, but not overtly Communist, publishing house.[61] The press distribution was modeled after the French newspaper chain *Hachette*. After one year, the *Czytelnik* network covered the entire country. By the end of 1946, it sent newspapers to about 18,000 newsstands.

Czytelnik's charter, enacted in 1946, stated that "the goal of the cooperative is publishing, educational, and propagandistic activity, based on democratic and progressive principles, aiming to raise the general level of social-political knowledge in Poland."[62] Its press was addressed to the non-Communist intelligentsia, catering to the tastes of middle classes, especially women and prewar clerks.

Such an "independent" agency for the production, publication, and distribution of such propaganda was invented by Jerzy Borejsza, a vigorous and resourceful emigré from the Soviet Union, who became its chairman.[63] His "united national front" approach, vast political contacts, and positive attitude toward prewar journalists worked well in the mid-1940s. The political formula of the "mild revolution" was reinforced by employing some prominent prewar journalists and editors and by using the best journalistic techniques. The aim was to win the hostile population by using an indirect, soft approach. Instead of traditional, heavy Communist propaganda, new journalism used sophisticated arguments and even entertainment to attract obstinate audiences.

Czytelnik press was lively, interesting, and widely read—perhaps too widely. After 1948, when the Communist party decided to abandon all appearances of political pluralism, *Czytelnik* became the first victim. It had fulfilled its role as a publishing newspaper chain and the time had come for it to be eliminated as a rival of the PZPR press. As early as in

1947 its newspapers were reprimanded for their pseudo-objectivity, pseudo-neutralism, and lack of a political program. They were, therefore, criticized for the very purposes they were designed to serve. The accusations were repeated in the September 1948 resolution of the PPR Secretariat, which decision sealed the fate of the cooperative. The resolution and the subsequent guidance of the Press Commission of the Central Committee of the PPR were the first documents that spelled out the position of the Communist party regarding the new journalism and the press.[64] They resulted in a call for a change in the media personnel, all of whom had to be trusted party members or proregime loyalists.

Borejsza's empire was openly criticized and was soon seized by the PPR. The Communist press growth was assured by administrative privileges. Many of *Czytelnik*'s dailies and weeklies continued to be published as editions of the Communist party publishing house, the RSW *Prasa*. It was set up on May 10, 1947, as a small cooperative, which printed eight dailies and four magazines. From the beginning it was an unusual institution—a cooperative with about one thousand shares of which a few were owned by private citizens who in fact were senior party leaders. The rest of the shares were retained by the party.[65] The status of cooperative was therefore a foil to deceive readers about the nature of the Communist press.

The End of Limited Pluralism

In summary, the first, short-lived model of the Polish postwar press emerged in the period 1945-1947. Its core was the national and local press of *Czytelnik*. Among the party presses, the socialist papers were developing the most rapidly, which was strongly resented by the Communists. Other political groupings, even the largest party, the PSL, could only produce a very limited number of its papers. In addition, some independent Catholic weeklies continued to be published.

In 1948, there were 53 dailies and 564 other periodicals, with a total circulation of 1.5 million copies. Under the Communist system even selling newspapers was considered a political function of the greatest importance, and those engaged in it were treated as political agents. Before World War II, the distribution of the press on a national scale was organized by the *Ruch* ("Movement," the Polish Company of Railway Bookstores). It operated a large network of stands, mostly at railroad stations, to sell newspapers, periodicals, and books. After the war, such an independent company was not allowed to resume its activities. Circulation was organized by the publishers and by the network of *Czytelnik*. This was not acceptable to the Communist party in the long run. Therefore, in 1949, prewar *Ruch* was revived and reorganized as a state enterprise. Immediately, it began to build newsstands all over the country. Having its own fleet of trucks, combined with train delivery, it won a privileged position to distribute newspapers of any sort. Then, by the decree of July 27, 1950, it obtained the exclusive right to collect subscriptions and to distribute all newspapers, magazines, and periodicals, except for *Dziennik Ustaw* (Journal of Laws) and a few official governmental periodicals.

Thus, in the late 1940s, the basic core of the monocentric media system was created. It lacked only an openly monopolistic journalism doctrine because until 1948 the Communists still paid lip service to people's democracy and pluralism. By late 1948 they were firmly established in the government and the army and, above all, had completed organizing the security forces, directly supervised by the Russians. The organized opposition in the form of rival parties was totally suppressed, as was its media. The 1949 removal of Władysław Gomułka, the Communist who favored Polish ways, crowned the process.[66]

There was no longer any question about the fate of the press and of the journalist profession. A new professional elite came after 1948. Instead of the Polish People's army (Communist) commissars and prewar journalists who had staffed most of the newspapers, new journalistic cadres arrive in great numbers. These young men and women lacked professional experience, but they were graduates of the party evening schools. For them the press and radio offered a chance to make it, which they took eagerly.[67] In their turn, they made the media Stalinist.

Notes

1. Dana A. Schmidt, *The Anatomy of a Satellite* (London: Secker & Wartburg, 1053), p. 17.

2. The description of Hugh Seton-Watson's classification borrows from Jacques Rupnik, *The Other Europe* (London: Weidenfeld and Nicolson, 1988), pp. 73-74.

3. The PKWN was formed in Moscow, but it was disclosed in Lublin, the first major Polish city liberated by the Polish (Communist) army.

4. *Manifest Lipcowy* [The PKWN Manifesto] (Warszawa: Książka i Wiedza, 1974), p. 5.

5. This is supported by newly released files of the International Department of the Soviet Communist party. See Sergei Kudriashov, "Soviet Ideological Influence and Control over Eastern Europe, 1945-1953," paper presented at the Nobel Peace Institute Conference (Oslo, February 1992).

6. At that time, a civil war was going on in Poland. It was induced by the behavior of the Soviet security forces when the Red Army entered Polish territory. "By demanding total submission," writes Norman Davies in *God's Playground: A History of Poland* (Oxford: Clarendon Press, 1981), "they provoked armed resistance from thousands of Poles." Vol. 2, p. 560.

The Poles felt particularly threatened by treacherous Red Army conduct toward the Home army and other patriotic underground organizations. Thousands of Polish militants had been sent to Soviet gulags. The Poles responded with military actions. The end of this undeclared war came in February 1947, when forty thousand men laid down their arms in public, taking advantage of the proclaimed amnesty. Later, most were prosecuted and jailed under false accusations.

7. Stanisław Mikołajczyk, *The Pattern of Soviet Domination* (London: Sampson Low, Marston and Co., 1948), p. 266.

8. Ibid., p. 266.

9. Its position was, however, very strong, because the Soviet Union was a superpower in the region. On April 21, 1945, the Polish government signed the first Polish-Soviet Treaty of Friendship, Mutual Aid, and Co-Operation. The treaty confirmed Poland's borders and, in exchange, committed Poland to the Soviet camp for no less than twenty years.

10. In Yalta, the leaders of the United States, the United Kingdom, and the Soviet Union agreed that Poland would be run by a provisional government including "all democratic and anti-Nazi elements" until free elections could be held. In Poland this was called the "people's democracy" system of government, a system in which, although the Communists dominated, they had to share power with the accepted bourgeois parties.

The Yalta Agreement, in the words of Jacques Rupnik, was the "original sin," the founding myth of a divided Europe. It has become synonymous with Sovietization" (*The Other Europe*, p. 63.) However, Adam Michnik rightly commented in *Letters from Prison*: "The Yalta Agreement did not stipulate the rule of the Polish United Workers' Party—that rule was merely the consequence of terror, rigged elections and Stalin's violation of the agreement" (Berkeley: University of California Press, 1985), p. 124.

11. Edward Osóbka-Morawski became prime minister, Bolesław Bierut was later nominated for President.

12. Although a convinced Communist, Gomułka never was a "Comintern man," that is, a "Stalin's man." See, for instance, Neal Ascherson, *The Struggles for Poland* (London: Michael Joseph, 1989), p. 141.

13. Alicja Słomkowska, *Prasa w PRL: Szkice historyczne* [The Press in People's Poland: The Historical Essays] (Warszawa: PWN, 1980), p. 47.

14. Ibid., p. 45.

15. By the end of this period, there were 789 printing plants with 101 rotary presses, 1,606 flat presses, and 502 linotypes, not all state-run. The State Printing Industry managed only 258 plants, but these plants had most of the printing presses.

16. *Dziennik Świadczeń Rzeczowych* 3, December 18, 1944.

17. "Rafała Pragi głos" [Rafała Pragi's Speech], *Prasa Polska*, July-August 1947, p. 3.

18. Described in Denis MacShane, *Solidarity: Poland's Independent Trade Union* (Nottingham: Spokesman, 1981), p. 97.

19. Jan Golec, "Nielegalne pisma antykomunistyczne wobec referendum ludowego (1946) i wyborów do Sejmu Ustawodawczego (1947)" [Illegal Anti-Communist Papers], in Alina Słomkowska, ed., *Materiały pomocnicze do historii dziennikarstwa PRL*, vol. 12 (Warszawa: Uniwersytet Warszawski, 1988), pp. 55-73.

20. Mieczysław Ciećwierz, *Polityka prasowa. 1944-1948* [The Press Policy] (Warszawa: PWN, 1989), p. 89.

21. *Archives of the Central Committee*, Archive of New Records (AAN), collection PKWN, 233/14, k. 2.

22. Mikołajczyk, *The Pattern*, p. 266.

23. To reach an obstinate populace Communist publications were sometimes dropped down from airplanes.

24. Ciećwierz, *Polityka*, p. 72.

25. Initially, when the USSR tried to create an anti-Western Jewish state, the Polish government facilitated Jewish emigration to Israel and supported Zionist activities and aspirations. However, by late 1940s, Stalin's attitude radically changed. This was expressed in the form of Ilya Ehrenburg's (well-known Soviet writer of a Jewish origin) article in Moscow *Pravda* on September 28, 1948. He condemned Zionism as "mysticism" and denounced the bourgeoisie-governed state of Israel. For the Polish Communists, it was the clear and definite signal that the love affair with the Zionists was over. Since then, the Jewish culture and Jewish cultural work has been integrated with Polish socialist culture. For example, at the end of 1949, the Jewish cooperative movement *Solidarność* merged with its Polish counterpart.

26. Jaff Schatz, *The Generation: The Rise and Fall of the Jewish Communists in Poland* (Berkeley: University of California Press, 1991), p. 234.

27. Lucjan Blit, *The Anti-Jewish Campaign in Present-Day Poland: Facts, Documents, Reports* (London: Institute of Jewish Affairs, 1968), p. 60.

28. *Rzeczpospolita*, December 19, 1944, p. 1.

29. Jane Leftwich Curry, *Poland's Journalists: Professionalism and Politics* (Cambridge: Cambridge University Press, 1990), p. 16.

30. Andrzej Krawczyk, "Geneza i zarys działalności Resortu Informacji i Propagandy (1944-1947)" [Origins and Outline of Activity of the Ministry of Information and Propaganda], in Alina Słomkowska, ed., *Materiały pomocnicze* (Warszawa: Uniwersytet Warszawski, 1987), vol. 12, p. 11.

31. The first decision concerning such a division was made in Moscow on July 18, 1944, by the presidium of the Communist emigres and the delegates of the Communist underground umbrella organization, the National Council (KRN).

32. Ciećwierz, *Polityka*, pp. 20-21.

33. See, for instance, Jacek Wasilewski, "Dilemmas and Controversies Concerning Leadership Recruitment in Eastern Europe," in Paul G. Lewis, ed., *Democracy and Civil Society in Eastern Europe* (London: Macmillan, 1992), pp. 113-114.

34. *Dekret PKWN* [The Decree of the PKWN] of September 7, 1944.

35. Ciećwierz, *Polityka*, p. 29.

36. *Dziennik Ustaw* no. 19, 1944, item 99.

37. Ciećwierz, *Polityka*, p. 21.

38. Ibid. p. 21.

39. Ibid. p. 21.

40. Censorship functions were initially exercised by Jerzy Borejsza. See Andrzej Kozieł, *Studium o polityce prasowej PZPR w latach 1948-1957* [The Study on the Press Policy of the PZPR] (Warszawa: Uniwersytet Warszawski, 1991), p. 39.

41. Ibid. p. 107.

42. Jerzy Myśliński, "Z działalności Resortu Informacji i Propagandy" [On Activities of the Department of the Information and Propaganda], *Rocznik Historii Czasopiśmienictwa Polskiego*, 1, 1967, p. 24.

43. In addition to preventive censorship, the Department of Information and Propaganda exercised the control of the mail, which was legalized by the December 28, 1944, decree of the PKWN. See Ciećwierz, *Polityka*, p. 39.

44. Ibid. p. 105.

45. In Sokołów Podlaski (eastern Poland). See ibid., p. 41.

46. Ibid., p. 171-172.

47. Ibid., p. 45.

48. W. Grosz, "W walce o prawdziwą wolność słowa" [In Struggle for a True Freedom of the Press], *Prasa Polska*, no. 12-13, 1948, pp. 12-23.

49. "The temporary Parliament was convened on September 20, 1946. One of the first speakers was our member, Madame Hanna Chorążyna. She gave a superb speech on freedom of the press. It was fully censored." Mikołajczyk, *The Pattern*, p. 194.

50. *Dziennik Ustaw* no. 34, 1946, item 210.

51. Ibid.

52. This particular point epitomizes, however, the very nature of formal state censorship as "a tool in the hands of authorities to shape and perpetuate an official version of `the truth´." See *International Encyclopedia of Communication* (New York: Oxford University Press), vol. 1, p. 243.

53. Ibid., p. 110.

54. Ciećwierz, *Polityka*, p. 101.

55. For example, *Gazeta Ludowa*. See ibid., p. 99.

56. Eventually, in the dramatic circumstances of an internal political fight between Yeltsin and Gorbachev, the former did what the latter could not do. Yeltsin revealed the most secret document in the Soviet archives: the signed decision of Stalin's Politburo to shoot Polish citizens captured after the Red Army invasion of Poland on September 17, 1942. The truth was even worse than former Polish accusations—not five thousand but more than twenty-three thousand persons, among them two hundred generals and four hundred colonels, were executed without due process of law, without martial court, with no interrogation. For the Poles, this order amounted to a liquidation (holocaust) of the Polish intelligentsia.

57. Mikołajczyk recalls the campaign using such examples: "There was little chance to protest widely in our party organs or in our mass meetings. For it took us from June of 1945 until October to gain a license from the Government to publish two Peasant Party weeklies, *Piast* and *Chłopski Sztandar*. We could not begin publication of our daily *Gazeta Ludowa* until November 1, 1945. Furthermore, all our publications were heavily censored." *The Pattern*, p. 166.

58. The leader of the PSL recorded: "We were not allowed to reach the street with a *Gazeta Ludowa* which showed bare white space where parts of stories and articles had been censored. The pages had to be filled as if no censorship had taken place. Typical censored items were news of international conferences, foreign options in Poland, stories of foreign credits for Poland in the United States, demands of Western powers for a free election, reports on the U.N. and the U.S. aid, stories of police murders or arrests, analyses of democracy, bits on activity of censors, any item considered unfriendly to the Government, examples of private enterprise, electoral cartoons, Jewish affairs, justice or the lack of it, Church messages, cartoons, announcements about missing persons, letters to the editors, poems, jokes, speeches by the Polish Peasant Party members in Parliament and articles bearing on the party past of the Peasant Party and its leaders." Ibid., p. 266.

59. Again I refer to Mikołajczyk's memoirs: "The entire pastoral letter was censored from *Gazeta Ludowa*. When we telephoned the censor, he barked: `For the time being I cannot stop the reading of such letters in the churches. But I'm sure the time will come when I'll be able to do something about that.'" Ibid., p. 253.

60. Ciećwierz, *Polityka*, p. 108.

61. The first members of the cooperative were Bolesław Bierut, a Stalin-man, and Edward Osóbka-Morawski, then the Prime Minister.

62. *Zasady działania Spółdzielni Wydawniczej "Czytelnik"* [The Rules of Operation of the Publishing Cooperative *Czytelnik*] (Warszawa: Czytelnik, 1946).

63. Stanisław Mikołajczyk mentioned him in his memoirs as follows: "a man named Goldberg, who calls himself Borejsza, is chairman of `The Reader'—under which all newspapers and publishing houses operated, a deputy of the Politburo member, his blood brother is colonel Różański, in the Security Police and chief of its Political Department," *The Pattern*, p. 258.

64. *Archives of the Central Committee*, AAN, 295-VII-5, k. 131-132.

65. Kozieł, *Studium o polityce*, p. 30.

66. Neal Ascherson, *The Struggles*, p. 96.

67. Curry, *Poland's Journalists*, p. 35.

6

Marching and Singing
to the Soviet Beat
December 1948 to December 1953

Stalin put Eastern Europe into a straightjacket. More correctly, into eight separate, but identical straightjackets. Nothing fit. But it did not deter Stalin. The straightjackets must fit.

—J.F. Brown, *Surge to Freedom*

By the end of the 1940s. Soviet-type regimes had been completely installed in Central and Eastern Europe. In Poland, the Stalinist era began in 1948 with the ousting of Gomułka and his associates from party leadership. The period lasted until 1954, reaching its peak from 1949 to 1953. In those years Poland, like the other countries in that region, suffered political terror, ideological subjugation, and the ludicrous cult of Stalinism.[1] The Iron Curtain became a reality—an impassable barrier to the flow of people and ideas.[2] All forms of communications with the West were cut off.[3]

Paradise Promised

Yet, at the outset, the Stalinist policy did not lack genuine supporters. The ability of the Polish Communists to offer something to talented young men and women and to make them members of a new elite was instrumental in creating a committed minority with enough members to help the authorities control all walks of life.[4]

When the horrors of World War II had ended, there was a great deal of enthusiasm to create a better world.[5] The Communists regarded themselves as the only organized political force able to lead the nation in its pursuit of happiness. The party had answers to all questions. It promised that tomorrow would be even better than today. Its propagandists sketched an image of communism using the allegory of the "desert and the Promised land."[6] This image was influential in deceiving the intellectuals, which perceived the Marxist-Leninist-Stalinist ideology as representing both liberation and a modernization program—as a scientific blueprint for building a flawless society, rid of poverty and injustice.[7]

In addition, the international prestige of the Soviet Union's victory over the Nazis and that of Stalin himself had an indisputable impact. Many writers and intellectuals were caught up in the excitement. In *The Polish Ordeal* Andrzej Szczypiorski succinctly observed: "The spiritual vacuum in the Polish graveyard could not last indefinitely. Stalinism filled that vacuum." And he explained: "Artists have to believe in something, otherwise they cannot be artists."[8] After several years, Czesław Miłosz, a Polish Nobel Prize-winning poet laureate, asked rhetorically: "The question had been not why so many were for, but why not all were for."[9] Even after many years an ideological legitimization of what was actually terrorist one-party rule was still used by former members of the Stalinist elite in Poland as self-justification.[10]

After the miseries of war, the Communists indeed offered something for all: land for peasants, full employment for workers and clerks, cheap housing for city dwellers, free education for youth, health services for senior citizens. Social mobility was promoted: Peasants could become workers, workers could become managers. Young writers and artists were lured with ample opportunities to publish, paint, and sculpt. Of course, they could do these things only in harmony with the doctrine of "social realism," or, in short, "socrealism."[11] This strange term meant seeing and depicting reality according to the party line and interpretation: the "beet and tractor literature," the Polish critics called it. Graphic arts degenerated into a Soviet-style series of poster contests, with orthodox pictures of smiling collective farmers covering museum walls from East Berlin to Moscow.

Initially, even such a debilitating aesthetic canon as socrealism seemed to offer certain intellectual values and artistic opportunities. Furthermore, the price was right: Intellectuals and artists for following the party aesthetics were well paid. Moreover, the apparently liberating ideology of Marxism-Leninism-Stalinism was enforced and sustained by using so-called administrative (police) methods. These were applied to both the so-called "enemies of the people" and the party intellectuals, although the latter perhaps could not realize the full scale of terror. However, it should be noted that Polish Stalinism, bad as it was, never reached the crescendo of terror that existed in the other East European states.

This partially explains why, despite discrepancies between the lofty aims of ideology and the cruel methods of the secret police, there were some perhaps genuine enthusiasts of the system. Caught up in the trap of ideology, many artists and intellectuals served as voluntary party controllers, media managers, commentators, creative writers, and even censors, willingly implementing Stalin's policy on reluctant masses. The ways of compelling and seducing the Polish intelligentsia to stick to the party line were astutely described in Czesław Miłosz's *The Captive Mind*.

Propaganda *Gleichschaltung*

Since the late 1940s and early 1950s the media policy had two goals: to win support from a hostile population for Communist rule in Poland and to emulate Soviet propaganda.[12] The former predominated in the late 1940s, whereas the latter rose to the fore in the early 1950s.

The pattern of political organization, including the media, had to follow the Soviet example, regardless of its applicability to Polish circumstances; this was Stalin's way of making Eastern European countries parallel parts of his empire. His Polish puppets applied the same standardized patterns in politics, in the army, and in the security forces.[13] In the early 1950s, all appearances of political pluralism disappeared. The basic division was between "us" and "them," between friend and foe. The Third Party Plenum (November 11-13, 1949) demanded "revolutionary" vigilance. Only those classified as allies had a right to participate in public life, all others were a priori excluded.

The proper political attitude, or rather its evaluation by the authorities, was critical in all walks of life. Therefore, for instance, the courts were instructed to take into account the political stance of a citizen when considering the accusation from article 22 of the *Little Penal Code* dealing with "crimes" of distributing seditious information, so-called whispered propaganda. The ruling of the Supreme Court on September 12, 1951, explained the difference between seditious and erroneous criticism by indicating not the content but a social status of the person who made it:

Not every critical remark, even objectively erroneous, is false news which can seriously harm the interests of the Polish People's Republic (PRL). Such a remark uttered by a class enemy, who wants in this way to act destructively, obviously may fulfill the provision of article 22. But the same remark, uttered by a citizen positively oriented toward the political system of the PRL, might be considered as mistaken supposition, which should be corrected or explained through discussion, or in an administrative or a party way.[14]

Nothing can better illustrate the very nature of the Stalinist system than this example. On the one hand, it was very brutal, condemning innocent people for such "crimes" as making an innocent remark about the system or a joke about Stalin. On the other, analytical articles were allowed to be published if they were written by true Communist believers and party members, rather than if written by nonparty associates, not to mention declared oppositionists. The critical utterances were treated very flexibly provided they were expressed by the "right" people.

Because the Polish political system had to be a clone of "Big brother's" political structure, the mass media could not be an exception. The media was standardized and Sovietized. Foreign news was usually directly translated from TASS (Soviet Press Agency) dispatches. Editorials from Moscow's *Pravda* served as ideological and political guides for the media, both printed and audiovisual—the press, radio, and newsreels. In its contents and layout the central Communist party daily, *Trybuna Ludu*, was a faithful copy of a prominent model in Moscow.

Some independent opinions that still could have been expressed shortly after the war, were now totally silenced. Freedom of speech, of the press, and of association, although guaranteed by the 1952 constitution of the Polish People's Republic, existed only on paper. By the end of the 1940s, the press and radio had already been reorganized along Soviet lines. Accordingly, in the 1950s there was no need for any radical changes. Only minor modifications, aiming to increase the centralization and monopolization of control over the media, were implemented in this period. In February 1949, the Polish Radio, already state-owned and operated, was incorporated as the Main Office of Radiophonisation. This new body was not only in charge of the production and transmission of all radio programs but also supervised the manufacturing of radio sets and oversaw the development of the cable radio networks.[15] The office was directly answerable to the presidium of the Council of Ministers.[16]

The decree of August 2, 1951, founded the Central Office of Publications, Graphic Industry, and Book Trade, which was to supervise all activities of the publishing houses and enterprises dealing with the printed media and book trade. The Central Office of Newsprint Distribution was established to administer all newsprint. The state-owned *Ruch* newsstand chain held a distribution monopoly on sale of all newspapers and periodicals, including Catholic publications.

In 1952 through a vague amendment to the decree of 1946, the scope of state censorship was extended. The ruling of the prime minister stated that the main office should oversee all phases of information production and distribution. The censors held control of duplicating machines and issued permits for the production of all posters. They even oversaw the manufacturing of rubber stamps.[17] The only component of the media system that was not yet fully controlled was journalists themselves. Many of them had worked in prewar bourgeois papers, and some continued to provide "objective" information. This oversight had to be corrected.

In May 1950, during a journalism seminar, a new and much more restrictive personnel policy was announced. The head of the Press Department, Stefan Staszewski, said that too many (namely, one-third) of the journalists had "prewar background."[18] He recommended hiring new cadres immediately and organizing intensive training for both old and new journalist staff. Consequently, an extensive cleansing operation was carried out among the journalist cadres.

The press was designed not only to serve as a propaganda instrument but also as an instrument of party control. The principle of a "proletarian nature" of the press was implemented by creating a network of worker-peasant correspondents. With their help, the press and the journalists who produced it became part of a "thread from the party through the newspaper that extends to all worker-peasant districts, without exception."[19] These people were expected to send letters to the editor expressing support for the party policy and unmasking the "enemies" of socialism. The Stalinist doctrine of the press called this "speak[ing] with the laboring class in its own vital language." The propaganda became remarkably servile to the USSR, imitating the primitive and brutal style of the Soviet media. In September 1951, a group of the top agitprop apparatchiks went to Moscow. Upon their return, they prepared three documents: "The Directives on How to Apply the Soviet Procedures of the Press," "The Recommendation on the Work of Editorial Boards," and "The Recommendation for Accepting the Contents to be Printed."[20]

From that time the press was directed like an orchestra by the Central Committee propaganda apparatus. The first violin, *Trybuna Ludu*, and the other performers could play only when the Department of Propaganda gave an appropriate signal. They had to obey its every order and respond to its every mood.

Propaganda glorified Stalin and portrayed him as the greatest ally of Poland. His images peppered almost every history textbook, class wall, and office. Huge portraits of him were carried in the May Day parades; small ones were printed on postage stamps. The best Polish poets were compelled to write poems glorifying him. Less talented, but perhaps more devoted or simply more opportunistic artists willingly wrote lyrics and essays, composed songs and symphonies, painted huge portraits, and sculpted effigies; all works praised Stalin's person and thoughts.[21]

By 1951, the heights of Stalinism were reached. In general, all literary and film products from the West were censored. With the exception of classical music and operas, all modern Western music was forbidden. In particular, U.S. jazz, country music, and especially popular boogie-woogie were blacklisted. On the radio, music of Polish composer Chopin and Russian composer Tchaikovsky were played constantly and were mixed with Polish and Russian folk songs and political propaganda programs.

In a manner that mirrored the pattern of the Soviet Union, an official cult of the first secretary of the Communist party, Bolesław Bierut, was forced upon an obstinate population. Like Stalin, Bierut also had to become a hero for every profession. To give but one example, the article "Comrade Bierut—Our Teacher," in the March-April 1952 issue of *Prasa Polska* (Polish Press) glorified him as the best guide for Polish journalists:

> His every utterance is for us—the workers with the printed word—an important occurrence. It shows new tasks—difficult, but how engaging. We, the journalists of the Polish People's Republic, can say with justified pride that considerations of comrade Bierut, his personal help, are the sources of every one of our steps forward, every achievement. Comrade Bierut gives us advice that always comes in good time and has an essential bearing on further raising the effectiveness of the influence of the press, in raising its role in the building of a new, wonderful nation.[22]

The style of this citation clearly epitomizes the servile attitude of official journalism toward the party guidance, which was so characteristic of Stalinism. In media, this meant following the so-called socialist realism, translated in journalistic practice as "socjournalism."

Newspapers, radio accounts, and film documentaries never tired of news, features, and photos of smiling workers achieving gigantic production feats. The preferred subject of socjournalism was the woman-hero of "socialist work," usually a tractor driver or a mechanist featured in a program entitled "Higher, Faster, Better." In addition, countless pictures of steel mills, shipyards, and mines were found in every newspaper. The positive, "life-affirming" attitude of the official media had to be adopted even when describing a catastrophe. For example, information about victims was not allowed; instead articles extolled the heroic struggles of fire fighters and militiamen. In one case of a cattle disease, it was announced only that a certain region was closed for tourism. Afterward, when the epidemic was successfully eliminated, the newest Soviet vaccine was usually praised for this success.

Following the lead of Soviet propaganda, the Polish media maintained that the government, the party, and the people were one. Accordingly, there could be no conflicts of interest, objectives, and attitudes within a society. Based on this assumption, which clearly tried to square the circle, it followed that if the media opposed the party or the government, it in fact opposed the people. Autonomous criticism from the part of the media was considered an illogical or a criminal act and was a priori excluded. However, there was one exception: Criticism was allowed if it was encouraged by the leadership and directed against negligence and laziness in fulfilling production plans, against the bureaucratic attitude of lower-ranking officials, and, in general, against "class enemies."

An example of such doctored criticism can be an anti-Roman Catholic church campaign in 1953. At the outset of the Stalinist period from 1950 to 1951, criticism of the Catholic religion was still guarded. However, even then some clergy were marked as targets of an anti-church campaign. It changed for worse in 1953. A radio commentary by Wanda Odolska, popularly called the "Walküre of the microphone," issued a warning that "a pulpit should not be a [political] tribune." Soon, the Polish primate, Cardinal Wyszyński, was personally assailed in the media. In September 1953, he was imprisoned.[23]

Semantics of Stalinist Propaganda

The force of Stalinism was based not solely on violence but also on perverted ideology. On the one hand, it praised peace, friendship, and brotherhood. On the other, it denounced all critics, labeling them as "class enemies" or "counterrevolutionaries," and threatened them with terror or, if they were out of reach, with the most brutal propaganda.

Orwell's well-known description of the "newspeak" could not be exaggerated as far as Stalinist propaganda was concerned. To convey their ideology, the Communists developed their own language, which, having the same grammar as a natural language, employed many verbal symbols, euphemisms, clichés, and terms with meanings different from those given by dictionaries or through traditional understanding. Words such as "democracy," "freedom," "party," and "election" meant different things in the Communist press than they did to Western journalists. For instance, the adjective "socialist" changed the meaning of the root word; the term "socialist democracy" meant not democracy in a normal Western sense but a so-called people's (or true) democracy—in fact no democracy at all.

The language of description in the Communist countries was filled with such generalities as "fraternal community," "proletarian vanguard," and "peace-loving nations of Socialism." These terms contrasted with the name calling used for Western countries. Stalinist propaganda loved such labels as "neocolonialism," "reactionary circles," "imperialists." Among the words most frequently used was warmongers.[24] Western journalists received a more colorful description: "praetorians of the dollar on the payroll of the press barons."

Stalin concocted the so-called theory of ever-intensifying class struggle, which demanded permanent vigilance against the "imperialists," especially the strongest and the worst of them—the Americans. This thesis laid ground for a propaganda campaign that fiercely attacked everything American, and urged the population to be constantly vigilant against the "aggressive plans" of the "imperialist West." This campaign had begun in Poland by the late 1940s.

Between 1948 and 1953, one could hardly find an issue of any daily or weekly paper that did not contain an anti-U.S. tirade or at least one political cartoon.[25] In a weekly magazine *Radio i Świat* (The Radio and the World), it was officially stated that "American imperialism poisons the air with the venom of hatred toward progress and democracy." At that time the most fiercely attacked foreign radio station was Voice of America, whose "multi-language hyena's howl was supported by the West German's and Tito's jackals."[26]

The motto of Voice of America, "We bring you news, good or bad, but always true," was publicly questioned, with examples, usually very naive, that acknowledged the unreliability of some facts or figures. On a more general level, the ideas of freedom and democracy (with the necessary adjective bourgeois) were challenged in *Trybuna Ludu* editorials and in radio commentaries.

Polish radio, as the key political mass medium at that time, was involved in the strongest anti-U.S. propaganda. A special program, "Music and News" (*Muzyka i Aktualności*), was conceived to counteract the U.S. and Western radio propaganda.[27] To make its messages more dynamic and alluring to the young audiences, it was the only radio program allowed to play jazz and country music, and, mainly for this reason, it attracted a large audience.[28] Another such program, "Wave 49," developed a special style of aggressively reading malicious political commentaries. Here is an excerpt from a typical broadcast: "'Dear Wave 49,' a female listener wrote us, 'I violently hate all those obese American warmongers, who drink our workers' blood, and now they want to spill it to earn money.'" The program's reply was short and affirmative: "You are right, Comrade Jaworska."[29]

The propaganda style was black-and-white. It employed a contrasting technique, which is expressed in the opening words of a typical radio program, "While in the Soviet Union—" and then an example of a Soviet success was given. This was followed by "in the United States" and examples of alleged U.S. war atrocities or failures.[30]

Anti-U.S. and anti-Western propaganda cheerfully made use of political cartoons. The most popular figure was Uncle Sam: a plump person clothed in a formal dress-coat and top hat, with a cigar in its mouth, a sack of dollars in one hand, and a bomb or a missile in the other. Real political personalities were also portrayed in cartoons; favorites were President Truman, Generals MacArthur and Eisenhower, and Senators McCarthy and Marshall. They were, of course, depicted as embodiments of capitalist evil. In a typical issue of the satirical weekly *Szpilki* (Pins), one would find as many as twenty-four political cartoons and eight anti-U.S. texts.[31] The only Americans who were viewed favorably were those U.S. citizens who questioned U.S. politics and culture or, even better, who showed some sympathy toward the Soviet Union, communism, or Marxism.

The language of such propaganda was simple, repetitious, and brutal. However, the dullness of the single correct interpretation of events and the sameness of the language in all periodicals and in radio and television broadcasts rendered such propaganda highly ineffective. Almost immediately after Stalin's death, the imperial style of Soviet propaganda was toned down.

Journalists Domesticated

The Stalinist doctrine stressed the role of the journalist as a political propagandist rather than an independent agitator. The first rule for a successful journalist was, therefore, not to deviate from the current political line. Such an error could range from expressing a major ideological heresy to making minor mistakes in spelling or composition. All forms of lapses could not only end a journalist's career but could even result in the journalist's being sent to prison.

Newspeople were, therefore, very careful not to make mistakes that could be taken as expressions of a hostile attitude. These could occur even in such an innocent way as having headlines that were amusingly coincidental or placing an improper picture or caption within the text. A Polish journalist recalls a horrifying mishap that occurred regarding the central Communist paper *Trybuna Ludu*. In December 1949, the entire Soviet bloc celebrated the seventieth anniversary of Stalin's birth; a large photograph of the leader was fittingly placed in the center of the first page. However, this picture separated the headline: "Churchill said that Stalin would break a neck"—and here Stalin's photo was inserted—"that of Hitler." It is not difficult to imagine what happened next. All copies of the newspaper were confiscated, the printing house was closed, and all of the printers were arrested. They returned to work after several days.[32] This example clearly illustrates the difference between press control by a Communist editor, who always had to be concerned about the context of a publication, and that of his or her Western counterpart, who usually does not have to think about what is to be printed on the same or the next page.

The Stalinist press system minimized the professional autonomy of journalists. They were to be only adjuncts of the party, intermediaries between the leadership and the masses. Their professional talents as reporters or writers of prose were appreciated only if they produced innovatively and abundantly party propaganda.[33]

In order to achieve better control over the Polish intellectuals, the Soviet model of establishing only one compulsory organization for every creative profession was adopted. The prewar journalist trade union was transformed into the Association of Polish Journalists (SDP), which turned from advocating professional rights to sustaining political loyalty. Nonetheless, journalists occasionally used professional gatherings to discuss weaknesses in the training and educational programs, difficulties in government-press relations, and the plight of older journalists.[34] SDP membership, or in colloquial language the "having the card," was necessary for employment in party or state media and even for obtaining work as a free-lancer. It is little wonder that SDP membership doubled in three years.

The journalism profession grew remarkably rapidly in the Stalinist era. The new journalism needed new cadres. Workers, peasants, and women entered the profession in large numbers. The professional journal *Prasa Polska* stated in February 1950: "Reservoirs of journalism cadres are party and social activists, worker and peasant correspondents, young ZMP [the Communist youth organization] activists, and, most of all, young workers and peasants.[35] From 1950 to 1955, two-thirds of the students in journalism education programs came from the working class.[36] These Stalinist-era classes of the 1950s formed the core of the journalistic profession until the end of the 1970s.

Organization of the Communist Media

In the early 1950s the press and radio were absolutely controlled by the Communist party. The Polish constitution of 1952 guaranteed—as did the constitution of the USSR—freedom of the press. However, the practice in both countries ran contrary to this principle.[37] During this period the basic scheme for the political organization of the Polish mass media was adopted.

In order to keep the mass media and journalists under strict political control and subject to censorship administrative control— Stalin's system of assigning specific problems to two or-three member Politburo "subcommittees" was implemented. This system made it impossible for anyone but the triumvirate—composed of Bierut, Berman, Minc (Hilary, in charge of economy)—to be well informed on the total national situation. The media became fully centralized and manageable from above: On the practical lower level it was managed from Warsaw, but Moscow always had the final say.

The key figure in the control of journalists was Berman. He behaved like Goebbels in Nazi Germany but without his flair. On regular meetings with the press, he analyzed media performance, praised good journalists, and castigated bad ones. Everyday guidance and surveillance was carried out by Stefan Staszewski, head of the Department of the Press and Publication (later renamed the Propaganda Department) who issued detailed rules on the contents and layout of every newspaper. Priority was to be given to national news; regarding foreign news, only dispatches sent by TASS, the Soviet news agency, should be included.

All media matters were placed under the control of the Department of the Press, Radio and Publications of the Central Committee of the Polish United Workers' Party. The department's most important tasks were to define the propaganda line and establish guiding principles for ideological trends. It employed the instructors who were responsible for developing guidelines on how to treat the news and how to comment on events. Censors had to use the party guidelines when editing the contents of the news.[38] However, at that time censorship as such had limited importance, because journalists were eager to follow the party line, either voluntarily or because they feared violent recrimination. The censorship office was preoccupied with an allocation of newsprint to legal organizations and with supervising free-lance journalists, creative writers, and the Catholic press.

The ideology and practice of the Communist party were based on the principle of a monolithic structure of the entire system and of direct control of journalists by the party apparatus. This policy dictated the details of the contents of the press and sometimes even the form of the articles. The guidelines were to be followed by all newspapers and periodicals. The propaganda department had a decisive voice in the selection of the editorial staffs of newspapers and periodicals and the managing boards of publishing houses.

Radio was the easiest medium to mold into total submission. It operated within the confines of the Ministry of Telecommunications (transmission) and the Committee for Radiophonisation (programming and production). Because radio was under state control, no other organization could have direct access to its facilities or to the airwaves. Its legal situation was, therefore, different from that of the printed media, where the role of the state was small and public organizations and institutions could own their journals. Prior to World War II, eleven Polish radio stations operated for a listenership that owned about 1 million registered radio sets, a number that was reached again ten years later. In the early 1950s, the government launched a crash program to increase the reach of Polish Radio. Although the number of radio sets had doubled, the authorities were not satisfied: This was still not enough for propaganda needs. Drawing from past Soviet experience, cable radio networks were started, with the primary intent of isolating the population from foreign radio information. Such a network had a potent receiver connected through cables, with single loudspeakers, placed in private apartments and peasants' houses. The studios were operated by dedicated party activists, who had their own network of "peasant-worker correspondents" to collect local news and commentaries, always following the current party line.

Chaining the Press

In the early 1950s, the Communist party press assured its dominant position over the press by implementing various administrative measures. After the elimination of the PSL and its vigorous press in 1947, the only serious rival of the Communists was the Polish Socialist party. As was described in Chapter 5, the Socialist party was swallowed up by Communists in 1948 through the so-called unifying process. After 1948, the Communists, who enjoyed a hegemonic position, allowed only two other parties or political alliances to exist: the United Peasant Alliance (ZSL) and, after 1950, the Democratic Alliance (SD).[39] Shortly thereafter, three political organizations of Catholic nature came into being: first the PAX Association, then the Christian Social Association (ChSS), and finally the Polish Union of Lay Catholics (PZKS, sometimes refereed to as ZNAK). Only the last of these enjoyed any sort of limited autonomy and independence. The PAX Association, also called "Progressive Catholics," was in reality a front organization for the Communist party, a Trojan horse among the ranks of Catholics. All of these groups were allowed to have their own presses, but censors limited them severely in both circulation and content.

The main rival of the Communist party press in the early 1950s remained, paradoxically, the *Czytelnik* press, which, as was shown in Chapter 5, had been created by the Communists some years earlier to mask their control over the media. When *Czytelnik* had fulfilled its role as a cover organization, its network of newspapers was gradually pruned. Thus, in the 1950s there were fewer dailies and magazines than there had been in the late 1940s. There were approximately four hundred periodicals and forty-three daily newspapers. In comparison to prewar Poland, the press had fewer titles but a larger circulation. Among the daily newspapers, *Trybuna Ludu* (People's Tribune), the organ of the Central Committee of the party, had the largest readership, printing about 500,000 copies. Among other periodicals, the most heavily distributed was *Przyjaciółka* (Woman's Companion), a woman's weekly with a run of 2,000,000 copies.

The nucleus of the Communist party press was its publishing institution RSW *Prasa* (Workers' Publishing Cooperative), which set up in 1947. From the start its readership was modest, which was a direct consequence of the weak standing of the Communists in Polish society. RSW's only strength came from support of the state authorities and, especially, security services. After an imposed unification of the socialist and Communist parties in December 1948, RSW *Prasa* first absorbed the socialist press. The next Communist party move was a takeover of the *Czytelnik* press by RSW *Prasa* in 1951.[40] This was insufficient for the total control of the media. Thus, on July 27, 1950, the exclusive right to distribution of the press was granted to the newly developed State Enterprise of Press Circulation, *Ruch*. In the next few years it became a distribution giant.

Paradise Lost

The commitments made by the Communists when they took power in the 1940s were obviously unrealistic. The Soviet system was never able to fulfill its promises. In Poland, the economic hardships were evident almost from the beginning and were aggravated in the early 1950s. The period of the so-called Six-Year Plan was characterized by the deteriorating quality of consumer goods, the lengthening of food queues, and a lowering of the standard of living. The party had to adopt a more cautious propaganda line. It warned overzealous journalists against promising a future Communist paradise or at least a Communist welfare state, and it ordered them to emphasize other issues.

In mid-1952, during the Seventh Plenum of the Central Committee, rosy propaganda (a prototype of the "propaganda of success" in the 1970s) was condemned as being too simplistic. This was the first major revision of the party propaganda line since 1949. It meant that the Communist party was experiencing major and real problems. The new line, which called for more criticism and less candied propaganda, was sounded on all party caucuses. In addition, an increased vigilance against imperialism, clericalism, and internal enemies was recommended, even demanded. Nevertheless, in October 1953, the president and party leader, Bolesław Bierut, had to admit some failure in raising "material and cultural levels of the living standard of the masses," conceding that the party leadership had made mistakes in its economic policy. Although such a public confession was in tune with the Stalinist style of criticism and self-criticism, it opened the way to a review of all Communist policies. Disillusionment with the results of the Soviet model turned many former enthusiasts into bitter opponents of Stalinism. The monolith showed its first cracks, which quickly became increasingly visible. These new developments open the next chapter in the history of the Polish media.

Notes

1. Within his empire Stalin was usually called The Great Revolutionary, Our Soso, the Second Great Leader of the Bolshevik Revolution, the Most Prominent Organizer of the October Revolution, the Civil War Fighter, or the Eminent Marxist Theorizer. The traditional allusion to his "steel" character was used so often that only the comparison of him to a "mountain eagle" by Demyan Bedny, a well-known poet, did render him justice.

The cult of Stalin was even spread by some Western intellectuals. H.G. Wells felt Stalin owed his position to the fact that "no one is afraid of him and everyone trusts him." Barbusse, Roland, Feuchwangner, and many others praised Stalin as a "modest, impersonal man" nevertheless a great ruler who was leading his country to power, prosperity, and democracy. See Walter Laqueur, *Glasnost': Stalin Revelations* (London: Hyman, 1990), pp. 189-194.

2. In 1952 only two thousand Poles were allowed to travel to the West; of this number only fifty-one were private citizens visiting their families abroad. Zbysław Rykowski and Władysław Władyka, *Polska Próba: Październik '56* [The Polish Attempt: October 1956] (Kraków: Wydawnictwo Literackie, 1989), p. 23.

3. In the prewar period, and even in the late 1940s, U.S. movies were very popular and frequently shown in Poland. This tradition ended in the Stalinist era. Between 1948 and 1958 only one U.S. film was screened: *The Adventures of Martin Eden* (1942, directed by S. Salkow), a story of a sailor who, as a member of a trade union, fights against the capitalist system. Wojciech Lipoński, "Political Cartoons and Anti-American Propaganda in Poland from 1949 to 1954" (typescript, Wrocław, 1990), p. 4.

4. Peter Kenez, *The Birth of the Propaganda State: Soviet Methods of Mass Mobilization, 1917-1929* (Cambridge: Cambridge University Press, 1985), p. 53.

5. Z.A.B. Zeman, *Pursued by a Bear: The Making of Eastern Europe* (London: Chatto and Windus, 1987), p. 7.

6. At this point it becomes relevant to mention an unusual justification for the reintroduction of censorship in Soviet Russia. In December 1921, Anatolii Lunacharskii, the commissar for Education, a bright and educated man, explained the establishing of a censoring agency, *Glavlit*, as follows: "We were not in the least afraid to censor even artistic literature; for beneath its flag, beneath its artistic exterior, we might be injecting the poison into the as yet naive and unenlightened soul of the vast masses, who—because of the all too numerous ordeals of the journey—are daily on the verge of staggering and of pushing aside the hand which is leading them through the desert to the Promised land." A.V. Lunacharskii, *Sobranie sochinenii*, vol. 7 (Moscow: Polizdat, 1967), p. 241.

7. David W. Benn, *Persuasion & Soviet Politics* (Oxford: Blackwell, 1989), p. 62.

8. Andrzej Szczypiorski, *The Polish Ordeal: The View from Within* (London: Croom Helm, 1982), p. 55.

9. Interview with Czesław Miłosz in *Gazeta Wyborcza*, January 3, 1993, p. 11.

10. See Teresa Torańska, *Them: Stalin's Polish Puppets* (New York: Harper & Row, 1987), particularly the interview with Jakub Berman.

11. In major English-language encyclopedias, definitions of "socialist realism" are rare, because it has been of little concern to the Western world. In Eastern Europe, however, it shaped the landscape of urban downtowns, and politicized art. Its roots go back to 1926, when a resolution called "The Party's Policies in Connection with Literature" was adopted by the Central Committee, headed by Stalin. Then in 1932, in an informal discussion group composed of Stalin and Communist writers, the name "socialist realism" was selected for the new literary style. Its realism involved adhering to an ideal at the expense of belying the present. Not only writers (who Stalin called the "engineers of the soul") were obliged to follow the rules; all creative artists, including musicians and, above all, journalists were enlisted. Their reports had to stress optimistic developments, and find "embryos of the future" in even the gloomiest situations. Their investigative reporting had to lead to the unmasking of the "enemies of the people," whom were to blame for all shortages and shortcomings.

Socialist realism was also a framework for propaganda in general. Its guidelines even regulated the layout of shop windows. They were to be dressed in such a way as to offer material proof of the advance of socialism and, at the same time, to scorn the myth of consumption for its own sake, which was no mean achievement considering that most shops were nearly empty. The main political festival was the May Day Parade. For this occasion, tribunes were erected to allow people to demonstrate before their beloved leaders. There were handbooks setting down in minutest detail which portraits should be carried and in what order (those of Marx, Engels, Lenin, Stalin, and, in Poland, Bierut). See Marek Bialoruski, "Rytuał pochodu 1-majowego w Polsce 1949-1981" [Ritual of the May Day Parade in Poland], *Państwo i Kultura Polityczna* 3, 1988, pp. 184-200.

12. Jane Leftwich Curry, *Poland's Journalists: Professionalism and Politics* (Cambridge: Cambridge University Press, 1990), p. 39.

13. Flora Lewis, *A Case History of Hope: The Story of Poland's Peaceful Revolutions* (New York: Doubleday, 1958), p. 29.

14. *Zbiór orzeczeń Sądu Najwyższego z 1952* [The Collection of the Ruling of the Supreme Court, 1952] (Warszawa: Sąd Najwyższy, 1953), p. 25.

15. The cable radio networks were usually called *kolhozniks* after the Russian word for loudspeakers transmitting centrally fed program to peasants' homes [*kolhoznik* means a collective farmer]. This system was propagated by the Soviet Union as a cheaper form of making radio a mass propaganda medium and eliminating the danger of people listening to foreign radio stations.

16. *Dziennik Ustaw* 9, 1949, item 50.

17. *Dziennik Ustaw* 19, 1952, items 114 and 124.

18. He mentioned two thousand working journalists, whereas in 1947 there were half this number. One third of the personnel had already been fired from the profession, particularly journalists from "hostile organizations," meaning the Home army and other non-Communist underground organizations. See the *Archives of the Central Committee*, Archives of New Records (AAN), VI 237/XIX/2.

19. Mark Hopkins, *Mass Media in the Soviet Union* (New York: Pegasus, 1970), p. 20.

20. *Archives of the Central Committee*, AAN, collection Press Department, 237/XIX, files 3 and 10.

21. The day of Stalin's death became a day of national mourning. A radio commentator, Wanda Odolska, in tears, swore that although he was gone, the party he created was a "granite force, a collective of brains, taking care of everything, will last forever." Jerzy Myśliński, *Mikrofon i polityka. Z dziejów radiofonii polskiej: 1944-1960* [Microphone and Politics: From the History of Polish Radio, 1944-1960] (Warszawa: Instytut Badań Literackich, 1990), p. 200.

22. *Prasa Polska*, March-April 1952, p. 2.

23. "The press is the most powerful instrument with which the party daily, hourly, speaks with the laboring class in its own vital language." Quoted in ibid., p. 74.

24. Michał Głowiński, *Nowomowa po polsku* [Newspeak, Polish-style] (Warszawa: Pen, 1990).

25. Ibid., p. 3.

26. *Radio i Świat* 2 (1951), p. 1. In later years, until the end of the 1980s, the most frequently and fervently attacked medium was Radio Free Europe.

27. This was announced by the chairman of Polish Radio, W. Billig, during the program conference of September 6-7, 1949. The program was modeled on the East German pattern, *schwarz Kanal* (black channel). *The Archive of the Polish Radio*, collection ADA/Dyrekcja Planowania 290, p. 1.

28. Marcin Czerwiński, *Telewizja, radio, ludzie* [Television, Radio, and the People] (Warszawa: PIW, 1979), p. 87.

29. Myśliński, *Mikrofon*, p. 213.

30. Ibid., p. 216.

31. Lipoński, "Political Cartoons," p. 6.

32. Kazimierz R. Trager in the Polish weekly *Skandale*, January 10, 1991, p. 2.

33. Ibid., p. 39.

34. Ibid., pp. 37-38.

35. Tadeusz Kupis, *Zawód dziennikarza w Polsce Ludowej* [The Journalistic Profession in Poland] (Warszawa: PWN, 1966), p. 53.

36. Curry, *Poland's Journalists*, p. 25.

37. In Polish archives a copy of a draft of the constitution with Stalin's handwritten remarks has been preserved. It shows clearly that the 1952 constitution was modeled on the Soviet constitution of 1936 and that Stalin made about fifty alterations to the draft. He added the sentence stating that the Poles have the right to the freedom of the press. That right was evidently forgotten by the Polish Communist lawyers; Stalin corrected their omission. See Janina Zakrzewska and Andrzej Garlicki, "Zatwierdzenie Konstytucji PRL" [The Approval of the Polish Constitution], *Polityka*, July 14, 1990, p. 6.

38. *Archives of the Central Committee*, AAN, Department of the Press and Publications, 237/XIX/10.

39. Jerzy J. Wiatr termed the Communist system in Poland a hegemonic party system, because the PZPR leadership was imposed upon the entire system (this was called the leading role of the PZPR). See Jerzy J. Wiatr, "The Hegemonic Party System in Poland," in Eric Allard and Stein Rokkan, eds., *Mass Politics: Studies in Political Sociology* (New York: Free Press, 1970), pp. 312-321.

40. *Czytelnik* became a state-controlled book publishing house. Considering its origins and pro-Communist role, it was very ironic when in 1991, Stefan Bratkowski, the dissident chairman of the journalist association, was nominated to be its new president.

7

New Themes, Instruments, and Players
December 1953 to October 1956

The great attraction for us is papers, of which we get Świat, Przekrój, Stolica. All this is a revelation for us. How could it be that it is possible to speak, without any shame, about the faults in the police, the kolhozs, and the bankruptcy of the Communist Youth Union? Two years ago even such thinking was forbidden.
—Stefan Wyszyński, Polish primate, in prison

Poles have had such long exposure to political blackout that they can sniff a change. Very quickly after Stalin's death, there was a faint whiff of something.
—Flora Lewis, *A Case History of Hope*

Never in the history of Poland had the press played such a crucial political role as in October 1956—during the first Polish revolt challenging the Stalinist model. However, the ferment among journalists began much earlier; moreover, this was in many respects a vanguard of the social and political turmoil of 1956.

Harbingers of Change

The frustration felt throughout Eastern Europe exploded in the wake of Stalin's death. In May 1953, a series of workers' strikes led to a demonstration in Pilzen, Czechoslovakia. In June of that year, a Berlin workers' uprising was crushed with tanks. The revolts only increased the vigilance of the Polish regime. The Stalinist doctrine of ever-increasing class struggle was still valid. Poland remained terrorized and was, therefore, quiet in the summer of 1953. Political oppression and control, as epitomized by the anti-church campaign, became more intense.[1] The target of oppression was initially Catholic publications.[2] Soon thereafter, on September 25, 1953, the primate, Cardinal Stefan Wyszyński, was arrested—an act that had no historical precedent in Poland.[3] However, the people used to reading between the lines discerned signs of pending political change. In the newspapers Stalin's name suddenly appeared less. The secret police became more tolerant of political jokes. Under a totalitarian regime, small changes such as these really mattered.

When, at the end of June 1953, high ranking senior party editors gathered for a regular caucus at the Department of Propaganda, the department officers were nervous and did not, as was normal practice, give directives. Instead, they asked for advice on how to improve propaganda, especially that directed toward young workers.[4] Some of those invited immediately pushed for more honest reporting.[5] They even dared to suggest that since the official press had hardly any credibility, the confidence of the people must be won. Such an objective could be achieved by expanding the scope of public information. Journalists, it was proposed, should be allowed to write about so-called "blank spots"—issues about which everyone knew but that no one risked discussing.

To understand this timid defense of professional values, one must realize that in the early 1950s, practicing honest journalism, even on neutral or harmless issues, was virtually impossible. The media portrayal of events was so distant from reality that it caused a kind of mental schizophrenia within the journalism profession. A poet likened journalists to people at sea who were told that they were surrounded by an ocean of lemonade and, in turn, had to call it lemonade. Such discrepancies virtually forced more idealistic journalists to push for "writing the truth."[6]

The party yielded somewhat to the journalists' demands, and after that meeting critical articles began to appear in the press. As early as July 1953, in Cracow, "angry young men" started *Przedpole* (Foreground), a literary supplement to the Communist youth daily *Sztandar Młodych* (Banner of Youth). A political retreat from Stalinism commenced in October of the same year. An eminent party writer, Jerzy Putrament, expressed in a veiled way the discontent that had swept through the writers' and journalists' associations. He focused on the shortcomings of the press and mentioned poor reporting and the lack of authentic discussions.[7]

At the meetings of local branches of the SDP (the journalists' association), more serious concerns and definite demands for changes in journalistic style were frequently voiced.[8] The first sign of the growing unrest occurred at a journalists' meeting in Warsaw on November 28, 1953. In a keynote address, Henryk Korotyński, chairman of the journalists' association, dared to depart from the official line. He called for professional skills rather than political reliability to determine the qualities of the journalism profession. This was a major apostasy of the Stalinist doctrine. Moreover, some other members of the presidium of the journalists' association supported his position and voiced their criticism of the poor press performance.[9]

Journalists were not the only group that had grounds to be upset. The youth complained that life was dull and offered no future. Their dissatisfaction became clear by the end of 1953. In a provincial town near Cracow, young workers organized a protest march, carrying black flags. The government and the party were shocked at this manifestation of discontent. Therefore, they allowed journalists from *Sztandar Młodych* to make inquiries and report on conditions in workers' hostels. This immediately opened a flood of criticism from people from all walks of life. A student weekly, *Po prostu* (Quite Simply), initiated a discussion on the compulsory courses on Marxism-Leninism-Stalinism. To the horror of Communist officials, it was even suggested that some changes should take place in the curriculum.

Alarmed, the party went on the defensive. The main event in official political life was the Second Party Congress on March 10-16, 1954. However, its attenders only reelected the party's old leadership and reconfirmed the basic political assumptions. Stalin was dead, but Poland was still Stalinist. The party reprimanded journalistic performance, and suggested more ideological vigilance as a remedy.[10] No new ideas about the role of the media were discussed. President Bierut admitted only that the press was "dull, grey and distant from reality." More important, in a meeting after the congress between Bierut and prominent party journalists and editors, the latter group demanded some professional freedom; of course, it justified this request with the need to improve party propaganda.[11]

The next call for political reforms was voiced during the eleventh session of the state Council of Art in April 1954; this time it came in the form of an abstract discussion of the theory of art. Minister of Culture Włodzimierz Sokorski, formerly an eloquent advocate of the doctrine and practice of socrealism in art, unexpectedly criticized its "dogmatic" understanding and implementation.[12] Under the Communist system, this was a very portentous policy statement, and, as such, it could not have been uttered without tacit authorization from the highest ideological authority—the Politburo.[13]

By the beginning of 1954, the erosion of party power and revisions of its policy had become self-evident. The most fanatical Stalinist writers lost their trust; a few began to work for change within the party. Many intellectuals, especially nonparty members, were making efforts to renew

Poland's traditional cultural ties with the West. After so many years of Stalinist terror and isolation, Polish intellectuals began to recover their lost confidence. The new atmosphere in Poland was fostered largely by the press. This development attracted the attention of the primate, Stefan Wyszyński. On August 9, 1955, he wrote in his prison diary: "Something important in the tactical line [of the party] had to occur so that public opinion could get its voice."[14] Soon, more was to be heard.

The Second National Congress of the journalists association opened in a changed political climate. In the official keynote address, Jerzy Morawski, head of the Department of Propaganda and Agitation, took a cautious tone and warned that the press should not flatter the audience nor cater to the lowest level of taste.[15] Nevertheless, Korotyński and his colleagues were not intimidated; rather, they became bolder than ever before.[16] They criticized the journalists' output for being alien to readers' interests, mentioning "half-truths that do not actually explain anything," and for being forced to remain "silent about many topics." They complained that critical articles were considered to be a negative influence; their authors were accused by the party apparatus of helping enemies of socialism, which at the time was a serious charge.[17] Even the sacrosanct system of worker-peasant correspondents was castigated, as the journalists demanded that a distinction be made between professional reporters and ordinary readers who sent letters to the editor.[18] Consequently, another dogma of Leninist-Stalinist press doctrine and practice had been questioned: In plain words, the profession demanded modifications of the information policy.

Influenced by unrest among the intellectuals, students joined the chorus of complaints: Life was boring, their dormitories were awful, and the compulsory lecture system was overloaded with Marxism-Leninism classes. They accused the Union of the Polish Youth (ZMP) [Communist youth organization] of neglecting the needs of the young people. The organization engaged in soul-searching, allowing its more analytical members to verbalize and print their objections in its newspapers and magazines. As a result, the youth press was the first to change the style and content of Polish postwar journalism.

Influence of Foreign Radio

Excessive control of the press always brings the loss of its credibility; consequently, people are forced to look for alternative sources of information. Stalinist Poland was no exception to this rule. When independent communications were virtually shut down, rumor mills and grapevines replaced news bulletins.[19] Fortunately, more reliable news sources were also available. Certain professionals—such as scholars, journalists, and, particularly, international news editors—had access to foreign books and some Western magazines. The remainder of the population could listen to foreign radio stations. The most popular of these was the BBC, whose tradition of relaying its information went back to the time of the war. The BBC news service was supplemented in the early 1950s by two newly founded U.S. radio stations: Radio Free Europe and Voice of America.[20] They were, of course, jammed, but not all words could be obliterated.[21] Although reliable radio sets were difficult to obtain, doing so was not an insurmountable obstacle for those interested in politics.

Despite a fierce propaganda campaign against foreign stations, the Poles spent countless hours listening to them. In those days, it was dangerous to publicly contradict the official propaganda. However, when people received information from foreign radio stations, they usually whispered the news to others. A prime example of the influence of uncensored information was the Radio Free Europe programs that carried revelations of an important Polish defector.

In December 1953, a senior official at the Ministry of Public Security, Lieutenant-Colonel Józef Światło, escaped to the West. His confessions were used as material for a massive and sophisticated radio propaganda campaign. Week after week, Światło reported on the Radio Free Europe airwaves details of torture and blackmail and of Soviet interference in Polish affairs. He named informers and quoted their reports. The people involved recognized their cases and gave credence to the rest. Flora Lewis recorded in her notes: "People stayed awake late at night when radio jamming was least effective to catch another fragment of the broadcast. In the morning the latest shocking details were whispered word for word in every factory and office."[22]

Between September 28 and December 31, 1954, Radio Free Europe featured Światło on more than one hundred broadcasts,[23] which were undoubtedly tailored to the U.S. political strategy of the day. Światło deliberately highlighted the issues of national independence, going so far as to hint at the unjust fate and courageous behavior of the imprisoned Communist leader, Władysław Gomułka. He presented him as a true Polish patriot, helping to keep the memory alive and building a legend in party circles about his resistance to Soviet communism.[24]

Although Światło's reports documented what everyone, even the party propagandists, already knew, they were precise in describing all the details and the extent of atrocities. Everyone was shocked, but, ironically, the Communists were particularly affected. The reason was very simple: At that time, radio receivers were still a rarity, and their owners were mainly wealthy urban people, of which a majority were party members. The terror exposed by Światło was not directed against the "enemies of the people" but against those most faithful to communism. Consequently, the broadcasts set off a chain of events that shook the entire police apparatus. The Stalinist system depended on secrecy, and Światło broke it.

The regime, which had previously tried to cover Światło's defection by silence, was eventually forced to react. Initially, he was accused of being an "American agent and provocateur,"[25] charges no one believed. Then, the government announced that some senior personnel changes would take place within the hated Ministry of Public Security. Yet, this was not enough; the outrage was too profound and widespread. It became obvious that official press and radio lost what plausibility they had.

The Stalinist paranoiac secrecy made the media totally incredible and unconvincing. The party decided to abandon its most harmful elements and to revise the information policy. At the Third Plenum of the Central Committee on January 21, 1955, participants demanded the truth about Gomułka. Ironically, in a damage-limitation speech, Bierut pointed out the defects of the press, which were caused by following the party guidelines on journalism. As a remedy, he demanded more competent and practical journalism.[26] In the final resolution, the Central Committee named the press as "the most important tool of influence on the masses" and expressed its function as "the tribune for public opinion."[27]

On March 8, 1955, a caucus of leading commentators, editors, and heads of regional propaganda departments asked for implementation of the "Leninist norms of the party." In a kind of veiled Stalinist style, the leadership of the Propaganda Department criticized itself. It admitted that the department, neglecting the "Leninist norms," had issued orders instead of consulting guidelines with editors. This was to be changed. The department would cooperate closely with journalists. Its goals would be to better inform, invigorate, and, eventually, analyze and evaluate the press.[28]

Such assurances heartened even the most reserved; the profession was promised a certain degree of independence. Upon receiving clearance, journalists began to write more boldly, which their readers enjoyed. For insiders, however, it was obvious that this change was authorized from above. A poet and a jester, Antoni Słonimski, sarcastically portrayed these new champions of criticism in journalism:

We should be courageous.
Because we may.
We are courageous.
Because we were ordered to.[29]

As the French know, appetites grow with eating. At the next central party gathering in July 1955, a direct call for "more openness" in public life was restated; of course, its traditional justification was based on the need for "further development of socialism."[30] The call for more openness was answered sooner than the party reformers expected.

A Window to the West: The World Festival

The occasion to break Poland's isolation happened during a rather ritualistic event—a Communist youth festival. In 1955, Stalin was dead, the Korean War had ended, the Geneva peace talks had begun. Ten years after the war, the Communists declared a decade for socialism, considering the younger generation mature enough to disseminate their ideas. Thus, in the summer of 1955, the Fifth World Youth Festival opened in Warsaw in a new mood of détente and coexistence.

The carnival brought an invasion of young people from non-Communist countries.[31] In comparison to Poland's former isolation, the country was inundated with foreigners. To everybody's surprise, instead of the old rules of vigilance toward aliens, the Communist youth organization recommended friendliness. The Polish youngsters felt freer. Interested in news and ideas, they flooded the Westerners with questions.[32]

The feast lasted for two weeks. Joy was everywhere, and it was expressed by dancing in city squares. The festival broke Poland's separation from the rest of the world. Afterward, a craze for listening to jazz and rock music on Western radios spread over the country. Although jazz was still not approved, it had too many enthusiasts for indictment.[33]

In the long run, the jamboree had consequences for the orthodox Communist regime that were even worse than those of Światło's broadcasts. Radio Free Europe was listened to mainly by people interested in politics—either party members or those who were already anti-Communists. The "straight" Western propaganda had, therefore, a restricted influence: It strengthened rather than changed attitudes.[34] What was more, seeing was believing. Radio Free Europe propaganda was bleak in comparison with the impression made by the relaxed Western students and young workers. They spoke freely, they showed new ways of living.

The political developments related to de-Stalinization inspired not only the youth, but also intellectuals and artists. When a Polish translation of a novel by Ilya Ehrenburg, *The Thaw*, was published, it became an instant best-seller and gave its title to an ongoing political and cultural liberalization.[35] The security forces were in disarray and the party could not keep the reigns so firmly as in the past.

A Poem Not for Adults Only

The next blow to Communist taboos was executed by a poet. On August 21, 1955, Adam Ważyk published "Poem for Adults" in the weekly *Nowa Kultura*, an organ of the Union of Polish Writers. He managed to get his poem printed after long quarrels with both his editor and a censor. The latter eventually limited his demands to transposing the poem from the first to the third page of the paper, which few people read.

The poem was long and filled with allusions that were clear only in the Poland of 1955. Today they can be difficult to grasp. However, at that time they were like lightning illuminating a new landscape, totally different from the rosy picture of socjournalism.

> There are people overworked
> There are girls forced to lie,
> There are boys forced to lie . . .
> There are people who wait for justice,
> There are people who have been waiting very long . . .

The public printing of such simple and truthful words had previously been unimaginable. The poet abandoned all ideological pretenses and admonished the delinquency and shortcomings that everyone knew existed, but that no one had gathered the courage to denounce until now.[36] Ważyk was a reputable literary figure in Poland. He was one of the founders of the literary weekly *Kuźnica*, a Marxist, although somewhat revisionist, paper; and now, he insisted:

> We ask for this on earth:
> For people who work hard,
> For keys to open doors . . .
> For a clear truth,
> For the bread of freedom,
> For ardent reason.
> We demand this every day.[37]

His angry tone was not softened by the poem's last line, which stressed his Communist loyalty: "We demand [this] through the party."

Copies of the poem were getting hefty black-market prices, and handwritten versions were circulated throughout the country. Naturally, the authorities were furious.[38] The editor-in-chief of the weekly was fired immediately for daring to print the poem. The official press cranked up a series of denunciations ("a bad and cruel half-truth"), but no one paid much attention. By 1955 it was too late for such measures. The writers' union refused to expel the poet from the association. The fired editor-in-chief boldly declared: "Comrade Berman [ideological secretary] is usurping the right to judge what is good and what is bad in literature."[39] Yet, such a challenge to the orthodox doctrine of Communist control over art went unpunished.[40] The editor was offered another position.

The controversy had become so "hot" that a youth daily, *Sztandar Młodych*, sent a reporter to Nowa Huta (New Forge), the dark new industrial city the poet described. The reporter met with young workers and read them the poem. Expecting shouts of outrage, the journalist found to his surprise that the audience applauded. "Ważyk is right," they said. "At last the newspapers have published something worth reading."[41]

By mid-1955, journalists had begun to talk critically among themselves and to seek more information. After the party plenum in July 1955, the propaganda apparatus granted certain freedoms to editorial boards. This in turn resulted in more critical reporting but it also sounded an alarm in specific party milieus. During the national caucus of provincial editors, held on December 3, 1955, the head of the propaganda department, Jerzy Kowalewski, called for restraint. He praised the criticism exercised by the press, but, in order to redress the balance, simultaneously demanded that such criticism should serve the party, and not be directed against it. In his words: "We do need less criticism, but better criticism. It cannot create an impression that the only institution in Poland that is credible is the newspaper. In such circumstances, the press acts not as a party's weapon, but as a party's adversary."[42]

By the end of 1955, the party was trying to limit the damage caused by too much openness. This again induced certain trepidations among journalists. Some were afraid of renewed rigorous party control. However, most realized that in the post-Stalinist period it was too late for a return to "old" measures. The time was ripe for change. A sixteen-year-old girl wrote a letter to a newspaper saying that her life was empty; the only ideal she could find was in Western literature. Others expressed similar feelings. These attitudes came as a shock to the official propagandists, who were still filled with disdain for the Western commercial, imperialistic culture. Intellectuals began again to speak of "Vitamin I," I for information.

Quite Simply Journalism

Young journalists were the first to become infused with the new social mood. This is not surprising: They were educated to think in political terms and were better informed about the extent of unrest among the youth. The party, in turn, blamed them for adding fuel to the discontent. As "agents of the party," they had access to party documents, which occasionally contained some truths, although veiled, about the real issues, mixed with a lot of promises and lofty words. In addition, as "transmission belts" to the population, they were subjected to questions they could not answer. Paradoxically, despite their knowledge of Polish realities, some believed in the vision of a better future. They were against "distortions of socialism," and favored Polish socialism with a human face.

By the end of 1955, a group of dedicated Communist journalists had managed to take over an obscure student weekly called *Po prostu* (Quite Simply) and to transform it into their own tribune. Eligiusz Lasota, the editor-in-chief, secured permission from censorship officials to produce a paper students could read. The party leadership realized that a way had to be found to revitalize the socialist commitment of the youth.

Lasota assembled a new staff of untrained journalists on the premise that "it was easier to teach people how to write than to teach them how to think."[43] Although it was conventional, his plan for winning readers was unprecedented in the Communist media system. The paper should *quite simply* tell straightforward, everyday truths and stop denying or omitting what everyone could plainly see. However, seeing these truths in print came as a revelation for young people and teenagers who for the first time could read such open accounts. The staff journalists became celebrities. Among them was a young man named Jerzy Urban, a brilliant commentator, who was a born columnist. Later roller-coaster variations within his professional life are a prime illustration of the curved development of the Polish postwar press. In the mid-1950s, Urban was riding high on the wave of a new journalistic freedom.

Po prostu initiated critical investigations of Polish life under communism, not accusing the system, of course, but merely showing its most explicit defects. It carried articles describing the incompetence of bureaucrats, the corruption of the officials, the frustrations of teachers, and the decline of ethics of everyday life. It looked into the management of factories and discovered revelations about thoughtlessness that helped explain the country's shortages. The weekly soon became a major voice for radical democratic reforms. Its success was tremendous. Circulation grew from a few thousand to over 150,000, although even that growth was limited by the quantity of newsprint censorship officials allowed it to use.

Quite naturally, other papers and magazines followed the example of *Po prostu*, including the organ of the Central Committee, *Trybuna Ludu*, and jumped on the bandwagon. Their journalists also looked for readers and suffered the same professional grievances as those experienced by the *Po prostu* team. The main problem with information was not so much one of learning state secrets as it was of securing the right to make public what everyone knew anyway. Journalists could not find readers for their official propaganda; thus, the readership of newspapers was falling quickly. The new journalism came to the rescue.

The most agitated group of young Communist journalists was given the name "the enraged," after a faction in the French Revolution; they were indeed enraged at the state of affairs, present as well as past. *Po prostu* was more daring than the rest of the press, but the others did not fall far behind. The press sought cautiously to expand its narrow role as loudspeakers of authority. Those judged a bit too rebellious were fired from their jobs, but some parables and tabooed facts leaked into print.

Despite official claims of an egalitarian society, the Communist party staff enjoyed privileges (although jealously masked) such as being allowed to shop in special, better-supplied stores, usually called "shops with yellow curtains" (in their windows). The newspapers launched an attack on yellow curtains. It was limited and simple, thus satisfying the guidelines of approved criticism. The reports and editorials forced the authorities to liquidate the "yellow curtain shops." Journalists saw this as proof of their power; it was possible to get concrete results through protest writing. Moreover, the issue was popular among the readership, making for good copy.

This was a remarkable development. Polish journalists discovered the joy of investigative reporting and found their beat everywhere—in small villages and towns, in factories, in government offices, and in statistical distortions. They listened carefully and printed what they heard. The tolerance shown by the authorities encouraged journalists to step up their complaints. Writers and journalists managed at times to trick the censors into approving allusions and hints that could never have been voiced openly. These occasional successes increased their stock of criticism against the censors' arbitrariness and stupidity. A film reviewer, for example, complained that if he described a Soviet film, the censor always asked for a good review "as a matter of friendship."

Jane Curry explains this sudden revival of journalism as occurring because by late 1954 the young people who were taking over editorial positions were far from the ideal loyalists the system was bent on forming. They were professionals, not system loyalists. They were more loyal to each other, even to their fellow students who had left the profession and gone into government work, than they were to an abstract system.[44] These young intellectuals were the first to push for more changes.[45] But the party refused to approve the new demands. The weakening of the surveillance police apparatus and the disputes within the party, left an opening the young journalists could widen. In

November 1955, a resolution of the Politburo assessing the party daily, *Trybuna Ludu*, and the party theoretical journal, *Nowe Drogi*, restated the traditional party guidance.[46] Nonetheless, it was too late. Millions of Poles began to read and enjoy the metamorphosed newspapers.

Khrushchev's Not-So-Secret Speech of 1956

Then, in Moscow, in February 1956, a thunderbolt struck. Before the Twentieth Congress of the Communist Party of the Soviet Union, Nikita Khrushchev denounced Stalin's cult and Stalin's crimes. These and other admissions opened old wounds and provoked a veritable earthquake among Polish Communists. Moreover, Bierut's sudden death in Moscow on March 12 caused even more problems for them.

As was customary after major Communist assemblages, special meetings of party cells were convened to hear reports on the Soviet Communist party Congress.[47] Thus, the Polish party mimeographed Khrushchev's secret speech and distributed it widely. The Western press correspondents in Warsaw immediately obtained copies of the speech; soon after, it was broadcast on Radio Free Europe,[48] at which point everyone heard about it. The Communist youth were especially shocked. The revelations about Stalin broadened their minds. They began to learn why the system had been wrong, asking the most dangerous question in the world—why?

After the congress, the diehard members of the Polish leadership, who later were given the name "Natolin group" (also the conservatives and *beton*, i.e., concrete), asserted that "Stalinism" was truly a matter of a wicked individual and his errors. Their opponents, who became known as liberalizers, progressives, or the Puławy group (also *Puławians*), insisted that it was not one insane man but the system of rule that man had generated which was to blame. They called each other the Jews and the boors.[49]

At the Nineteenth Session of the Council for Art and Culture, held in March 1956, the intellectuals again raised their voices. Criticism of censorship practices was sharp. Antoni Słonimski spoke very bluntly against Soviet (Zhdanov) doctrine of socialist realism and went so far as to demand a return to the principle of freedom for citizens. In a passionate speech, he declared: "The freedom of speech is guaranteed by the constitution and cannot be a toy in the hands of anonymous, authoritarian institutions."[50] This represented a formal break with the entire program of socialist realism.

For the first time since the earliest days of Communist rule, the press spoke with many voices. So many startling revelations appeared that it would be impossible to name all the papers and writers who contributed.

The journalists printed what was on their minds. Student theaters in Gdańsk, Łódź, Wrocław, and Cracow created a kind of talking newspaper with biting satirical revues. Monopoly of the written word had been broken, although it was still shrewdly guarded by the party.

The spring of 1956 was a time for discovering the facts about the other Poland. A *Po prostu* article, which appeared in the May 6 issue, entitled "Not only Zheran" (a car factory), was one of the bluntest attacks on the dreadful waste and inefficiency within the Polish economy. It opened a lively debate in the entire press.

The aftermath of the Moscow congress became evident when in May 1956 Jakub Berman, who for ten years had been the all-powerful man in charge of propaganda, ideology, and security forces, was expelled from the Politburo. He was accused of being a helper of Stalin in Poland; in addition, Berman was a Jew.[51] Ironically, some Polish orthodox Communists began to accuse their Jewish colleagues of being too liberal; in all probability, the Soviets advanced this idea. Flora Lewis noted at the time: "[Soviet] Ambassador Ponomarenko in a seven-hour harangue to a Polish journalist blamed the liveliness of the press on `the clique of Jews who control it.'"[52] The ruse, however, did not work. At least not at the time.

Despite all appearances of editorial freedom, the columns of the press were not made available to anti-Communists, nor to the Communist conservatives, especially those who were labeled Stalinists. There were several reasons for this. First, their views were not popular; second, newspaper editors and writers strongly favored reform and democratization. Third, and the most important, the reform wing of the party controlled the Department of Propaganda. It was almost impossible for an orthodox Communist to break into print in his or her own party's publication.[53]

The centrists in the party demanded moderation from the "enraged," but they were actually somewhat happy to see a new enthusiasm emerging within the Communist youth. More orthodox Communists had reservations about the explosive dynamism of the press and sought to impose restraints. The party's right felt the press was to blame for stirring up Poland. Older party apparatchiks were horrified. They argued that such freewheeling criticism and fierce attacks on all that had been achieved were merely serving to increase the nation's discontent. The press, they said, turned workers against the party with its exposés of the stupidity of factory management. The press was making people pessimistic with its disclosures of the dreadful state of the national economy, was making them envious with its accounts of the fleshpots in the West and was destroying their pride in the great things Communism had done for Poland. The journalists became a prime target of the party right.

In April 1956, First Secretary Ochab, a middle-of-the-roader, voiced demands that the new vitality must be curbed before the press went too far. In a speech, he joined the diehards:

> Some comrades lose their balance of mind and begin to lose proportion in judging what is right criticism and what is wrong. This has also happened in the columns of the press. The fact that they are writing against the party in the press is evidence of an unhealthy phenomenon, of a lost sense of party responsibility, of confusion of opinions. The words express concern for the party, but the meaning is attacks on the party.[54]

Some newspeople answered these dogmatic attacks at party meetings. The press invented nothing, they said, it was only reporting truths. It was not news to the workers that factories ran on impossible schedules, nor was it news to provincial Communists that their local party secretaries behaved like tyrants. But, they argued, publication of these facts was helping to restore popular confidence in the party press, and, consequently, in the party itself.

The solution for the survival of the party in such an embarrassing situation was found in a conception of "democratization" of the party and of public life. The idea of democratization was presented in extended form in an article significantly entitled "The Lessons of the Twentieth Congress," written by Jerzy Morawski, then secretary in charge of party propaganda.[55] In his words, the main role of propaganda was to "help people to think more independently, to strengthen their social responsibility and to assist them in better cultural living and in better, more efficient work."[56] Democratization was a concept of preserving party hegemony in a new political situation. It allowed a gradual reducing of the Stalinist practice of total power through partial acceptance of some legitimate social aspirations, a gradual "loosening up" in the press and in the arts, and an acknowledgment that individuals should have a certain autonomy and spontaneity of actions.[57]

The press was assessed in an unprecedented way during the plenary session of the Polish Parliament on April 23-24, 1956. In a parliamentary debate, Korotyński and Edmund Osmańczyk, both seasoned journalists with prewar experience, enlarged the issue of liberalization of the press. They stressed the role of the press as a medium for public opinion and demanded more information in newspapers. Józef Cyrankiewicz, the prime minister and a member of the Politburo, proclaimed "openness as an inseparable element of democratization." A reborn liberal, Cyrankiewicz gave the same reason that would be given by Mikhail Gorbachev thirty years later" [The] Better informed citizen better fulfills his duties."[58]

Cyrankiewicz's exposé was not accidental. A special letter from the secretariat of the Central Committee was issued to editors and provincial secretaries of propaganda: "Newspapers have to explain the party policy, but also to deal with and explain problems of everyday life, to deal with and generalize the justified demands of the working masses, which can help in improving leadership decisions."[59] This letter was well received by journalists; they saw it as an incentive for keeping their leading role in the process of democratization.

From June to October

In spring of 1956, the mood of the Poles shifted. Reports throughout the country showed a state of unrest.[60] The city of Poznań emerged as the center of particularly strong discontent. Throughout April and May a local newspaper, *Gazeta Poznańska*, protested against the shortage of consumer goods, low wages, and the miserable housing situation. The workers of ZISPO (locomotive works named after Stalin), the largest and oldest industrial establishment in Poznań, were unhappy with management. The intellectual climate of the thaw allowed them to protest, but, according to *Gazeta Poznańska*, their protests were ignored. On June, 28, 1956, the desperate workers prepared banners announcing their demands, which were simple—Bread and Freedom—but impossible to fulfill. The protest demonstration at the local Communist party headquarters ended in a clash with police and resulted in the death of several persons, including a young boy. The news of the fighting could not be hidden from fellow Poles. A brief radio communiqué could not forestall the spread of wild rumors throughout the country.

In the next days, the press, especially *Trybuna Ludu*, behaved in typical Communist fashion, accusing workers of irresponsible behavior, mentioning "anarchic elements," insinuating that there had been provocateurs, the U.S. and West German agents. After a few days, it began, however, to allude to the justified demands and "lost ties with the toiling masses." Nevertheless, when *Trybuna Ludu* published an editorial in this spirit, its editor-in-chief, Morawski, immediately lost his job. He was at odds with *Pravda*, which interpreted the news from Poland differently.

This was a clear sign that the leadership was divided and could not decide which tactics to follow: those of conciliation or confrontation. Furthermore, the leaders were not even clear as to the causes of the workers' protest. In a report of the special commission of the Politburo, the press was accused of being responsible for creating a climate of general social discontent and causing subversion of party authority.[61] A crackdown on the press was ordered. Eligiusz Lasota of *Po prostu* and

Irena Tarnowska, editor of the crusading youth daily *Sztandar Młodych*, were fired immediately. They protested to the leadership, and, surprisingly, the divided Politburo decided to reinstate them. However, the two were not grateful and did not change the tone of their papers; on the contrary, they published even sharper barbs in the next issues. Surprisingly, they had little trouble with censorship.

How was it that the editors who just had saved their skins, dared to press their penetrating attack? Evidently somewhere in the highest ranks of the party there were patrons of the critics. One of these was Jerzy Morawski, then editor-in-chief of *Trybuna Ludu*. He retained his influential post as a secretary of the Central Committee, and, therefore, could act as a protector of the reform faction. This, of course, does not discount the courage and determination of the journalists, but it places their actions in a proper context.

At the Seventh Plenum of the Central Committee, June 18 to 28, 1956, the longest in the party history, press performance was frequently, and passionately debated.[62] A main division appeared regarding the means to control the press: Should it be traditional and directive, or, rather, more flexible and cooperative. There was no question of true freedom of the press. Even when censorship was criticized, as in the case of Jerzy Putrament's speech, it was done so from the point of view of its rigidity and pettiness, not with the goal of attaining a free press.[63] Attitudes toward the press revealed much more fundamental political differences: those of how to exercise power—in a more authoritarian or a more consensual way. In a letter addressed to all local party organizations, the secretariat explained and interpreted its conclusion. Regarding the press, it stressed that party criticism was justified but that "certain papers" engaged in antiparty attacks or did not show enough vigilance against "alien and false opinions." Moreover, some disputants went too far in criticizing journalism, and they did not understand the process of democratization. Consequently, the highest party executive committee leaned toward strengthening party control over the press, yet without returning to Stalinist methods and propaganda.[64]

With Soviet support, and under the leadership of Politburo member Zenon Nowak, the Natolin group tried to transform the reformist mood into a programmable anti-Jewish purge. Nowak singled out several Stalinists of Jewish origin and blamed them for past failures and repressions. This time, however, the ploy did not work. Lacking definite official sanction and counteracted by the still influential Puławy group, the Natolin propaganda had only limited effect. However, some related incidents did occur: there were several instances of Jews being beaten up or abused in the streets. The intellectuals and the *Puławska*-allied liberal press took a stand against this anti-Jewish mood. The anti-Jewish Stalinist propaganda that was fostered throughout the entire Eastern bloc was less intense in Poland than elsewhere, probably because of the composition of the core of the Polish party. In Poland there were no anti-Jewish show trials, and the purges of Jews took place quietly.[65]

The internal evaluation of media performance, completed by the propaganda department that autumn, found that the resolutions of the Seventh Plenum and the contents of the letter to journalists paralyzed the editorial boards of major newspapers. The party did not want to go that far. Therefore, the next policy memo from the head of the department called for more "criticism in the press" and the intensification of "the battle for democratization." This example reveals the party method of operating like the driver of a car who pushes and releases the gas pedal.[66]

However, in real life such mechanical control does not work. The journalists continued to push for more freedom. The next occasion came at a plenary meeting in September of the presidium of the SDP. Those gathered formulated many recommendations in regard to the style of party leadership, local party organization, and even censorship. They demanded party support for journalistic criticism of the negative social phenomena. The journalist association sent an appeal to the Council of Ministers to set up a commission to assess censorship, because, it stated, "erroneous decisions of the Main Office of Press Control [censorship] cannot be excused from public scrutiny." Therefore, the SDP went further than the official party line and openly supported those within the party leadership who opted for more liberalization of the press. After this, the division of leadership between the more liberal (*Puławian*) group and the more conservative (*Natolin*) one was well established.

Even more important than journalist discontent was the silent revolt of young people. They simply began to behave in a normal, easy way. And in such a simple way, a spontaneous social movement gradually eroded the official doctrine of how the youth should behave, what they should wear, and what music they should listen to. This meant a fundamental retreat from the Stalinist aspiration to have total control of the society.

October

The Poznań events of June 1956 intensified the intraparty struggle, in which *Po prostu*'s journalists effectively supported the democratic changes. They asked for the "elimination of spheres of silence in the press and in public life"—using Gorbachev's term, they demanded glasnost. They soon found followers. In autumn, the popular unrest swept the country. Radical intellectuals, especially those of the clubs founded by *Po prostu*, talked about revolution. Poland was in ferment: "No Bread Without Freedom, No Freedom Without Bread" was the headline of an account of a rally posted on the bulletin boards at Warsaw University.

People insisted on more radical reforms in all walks of life. The most radical request was for the abolition of press censorship. On September 20, 1956, the executive committee of the Association of Polish Journalists passed a resolution against "the unjust and unjustifiable" interference of the Main Office of Press Control. The creation of a committee of journalists whose function would be to oversee the activities of the main office was proposed. The association also denounced interference by some party organs in editorial affairs, their lack of comprehension of the new role of the press, and, above all, their hostility toward journalists.[67]

On October 18, the vice-chairman of the Peasant party went so far as to call for the abolition of censorship. The Warsaw branch of the Communist youth organization made the same demand. This option had sympathizers even within the Main Office of Press Control. The Poznań censors voted in a resolution urging that they be disbanded. Warsaw censors adopted a similar proclamation; however, their declaration was censored from the newspapers by the highest censorship authorities.[68]

In this revolutionary mood of the country and the party, the Eighth Plenum of the Central Committee opened; it was later known as the October Plenum. The meeting began on October 19, 1956. By then, the reform leaders were in touch with the former party leader, Władysław Gomułka, who had been deposed in 1949. He was perhaps the only person who could control the deeply divided party.

The next twenty-four hours brought Poland to the brink of catastrophe. At the Warsaw City Party Committee, Stefan Staszewski drew up plans in case of an emergency. Communications had to be direct, for there could be no risk of treacherous jamming of normal party channels. He had no trouble finding volunteers to serve as messengers, speakers at mass meetings, and organizers. The journalists who had called themselves enraged were ready and eager to help. People stayed by the radio and grabbed newspapers as they arrived at the kiosks.

At the plenum, which was attended by the uninvited Soviet leader Khrushchev, accompanied by some dozen generals and senior apparatchiks, the confrontation went on all night. Khrushchev was particularly infuriated by the freedom of the Polish press; he observed that *Po prostu* had become the voice of anti-Soviet propaganda. His tone was angry, and rumors spread that the Red Army was marching toward Warsaw. Gomułka in turn threatened to broadcast Khrushchev's speech on the radio. Word was sent to the Warsaw radio station alerting the staff to prepare for a possible broadcast. Both sides knew what this could mean—at the least, a nationwide demonstration against the Soviet Union and possibly a war between Poland and the USSR. The Polish army announced its combat readiness. Therefore, when eventually Gomułka assured the Soviet delegation that attacks on the Soviet Union in the Polish press would soon be curbed, Khrushchev backed down from his threats, and an agreement was reached. He flew home to Moscow; Gomułka was elected first secretary of the Communist party. On October 20, when Gomułka appeared in public to accept the cheers of the crowds of Warsaw citizens, Lasota, the twenty-six-year-old editor of *Po prostu*, was at his side.

On Sunday evening, October 22, the newspapers put out special editions to announce the results of the plenum. Hundreds of taxi drivers volunteered to take copies to distribution points in the city and to railroad stations for shipment to the provinces. The papers were free. When the official press could not carry certain kinds of information, it was spread among the people by Radio Free Europe (RFE). At times its bulletins were pinned on university bulletin boards, which became rallying points for the entire city.[69] What the censors took out of the newspapers, the students put up on the boards.

Immediately after the October Plenum the press set out to prove that Poland was a nation of many voices. Within the profession, divisions between conservatives and liberals emerged in open warfare. The annual plenary assembly of the journalists' association, which meet from November 30 to December 2, 1956, adopted a resolution for a more open spirit. The liberal majority in the regional SDP executive boards was overwhelming. Journalists advocated the dissolution of the monopolistic party publishing house in favor of new smaller, independent publishers. Some pressed the SDP to prepare a draft of a press law controlling censorship in Poland; others felt such a law would only lead to increased party control over the profession.[70] In general, they were concerned with developing regulations to keep unskilled and unethical individuals out of journalism.

From the onset of new rule, Gomułka made it clear that the press might be an instrument of democratization but only under vigilant party guidance. The first occasion for such a reminder was a caucus of editors held on October 29, 1956. Gomułka told them that the press could be a "vanguard of democratization," but because it should now ease the tensions, it should "present facts in a reasonable, balanced way."[71] On December 10, 1956, Gomułka met with leading journalists. The new chairman of the SDP, Stanisław Brodski, demanded more independence and autonomy.[72] In response Gomułka stressed the role of party leadership,[73] which was received negatively by the journalists. He stiffened his position even further in a speech to the Central Commission of Party Control. At a meeting in December 1956, he emphasized the accountability of party journalists to the party organization, which ended their short period of relative independence.

Cooling Down

In these years of struggle within the Communist bloc, the angry intellectuals in Poland acted as a focus for the general discontent. Just as Gomułka had influenced the remainder of the Communist leadership, so the Warsaw intellectuals had powerfully influenced every member of the intelligentsia behind the Iron Curtain.[74]

For professional journalists October was a period in which they could achieve celebrity status. They felt they had real power within the contexts of both the party and the population at large. In some communities, journalists headed party committees, were dominant in the regional government council, or were leaders of newly organized intelligentsia associations. A myth about the role of the profession grew to the point of creating two contradictory images of their dependence.[75] One image presented journalists as chess figures in the hands of certain political players with assigned roles, even those of "revolutionaries" and "democrats." The second perceived image was that of a journalist profession characterized by total spontaneity. Journalists allegedly acted as representatives of society and oppressed masses, as an independent force on the Polish political scene, and almost as a prime mover of the revolutionary changes of 1956.

It seems that both images were false. Journalists were neither fully independent nor solely instruments of politics. But if they played a definite role, they played it well and for the benefit of the country. The easing of press restrictions was not the result of calculated efforts of the press. It was, rather, an optional historical accident. For a brief period, the Communist party was split into openly competing factions.

The fragmentation of power after Stalin's death was actually a momentary crack in the steady centralization of control and stabilization of authority that characterized the advance of communism in Poland. Gomułka found this split intolerable. After the October fever, he remained a popular hero in Poland. He promised changes in politics, the economy, and culture. However, immediately upon receiving mass support in the January 1957 elections, he began to brake. As Frank Gibney picturesquely described in *The Frozen Revolution*, "In his condition of constant political weighting and juggling, Gomułka welcomed the angry young intellectuals as cordially as a veteran tight-rope walker greets a couple of friendly helpers who insist on testing the strength of the wire by jumping on it in the middle of the act.[76] But young party intellectuals and journalists had no desire to stop the reforms. They had a vision of an open, pluralistic form of Marxist socialism, a self-governing workers' democracy. The pages of *Po prostu*, especially from October 1956 to June 1957, made fascinating and lively reading. The party hierarchy did not feel at ease with the incisive commentaries of the "Heretic," which appeared under the title "2 + 2 = 4." It did stop asking the provocative question, Would it not be best to dissolve the entire Communist party? In reality, it was the weekly that was dissolved.

In order to do so, so-called administrative measures were necessary. Administrative measures, in contrast to so-called party measures, meant using the repressive law, especially the police, the courts, and censorship. Censorship during the heights of Stalinism was less necessary than it had been in the 1940s. It was even useful for media personnel as a means to protect journalists and printers from their mistakes, the consequences of which at that time could be very dangerous and far-reaching.[77] The editors and journalists were so afraid and so dedicated that they censored themselves.

By the end of 1956 the struggle for suppression or substantial reduction of press control remained undecided. From October 1956 until autumn 1957, the functions of censorship were restricted to a very few, definite topics: (1) military information, (2) news concerning foreign affairs liable to provoke the Soviet Union, and (3) expression of opinions openly opposed to communism as a philosophy and a political system, as well as attacks against the government and its members.[78] The tactical retreat from strict party control and censorship was, however, short-lived. By autumn of 1957, the party embarked cautiously but firmly on a new policy of taking control over the press into its own hands. Poland was to cool down, the press was not to heat the public mood, and journalists had to be cooled, too. When the still-divided party was unable to enforce straight direction and control, censorship again became the major tool for keeping the press in line.

More important were the changes in society. Young people enjoyed vanguard paintings, cabarets, existential theater and philosophy, records, art, and occasionally Coca-Cola. The Union of Polish Youth (ZMP) had 3 million members in mid-1956; after October of that year its membership was barely thirty thousand.

Contacts with the West were partially restored; the jamming stations were silent. University libraries received foreign books and periodicals; movie theaters again screened Hollywood and Western films; theaters played the newest Paris dramas. Some Western newspapers, such as the *Times* (London) or *Le Monde*, could either be purchased or were available in public reading rooms. Throughout 1956 the cultural life in Poland remained freer than at any time since the Communist takeover.

Censorship eased and the social sciences discovered new topics that could be investigated. New public opinion research centers were also established, and the results were published.

Notes

1. The Catholic church was attacked less for ideological reasons of being a bridge to the other world than for political reasons stemming from its attachment to the Vatican, a part of the Western world.

2. The Cracow *Tygodnik Powszechny*, the most prestigious of the Catholic periodicals of the day, refused to print a large funeral photograph of Stalin and was relocated to Warsaw where the proregime PAX organization, which had been excommunicated by the church, continued with its publication.

3. Even at the height of the Stalinist era, the Polish Communists had to compromise with the church. A 1950 agreement guaranteed freedom of worship, religious education, and the existence of a church press. It is hardly necessary to add that these promises were not kept. However, the agreement constituted a certain precedent for mutual coexistence between the Communist state and the church. When all appearances of observance of the agreement by the authorities disappeared, Cardinal Wyszyński proclaimed *Non Possumus*—in plain words, enough is enough—which led to his imprisonment.

4. Flora Lewis, *A Case History of Hope: The Story of Poland's Peaceful Revolutions* (New York: Doubleday, 1958), p. 11.

5. *Archives of the Central Committee*, Archives of New Records (AAN), VI 237/XIX: 4, k. 37.

6. Adam Przeworski notes that this is why in Eastern Europe the call for "truth" had become at least as important as the demand for bread. "The 'East' Becomes the 'South'. The 'Autumn of the People,'" *PS Political Science and Politics* 1, March 1991, p. 21.

7. Putrament's address followed the party line, nevertheless, it added new elements. He was familiar with the situation in the Soviet Union and as a writer was more susceptible to the incoming changes. However, rather than being a party maverick, he merely ran in front of the wagon. Ironically, Putrament was one of the four "captive" intellectuals portrayed in Miłosz's essay "The Captive Mind." See Jerzy Putrament, "Wystąpienie na IX Plenum" [Address to the Ninth Plenum], *Nowe Drogi* 10, 1953, pp. 155-156.

8. "Narady wojewódzkie i zebrania redakcyjne" [Voivodship's Consultations and Editorial Boards' Meetings], *Prasa Polska* 7, 1953, p. 1.

9. It is significant that as Korotyński recalls, "the journalists' demands for Vitamin I [I for Information] were supported and even suggested by the deputy head of the Press Department, Jerzy Kowalewski. For such an action, he had to at least have Berman's approval." Henryk Korotyński, *Trzy czwarte prawdy* [Three-Fourths of the Truth] (Kraków: Wydawnictwo Literackie, 1987), p. 132.

10. The keynote address by Bolesław Bierut and a speech by Jakub Berman were printed in *Nowe Drogi* 3, 1954, pp. 73 ff and p. 393 ff.

11. *Archives of the Central Committee*, AAN, VI 237/V-196, k. 1-23.

12. *Nowa Kultura* 17, 1954, p. 3.

13. The next occasion for criticism of socialist realism came in Warsaw in June 1954 at the Sixth Congress of the Union of Polish Writers. A writer and historian, Paweł Jasienica, using somewhat Aesopian language, unveiled the shortcomings of the allegedly perfect "socialist" reality. This was understood as a call for more ethical writing and less censorship.

14. See note 1 above.

15. *Prasa Polska* 5, 1954, p. 6.

16. Jane Leftwich Curry, *Poland's Journalists: Professionalism and Politics* (Cambridge: Cambridge University Press, 1990), p. 48

17. Stefan Bankowski, *Stenogram Zjazdu SDP* [The Minutes of the Congress of the SDP], typescript, Warsaw, May 1954, p. 125.

18. Curry, *Poland's Journalists*, p. 43.

19. The gap between the official vision of socialism and the gloomy reality provoked widespread frustration, outrage, and distrust of the authorities; these feelings were sustained by the news from the foreign radio stations.

20. Radio Free Europe was established by a group of private citizens in December 1948 for the purpose of conducting a propaganda campaign against six Soviet-dominated countries in Central and Eastern Europe. Robert Holt explained the purpose of the station: "When it went on the air, RFE had for a goal the liberation of captive nations. It was explicitly engaged in a campaign of `psychological warfare'." Robert T. Holt, *Radio Free Europe* (Minneapolis: University of Minnesota Press, 1958), p. 14.

Donald R. Browne called RFE a "part of the U.S. Cold War arsenal," stressing that it was "charged with the task of encouraging and exploiting the discontent in Communist nations." To support this thesis, he reminded his reader that the sister radio station, Radio Liberty, which broadcast to the USSR, was initially named "Radio Liberation from Bolshevism." Donald R. Browne, *International Radio Broadcasting: The Limits of the Limitless Medium* (New York: Praeger, 1982), p. 135.

21. By 1955, Radio Free Europe had twenty-nine transmitters with a total power of more than a million watts. Browne, *International Radio Broadcasting*, p. 136. Holt explains why the jamming was not being able to eliminate RFE: "In order to effectively blot out RFE's short-wave transmitters operating on twenty-one different frequencies on an almost around-the-clock basis, year in and year out, the Soviets would need about twenty times that number of sky-wave jammers plus many local jammers. Even if they forgot about all other Western broadcasts, they could not marshal the necessary transmitters to accomplish this task." Holt, *Radio Free Europe*, p. 119.

22. Lewis, *A Case History*, p. 43.

23. Allegedly, the tapes of Światło's testimony appeared by chance on the desk of the director of the RFE, Jan Nowak-Jeziorański. See his memoirs, *Wojna w eterze* [War on the Airwaves] (London: Odnowa, 1988), p. 132.

24. Lewis explained: "Światło has worked personally on the case of Władysław Gomułka. It was Światło who arrested the fallen leader in August 1951, and Światło took part in the interrogations. In his broadcasts, the defector told of the efforts to frame the erstwhile party chief and to extract a confession, and he told

of Gomułka's stubborn refusal to capitulate." Lewis, *A Case History*, p. 43.

25. The transcripts of Światło's confessions were even dropped from special balloons sent in the direction of Poland.

26. RFE itself drew such conclusions about the impact of the Światło broadcasts: "It appears unlikely that Światło's broadcasts `forced´ the regime to carry out a re-organization which in any case followed a pattern set by the USSR. However, it seems reasonable to conclude that the Światło broadcasts were an important factor both in the timing of these actions and in the selection and punishment of scapegoats. The regime was anxious to provide the public with an official explanation for his revelations and convince party members that those responsible would be punished. These actions are explicable only on the assumption that a large part of the Polish people were aware of the Światło broadcasts." "Poland: Regime Press and Radio Response to Western Broadcasts, September-December 1954," *RFE Report* 9, March 1955, p. 22.

27. *Uchwały Komitetu Centralnego PZPR od II do III Zjazdu* [The Resolutions of the Central Committee of the Polish United Workers Party from the Second to the Third Congress] (Warszawa Książka i Wiedza, 1959), p. 60.

28. *Archives of the Central Committee*, AAN, IV 237/V 213, k. 26.

29. Quoted in A. Tel, "Bęben i nokturny Szopena" [A Drum and Chopin's Nocturnes], *Prasa Polska* 2, 1955, p. 25.

30. The calls for *jawność* (openness, publicity), a Polish equivalent of glasnost, had been voiced sporadically since the end of 1953.

31. More than one thousand young Frenchmen, over three thousand Englishmen, thousands of Germans, Swedes, and Danes, several hundred Egyptians and Indians—more than thirty thousand young people came from 114 countries.

32. Lewis described a very meaningful visit of three young Warsaw workers who were party members to the offices of *Sztandar Młodych*, the official Communist youth paper. They marched in and demanded to see the editor, asking: "We want to know why do you lie?" As they later explained, young workers from the Renault factory told them they were much better off than Polish workers. Hence, they asked, why had the paper written for years that workers in the West were oppressed and poverty-stricken by capitalism when obviously they lived much better than the Poles. Lewis, *A Case History*, p. 58.

33. Students procured X-ray plates from laboratories to make music recordings on home-built machines.

34. Moreover, for the overwhelming amount of propaganda in their lives, Polish listeners, paradoxically, developed a certain insusceptibility to tirades and persuasion, even on the value of Western democracy.

35. See Ilya Ehrenburg, *The Thaw* (English edition, London: MacGibbon & Kee, 1961).

36. Walter Laqueur, *Europe in Our Time: A History, 1945-1992* (New York: Viking, 1992), p. 302.

37. Translation in Lewis, *A Case History*, p. 76.

38. It was told that Berman leaped from his desk when he read the poem, shouting "I will teach him [Ważyk] a lesson. I will run him out of the party." Lewis, *A Case History*, p. 76.

39. Ibid., p. 77

40. This challenge was partially induced by Berman, when in 1954 the Council of Art and Culture promised, with Berman's encouragement or at least permission, that every artist is entitled to his or her own artistic truth.

41. Lewis, *A Case History*, p. 87-88.

42. Ibid., p. 87.

43. Ibid., p. 88

44. Curry, *Poland's Journalists*, p. 41.

45. Manuscripts that could not be printed were sometimes widely circulated in typewritten copies.

46. *Archives of the Central Committee*, AAN, VI 237/VIII-363, k. 54.

47. The plenum on March 20, 1956, elected a negotiated figure, a middle-of-the-roader, Edward Ochab, as first secretary. Two other candidates were Zenon Nowak, a hardliner, and Roman Zambrowski, a liberal.

48. In the battle for change within the PZPR, the reform Communists not only circulated the secret speech throughout the party but also handed its text to Western journalists who spread it across the front pages of the world newspapers.

49. Roman Zambrowski, a son of a rabbi, formed the *Puławy* group. See Lucjan Blit, *The Anti-Jewish Campaign in Present-Day Poland: Facts, Documents, Reports* (London: Institute of Jewish Affairs, 1986), p. 16.

50. Oscar Halecki, ed., *Poland* (New York and London: Praeger and Stevens & Sons, 1957), p. 571.

51. The Soviet Embassy contributed to this campaign of anti-semitism which was launched by certain hard-liners, who thought that "they could channel hatred for Communism into hatred for Jews." Lewis, *A Case History*, p. 121.

52. Ibid.

53. Ibid., p. 126.

54. Ibid., p. 137.

55. *Nowe Drogi* 3, 1956, p. 8.

56. Ibid.

57. Zbysław Rykowski and Wiesław Władyka, *Polska Próba. Październik '56* [The Polish Attempt: October 1956] (Kraków: Wydawnictwo Literackie, 1989), pp. 293-294.

58. "W Sejmie o prasie" [In the Parliament About the Press], *Prasa Polska* 5, 1956, p. 1.

59. *Archives of the Central Committee*, AAN, 233-XIX-68, k. 3.

60. Holt, *Radio Free Europe*, p. 174.

61. Gierek's *Report* and the minutes of the discussion about it; *Archives of the Central Committee*, AAN, VI 237/V-274.

62. Of eighty-six main speeches, fifty-three—almost two-thirds—mentioned or elaborated on press issues. One-third of these contained open attacks on "too liberal" journalism (especially the weekly *Po prostu*), one-third were balanced, and about one-third supported the press. Analysis done by J. Lubiński, *Zasady i cele polityki PZPR w dziedzinie komunikowania w latach 1948-1971* [The Principles and Goals of the Information Policy of the Polish United Workers Party in the Years 1948-1971], unpublished doctoral dissertation (Cracow: Jagiellonian University, 1988), vol. 1, p. 217.

63. Putrament said "Censorship is not a way to guide the press," meaning that it was too specific and too narrow-minded for the task. *Archives of the Central Committee,* AAN, VI 237/II, k. 748.

64. *Komitet Centralny—do wszystkich organizacji partyjnych* [The Central Committee to All Party Cells] (handout), August 1956, p. 3.

65. Jaff Schatz, *The Generation: The Rise and Fall of the Jewish Communists in Poland* (Berkeley: University of California Press, 1991), p. 262.

66. *Archives of the Central Committee,* AAN, VI 237-VIII-364, k. 107.

67. See Antoni Buzek, *How the Communist Press Works* (New York: Praeger, 1964), p. 145.

68. Ibid.

69. "In 1956, RFE felt that it was operating in an entirely new situation. It was broadcasting to a country in which the Communist Party had achieved substantial independence from Moscow and in which the Communist government was no longer looked upon by the people as a tool of foreign domination." Holt, *Radio Free Europe,* p. 198.

70. Jerzy Mond, "Uwagi i refleksje o terenie" [Observations and Remarks About the Provincial Situation] *Prasa Polska* 4, 1956, p. 2.

71. Henryk Korotyński, "Spotkania W. Gomułki z dziennikarzami: 1956-1957" [Meetings of Gomułka with Journalists, 1956-1957], *Zeszyty Prasoznawcze* 2, 1986, p. 52.

72. The resolution of the Third Congress of the SDP called for the press law, liberalization of censorship, and more autonomy for editorial boards.

73. *Archives of the Central Committee,* AAN, VI 327/VV-246, k. 195.

74. Frank Gibney, *The Frozen Revolution. Poland: A Study in Communist Decay* (New York: Farrar, Straus and Cudahy, 1959), p. 120.

75. Curry, *Poland's Journalists,* p. 62.

76. Gibney, *The Frozen Revolution,* p. 106.

77. Here is but one example. In the personal file of Jan Kalkowski, the reputed Cracow journalist, a letter of reprimand from September 11, 1952, has been preserved that pointed out that he made a "serious political mistake" by being careless with the arrangement of quotation marks in the headline "Appeal from the bastions of `socialism'" because the quotation marks were placed only around the word *socialism* and not around the phrase *bastions of socialism.* "Obituary of Jan Kalkowski," *Zeszyty Prasoznawcze* 4, 1989, p. 6.

78. Buzek, *How the Communist Press Works,* p. 146.

8

Under the Baton of Gomułka
January 1957 to March 1968

The second October was a minor tragedy of errors. The young writers on Po prostu *refused to abandon their belief that public opinion might yet buttress Gomułka against the ever-recurrent attacks from orthodoxy. "Irresponsible children," snorted the older party pundits.*

—Flora Lewis, *A Case History of Hope*

Post-war Polish history has run in cycles, each lasting between ten and fourteen years. The cycle begins with the arrival of a new party leadership, promising more democracy, more economic prosperity, and a grand extension of human liberty. Gradually the new authorities drift off course.

—Neal Ascherson, *The Struggles for Poland*

The public mood of October 1956 lasted much more than a month. The young journalists enjoyed investigative reporting and demanded further reforms. This was too much for the party leadership. The press was a symbol of the drive leading to the events of that October; later it became a self-appointed tribune of what those events were to mean.

Undoing October 1956

The closure of *Po prostu* in October 1957 marked the end of this mood and invited disillusionment with Władysław Gomułka. Despite the high hopes most Poles had for Gomułka, he was more a devoted Communist than a reformer. The journalists became his main hindrance in returning to Marxist-Leninist normalcy. Immediately after the January 1957 elections to the Polish parliament (which were overwhelmingly for Gomułka), he began an offensive against the undisciplined press and called for a return to the established information policy.

At the end of February, an assembly of the regional Communist organization in Wrocław violently attacked journalists for their emancipation from party control. Subsequently, the Politburo criticized the party daily, *Trybuna Ludu*, and ordered it to follow the party line more strictly. To make the paper more responsible, a new editor-in-chief was named immediately. In the same month a meeting of editors-in-chief of the main newspapers discussed the party style of guiding the press. Soon, by decision of the Politburo, a new political weekly, *Polityka*, was launched, designed to serve as anti-*Po prostu*.[1]

Gomułka took advantage of the party plenum to instigate an attack on "revisionists" within the party and the press. In the months that followed, new editors-in-chief were appointed for nearly all of the dailies, and a warning was issued to all journalists that freedom of the press did not include writing critically about the leadership.[2] In March, a regional party organization convention in Lublin viciously criticized the press. The same words were reiterated in April at a similar convention of the Warsaw branch of the Communist party. The antipress campaign went so far that the Ninth Plenum of the Central Committee, held in May, eventually felt obliged to defend journalists against local party dignitaries *if* their criticism were true and justified. Immediately after the plenum, the editors of *Po prostu* were instructed to change the name of the weekly and impose stricter self-censorship. Both orders were refused, which did not help them or the press in general.

The purge in the press and attacks on journalists became so widespread that even the timid presidium of the Association of Polish Journalists (SDP) felt it had to intervene. It sent a rather meek letter to Gomułka, defending its members and the press. Gomułka, however, was not impressed by this defense. On the contrary, he lost his temper and, on October 2, abruptly ordered the closing of *Po prostu*. No explanation was given, although officially it was announced as a ruling of censorship.

The ban seriously irritated the students, who still regarded the weekly as their true voice. A meeting to challenge the decision was called at Warsaw Polytechnic. Banners appeared calling for "Freedom of the Press." Unexpectedly, the gathered students were attacked by the police, who for the first time used new weapons—tear gas and clubs. The protesters responded with shouts of "The Gestapo" and "NKVD" (Soviet secret police), the most insulting words in the Polish language.[3] Despite brutal measures taken by the authorities, the unrest continued for several days. Not only students were upset. On October 4, a resolution of the Warsaw chapter of the Union of Polish Writers (ZLP) boldly protested the closure of the weekly as "a very serious limitation of the freedom of democratic criticism."[4] The case of *Po prostu* was generalized; it became a symbol both of press freedom and of its repression.[5]

Gomułka eventually met with a leading journalistic *aktiv* (a caucus including editors-in-chief, managing editors, and prominent columnists) However, instead of taking a conciliatory stand, he interpreted the letter of the journalist association as praise for the students' demonstration and as an open attack on his position and on that of the leadership of the party. He loudly demanded obedience: "It is the time of choice. The journalists should make a choice: either with the party or against the party. The discussions have ended. It is time now to draw conclusions—party and political."[6]

Polityka summed up *Po prostu*'s downfall in an editorial, with perhaps unintentional frankness: "There are people who declare: The liquidation of *Po prostu* means the suppression of freedom of speech, the stifling of criticism and a deviation from October. What can we say to this? Freedom of speech has defined boundaries in post-October Poland. These boundaries end where propaganda directed against the building of socialism in our country starts; they end where the vital interests of the state and nation start."[7]

Gomułka's ultimatum was an open warning and a demand for blind loyalty. This point of view was not accepted by all of the attending journalists. The distinguished prewar journalists of leftist orientation—including, among others, Stanisław Arski, Jan Strzelecki, and Szymon Dobrowolski—publicly objected to Gomułka's demand of absolute submission to the party and rejected his criterion of what constituted a dedicated journalist. Such an act of defiance could not be taken lightly. Gomułka, however, after initially fiercely scolding Dobrowolski, his long-time companion, eventually approached him, embraced him, and tried to explain his position.[8] However, his efforts were to no avail. The journalists had discovered the joy of independent writings and did not want to end it. Thus, the party took administrative measures against the maverick journalists. Ten columnists from the banned *Po prostu* were expelled from the Communist party; six others were officially reprimanded.[9]

Then, a series of structural adjustments inside the party chain, the RSW *Prasa*, strengthened its political control over the press. In May 1958, a new governmental Commission for Press Publication and Distribution was set up to "reorganize the press market." As a result of its action 225 papers disappeared, and 17 magazines were merged. These acts provoked protests from both journalists and writers. The convention of the Union of Polish Writers strongly criticized excessive censorship and unjustified restrictions on freedom of the press.

Despite such repression two years after October 1956, Poland still retained a freedom of access and expression unknown anywhere in the Communist world. During 1957 and 1958 several papers were banned, but still more appeared. About one hundred new periodicals emerged, including, among others, women's, youth, and satirical magazines. This was also the era of revival of the ethnic press. New titles appeared: the Ukrainian *Nasze Slovo* (Our Word), the Russian *Russkij Golos* (Russian Voice), the Byelorussian *Niva*, and the Czech and Slovak *Zhivot* (Life). Political parties that were allied with Communists were again allowed to publish their organs. Several new independent publishing initiatives were undertaken.[10] Some of these survived for only one or two issues, including a magazine on Russian culture, *Opinia*, which was instantly banned when it began to print *Doctor Zhivago*. The same fate met *Lewary*, a student newspaper in Częstochowa, for similar reasons. Most independent cultural publications had similar short lives, but a few have survived to outlive the regime.

Dormant for some time, censorship started again and was tightened further.[11] However, it was still under the prime minister's direct control, and at that time censors had to apply different, often opposing recommendations from both the party and different governmental agencies. It was therefore possible for writers and journalists to find a puissant patron and use his or her authority to influence or even sometimes reverse a censor's decision.

Thus, despite censorship and other political measures, some intellectual freedom did persist.[12] The Club of the Crooked Circle, a liberal revisionist gathering founded before October 1956, managed to survive for a few years. The universities enjoyed substantial academic freedom until March 1968. Clubs composed of Catholic intelligentsia and associations of creative artists and writers were also forums for the public defense of the idea and practice of freedom of speech.

Nevertheless, dangerous indications of new constraints on the freedom of expression appeared by the end of 1958. Hanna Rewska was put on trial for distributing publications of *Kultura*, the Literary Institute in Paris.[13] It was the first such trial after October 1956 and, therefore, threatened to set a judicial precedent. What was worse, it penalized access to the periodical, which, although not available in bookstores, was accessible in the major public libraries and was commonly borrowed from friends. The verdict sent a clear warning to the intellectual community: three years' imprisonment. To discourage nonparty intellectuals from sustaining professional contacts with the West, the authorities took an unprecedented step—they put on trial Anna Rudzińska, a respected and well-known translator of sociological literature. She was arrested and sentenced to one year's imprisonment for possessing a book that was to be translated and then published by *Kultura*.[14]

A party campaign against revisionism was launched after the Third Party Congress in March 1959. In April, the Press Commission of the

Central Committee discussed the issue of press criticism, especially the part of certain papers, such as *Polityka*, and *Życie Warszawy*. It stated that the press should not criticize the Communist system in general, but that it might criticize some particular concrete negative occurrences.[15]

Professional concerns changed. The consolidation of the press, the pressure on journals to be self-supporting, and the competition for positions within journals heightened journalists' concern with regulation.[16] However, the character of the profession itself did not change significantly. Only 153 members of the SDP, out of more than three thousand were expelled in the "verification" of credentials campaign (carried out in 1957 and 1958), which was designed to root out revisionist elements. Although most of the zealous Stalinist journalists had to leave the profession in 1955 and 1956, many soon returned to managerial positions in the profession or in media control institutions (both party and governmental).[17]

In the face of a deteriorating economic situation, censorship officials were instructed to ban articles criticizing shortages of goods. The press was ordered to help ease social tensions and to provide reasons for the unfortunate economic situation. In October 1959, the youth press was criticized for showing too much leniency toward the "Western culture" and for not having enough ideological vigilance. The Politburo denounced a situation "of ideological confusion and apathy" among journalists.[18] A popular weekly, *Dookoła świata*, was castigated as the magazine that was popularizing Western culture. Similar resolutions were taken with respect to periodicals such as *Przekrój* and *Świat*.

All of this showed that the party was preparing an ideological campaign targeted toward the youth. The main goal was to counter the growing church influence on young people with a more secular culture. The party demanded a change in the contents of the weeklies to make them more ideologically oriented. This was an impossible task, considering the party's simultaneous demand for popularization of the socialist culture which in fact did not exist. The Fourth Plenum of the Central Committee in January 1960 recommended turning the attention of the youth toward achievements in science and technology.[19] This pro-science orientation had an openly antireligious goal—to struggle, with the help of science, with "religious obscurantism, darkness, and spreading of nationalistic points of view."[20] This approach also did not work—the youth still practiced religion and attended optional religious classes organized by the church.

In April 1960, three important party documents concerning the media were adopted. The first, on the leading role of *Trybuna Ludu*, highlighted the need to explain ideological and economic problems. The second dealt with press criticism, demanding that criticism should be constructive and should give better answers to the major problems facing the party and the nation. The third document, for the first time in the party history, pointed to the importance of television and mentioned the tasks of the party in this regard.[21] It insisted that radio and television should limit or, when possible, eliminate all loud styles of music, such as rock and jazz. The broadcast media ought to develop solely as a serious, culture-filled, educational institution.[22] Later, in March 1962, the directive of the Press Bureau concerning information on white-collar crimes stated that whereas there was a need for more information, press emphasis should not be excessive and colored but proper and well-balanced.[23]

Inside the press, changes were taken to adjust its structure and to tighten control on deviating journalists. Two liberal weeklies, *Nowa Kultura* and *Przegląd Kulturalny*, were merged into one new publication entitled *Kultura*, a move that was met with understandable discontent. Only when an eminent editor-in-chief sent a letter of protest to the party leadership did Gomułka agree to meet with worried journalists. As on former occasions, he was not influenced by their arguments. The meeting, therefore, ended with his open warning: "If you want to collaborate [with the party], good, if not—also good."[24] Those gathered were well aware that refusal to cooperate with the party meant a definite loss of their jobs. In October 1960, the Polish Students' Union created an illustrated weekly, *ITD* (Etc.), a less political publication that was more oriented toward the arts. The party allowed it a special status, a so-called restricted independence, which meant that it was occasionally allowed to print articles that did not rigorously reflect the current party line on culture, art, and science. This experiment ended in March 1968, when the magazine was compelled to support the antistudents, anti-Semitic propaganda campaign.[25]

The Thirteenth Plenum in July 1963 was very important in setting the party's new media policy. The most urgent task was declared to be coordinating Polish media output with the worldwide Communist ideological struggle.[26] Party control over the press and cultural affairs increased radically, and censorship was again tightened. There was little or no trace of the victories won during the October struggles. When a hardliner, Artur Starewicz, replaced the more liberal head of the Propaganda Department, sweeping personnel changes followed.

The plenum established the ideological grounds for the Fourth Party Congress, scheduled for July the following year. Therefore, everything seemed perfectly planned and prepared in advance of this major party event. However, in early 1964, a portentous protest took the Communist leadership by surprise and changed the course of the well-defined media policy.

The Beginnings of Open Opposition

The tightening of censorship and the new restrictions on intellectual freedoms pushed intellectuals to action. On March 19, 1964, thirty-four prominent Polish writers, journalists, and academics delivered a letter of protest to the office of the prime minister. They objected to the doctored shortage of newsprint and demanded the implementation of the provisions and human rights that were guaranteed by the constitution of the Polish People's Republic.[27] Although the tone and style of the letter were serene and calm, the authorities reacted violently.

As a personal correspondence, the letter remained secret. However, one of the signatories, Jan J. Lipski, was suddenly arrested under the charge of collecting the signatures for this petition. In response, the intellectuals passed the letter to foreign correspondents in Warsaw, and it was immediately broadcast by Radio Free Europe (RFE).[28] Even then, the only "reply" the authors received was a secret instruction to censors and publishers forbidding them to print any material from the rebels.[29] Therefore, in typical Communist practice, in response to the unpublished letter of the group of thirty-four, the daily press carried a counterletter, signed by four times that number (to be precise—134) of loyal members of the writers' union. They were lamenting "the campaign of RFE and the Western press slandering Poland."

Not all intellectuals and journalists remained loyal to the party line. Some even dared to raise publicly their concerns about the lack of freedom of expression. An article in *Prawo i Życie* entitled "Interventions and Myths" defended the rights of journalists to generalize in their criticism and not be limited to a narrow, low-key approach. The article, which touched a delicate cord of professional responsibility, stirred a large response within the press and was placed on the agenda of a meeting of the Warsaw chapter of the journalists' association.[30] The letter from the group of thirty-four even provoked a peaceful demonstration by Warsaw students, who gathered to listen to the rector of the university and afterward dispersed peacefully. This was the only demonstration by Polish students between October 1957 and March 1968.

To all of these concerns, the official response was an endorsement of the strict communication policy adopted by the Thirteenth Plenum in 1963. At the Fourth Congress, the party once again asserted that the media was an adjunct of the party and that all spheres had to reflect party influence. Journalists were called upon to display more responsibility (that is, more partymindedness) and more offensiveness (that is, more attacks on the church).[31] Moreover, for the first time in party history, the final congress resolution, which was always a leading party document, directly addressed the mass media, placing it within the framework of the ideological struggle. The role of ideology was then appraised as being more important than that of the economy. There was no mention of dialogue or two-way communication. Much more was said about how the party press should influence public opinion. The screw of control was turned even tighter.

In the fall of 1964, a well-known Polish writer and journalist, Melchior Wańkowicz, was put on trial on the pretense "of spreading false information that could be harmful to the interests of the Polish state," although this "false information" was contained in a private letter to his daughter. Wańkowicz was sentenced to three years of imprisonment but as a celebrity was not sent to prison.[32] His trial served as a serious warning to any negligent letterwriter. Similar actions were taken against other intellectuals to discourage them from keeping contacts in the West.[33]

The party treated more rigorously dissenters within its own ranks. Thus, when two "then-revisionists," Jacek Kuroń and Karol Modzelewski, wrote a critical "Open Letter to Members of the Polish United Workers Party and the Union of Socialist [Communist] Youth of Warsaw University," they received a sentence of three years in prison, most of which they subsequently served.[34]

The trial had repercussions among the students, especially in Warsaw. During the 1966 and 1967 academic year tensions increased. When one of the most popular students, Adam Michnik, was suspended from the university, a mass petition in his defense was signed by over two hundred professors and one thousand students.[35] This action had even greater repercussions; in reality, it opened a new chapter in the history of the Polish media—one in which the party struggle with all kinds of deviators was intensified and the most repugnant. It will be discussed in Chapter 9.

The Media War Against the Church

Despite a tactical alliance formed between the party secretary, Gomułka, and the Polish primate, Stefan Wyszyński, in October of 1956, their relations soon disintegrated. The party and Gomułka himself still believed in the exclusive right of the party to control the entire public sphere, or, to use a Polish poet's expression, to "govern on the souls." However, this was the traditional role of the Roman Catholic church, which did not want to cede this power to the Communist party.

In 1957 the Catholic church had already begun preparations for the 1966 anniversary that would celebrate a millennium of christendom in Poland. The celebration, which was consistent with the centuries-long tradition of the Catholic faith, was a serious threat to the Communist party pretense of an ideological monopoly. Having lost any control of the mass media, the church was limited to its traditional sermons, pastoral letters which were read from thousands of pulpits, and mass pilgrimages to the holy shrine of the Black Madonna in Częstochowa.[36]

As part of the preparations, at Wyszyński's behest, a tour of a copy of the celebrated Black Madonna's icon from one village to another was arranged. This presented an occasion for crowded processions of believers to form, which demonstrated the perfect organization and resurgent influence of the church. Naturally, Gomułka was enraged.[37] On his order, the painting was seized and sent back to Częstochowa. The entire church establishment was livid. Bishops and priests found this act to be an excellent example of religious persecution, and they used it constantly in their sermons and pastoral letters. In response, Gomułka acted as a true Stalinist—Cardinal's passport was withdrawn, and he could not depart for Rome. Wyszyński was probably grateful for such a ridiculous move, because nothing could have better improved his standing both in Poland and the world. Information on the harassment of the church could only help to attract young people; in Poland, as everywhere, people were ready to support the weaker side.

The church discovered that such mild persecution could effectively serve to help it regain its traditional hold on society. With great energy, and nine years ahead of schedule, the church began to remind Poles about its thousand-year history during masses, processions, pilgrimages, vows, night vigils, and similar pious acts.

The party decided to sabotage these actions. In May 1959, relations between state and church were discussed by the top leadership. It was agreed not to launch open attacks against the church; instead a long-term campaign of secularization was contrived. Its principal task was to "unmask the conservative and reactionary activity" of the clergy. The tactic of the campaign was to challenge the goals of a nine-year church celebration. At the end of 1959, the regime went further and declared that "Polish atheism had to fight with the Catholic hierarchy for control over the souls of the whole nation."[38]

In December 1965, the secretariat of the Central Committee prepared guidelines for dealing with the church anniversary. The party found its remedy in a secular Polish tradition that had to be constantly emphasized. The media had to stress the idea that the "Polish People's Republic, not the Polish church, was a crowning achievement in the historical development of the Polish nation."[39]

Implementation of the guidelines was thoroughly monitored. A special research unit of the Press Bureau of the Central Committee did a content analysis covering the period December 1965 to February 1966. It calculated that the dailies published seventy-six and the weeklies fifty "important articles and editorials" classified as antichurch items. This was considered a fair result.[40]

The antichurch campaign increased after Gomułka's speech on January 14, 1966, in which he harshly criticized Jerzy Turowicz (the editor-in-chief of *Tygodnik Powszechny*) for his pro-bishop editorials. Attacks and slanders reached their peak in Poznań in April 1966, when Gomułka stated publicly that "the intellect of the chairman of the Polish Episcopate [the primate, Cardinal Wyszyński] is narrow-minded and without feeling for the state." Gomułka went so far as to describe the primate as "an irresponsible pastor, fighting with our state," who promoted "the crooked, anti-national idea of the *bulwark* of Christendom, driving Poland into conflict with the Soviet Union, and forgiving the Nazi murderers for extermination of the Polish nation."[41] This is just one example of the style of the antichurch propaganda of the day.

After this the press was ordered not to print information on millennium celebrations. The only exceptions were the official, short Polish Press Agency communiqués. Furthermore, in order to limit attendance at religious meetings, radio and television were directed to increase the attractiveness of their programs on all religious holidays and on those working days when church celebrations would take place.[42]

In October, apparatchiks from the Press Bureau of the Central Committee stated that it was necessary to differentiate between Wyszyński's supporters (allegedly the minority of Roman Catholics and mostly lesser-educated persons) and the rest of the believers and to try to influence the latter through the use of more sophisticated propaganda arguments.[43] In November 1966, the Press Bureau prepared a detailed plan of publication of church-related themes for the next three months. Even an apparently Catholic daily published by the PAX organization, *Słowo Powszechne*, was commanded to publish a series of statements by public figures condemning the U.S. war in Vietnam and praising the pope's appeal for peace, in such a way that Cardinal Wyszyński was accused indirectly of not supporting the pope's noble appeal. These arguments were to be reprinted in the mass-circulation weeklies, *Przekrój* and *Przyjaciółka* (Our Companion). The radio had to broadcast letters from "average, ordinary Catholics" condemning the Vietnam War and the stand of the Episcopate, especially in relation to the German question. *Panorama Śląska* (Silesian Review), a mass circulation magazine, was to present the "despotic, autocratic style of leadership of the primate." The rural biweekly *Gromada* (Community) was ordered to expose the primate's pro-Western orientation. Loyal party journalists were asked to uncover financial abuses by the clergy and even to discuss the working conditions of church organists. Television was compelled to show the medieval practices allegedly preserved in the Polish monasteries. The same theme was assigned to the youth press and illustrated magazines.[44] Of course, those guidelines were not to be publicly exposed. The regulations remained top secret, at least for rank-and-file journalists. The orchestration of the media was such that the press was played like a huge organ, with Gomułka performing the role of organist.

On November 18, 1966, the Polish bishops sent a historic letter of reconciliation to the West German Episcopate; in the letter the bishops implored: "we forgive and ask for forgiveness." This phrase and act sparked a furious reaction from the Communist party, particularly from Gomułka. The bishops were seen as trespassing on the government's monopoly on foreign policy.[45] Official propaganda began to refer to deeply rooted Polish resentment and anti-German stereotypes in its attack. Using the so-called technique of name-calling, the propagandists portrayed Wyszyński as a "Nazi-lover" who had forgiven the Germans for all the crimes committed in Poland during the war. This proved to be a smart propaganda maneuver: The veterans' organizations were enraged. In addition, popular opinion was unprepared for such a radical reconciliation with the Germans. The letter itself created a pretext for further intensification of the party-against-church war.

Yet, despite initial successes, the propaganda campaign soon backfired. Believers did not turn against the primate, and even fewer turned against the church. On the contrary, popular attitudes were strengthened. Each year churches were filled with increasing number of faithful. Wyszyński won the war with Gomułka. Eventually, after his death, Cardinal Wyszyński received the title, "the Primate of the Millennium." The name stresses his unquestioned role as the leader of the Polish church in its most difficult period and as the patron of a priest from Cracow, Karol Wojtyła, then a cardinal and later Pope John Paul II.

Nonetheless, in hindsight, Wyszyński's victory had its costs for the Polish church. The use of religious rituals and ceremonies— especially pilgrimages and the adoration of the Holy Mary—to strengthen Polish catholicism to make it strong enough to confront the atheist Communist state hindered the development of the deeper layer of religious life that deals with ethics, not with religious rites. Many Poles attended religious masses simply out of spite. Participation in religious life was an occasion to demonstrate (rather safely) disapproval of communism and to worship the Polish tradition. If this were true, a certain anarchization of Polish public life, a lack of so-called state instinct—"right or wrong, it's my country"—as well as a rather shallow religiousness, which expressed itself in mass participation but with superficial faith, proved a legacy of this Pyrrhic victory.

Tightening the Screw

One of the results of this war on the church, was an increased number of censorship interventions. During a party conference in January 1967, it was officially quoted that conflicts between journalists and censors had significantly increased.[46]

The party hierarchy also had every reason to believe that the ideological threat posed by the intellectuals was a serious one. Held under the banner "Shaping the Socialist Consciousness of Polish Society," the Eighth Plenum of the Central Committee in May 1967 stated that there should not be a peaceful coexistence with bourgeois ideology. The socialist countries were under a "mass psychological attack" by the Capitalist countries. It was, therefore, necessary to be vigilant and to counterattack. Recommendations for improving the technical base of radio and especially television were adopted to enlarge the range of party propaganda.[47] Zenon Kliszko, the secretary in charge of ideology, emphasized partymindedness and the importance of control of the media.[48] New press guidelines were prepared which recommended more aggressive propaganda. It was demanded that the press begin to unmask and refute the "pseudo-democratic bourgeois freedom" and engage in polemics with Radio Free Europe and emigré *Kultura*. It should rally around "politically mature" party cadres to stop bourgeois infiltration.[49] Journalists, above all, had to be party activists.

The Six-Day War in the Middle East in June of 1967 released a chain of events in the Soviet-bloc countries that took a pro-Arab stance. Speaking at the Fifth Congress of Trade Unions, Gomułka outlined the international policy of the party, hinting—in thoughts that were extremely important in the subsequent expression of anti-Semitism within the party—that the "Israeli aggression was met with applause in Zionist milieus of Poland's Jewish citizens." He emphasized that "one can have only one motherland." To conclude, he said: "The present situation demands of us more vigilance, cohesion, and discipline."[50]

The line was drawn for a new propaganda campaign. The Jewish enemy had been identified. No longer was the Roman Catholic church targeted; the target was now an international conspiracy of the Israeli Fifth Column allegedly operating in Poland. This time the enemy, or, in fact, the scapegoat, was much better chosen. It seemed plausible to revive old Polish (and Catholic) resentments of and prejudices toward the Jews, which had been dormant—especially among certain social strata and, more important, among the numerous party activists.[51]

On October 1, 1967, a party meeting of the editors of party dailies stressed that in general the press had taken an appropriate stance. Nevertheless, some papers were accused of having an "objective" approach, which allegedly caused ideological conflicts within editorial boards.[52] In November 1967, Stefan Olszowski, secretary in charge of party propaganda, emphasized the need to follow the example of the central papers in taking stands and positions.[53]

The 1967-1968 academic year began as a very turbulent season. Information about the Arab-Israeli conflict, economic reform in Yugoslavia and Hungary, and—above all—political liberalization in Czechoslovakia in January 1968 increased internal tensions in Poland. The leadership, was getting older and becoming more afraid; the intellectuals and students were greatly agitated.

Thus, again came the call for unity and orchestration of the media. This time the situation was different from that of a year ago. After the successful internal party campaign against revisionists, a new party faction emerged called the "Partisans"; it was formed around Mieczysław Moczar, the powerful minister of internal affairs.[54] An orthodox Communist, Moczar was nevertheless a passionate nationalist.[55] His faction secretly sought to oust Gomułka and impose Moczar's leadership. To increase their position, the "Partisans" cleverly made use of the traditional Polish hatred of Russians. But they were more authentically anti-Semitic, referring back to the strains of anti-Semitism that had existed in prewar Poland.[56] On their road to power, the Partisan faction needed not only the police but also the media. Thus, they secured the key positions in the major mass media, especially television and the weeklies. But not all media joined them. A striking exception was *Polityka*, whose editor-in-chief, Mieczysław Rakowski, was devoted to Gomułka but was even more indignant over nationalistic ideology and anti-Semitism.

In winter, the Warsaw party organization (dominated by the Moczar's faction) ordered a production of the nineteenth-century classic Polish play *Dziady* (Forefathers' Eve) to end because of its allegedly anti-Russian interpretation. The last performance on January 30, 1968, attracted some defiant students, who, after the standing ovation, left the theater with a banner that proclaimed "We want more performances." In an ensuing fight with police, some students were taken into custody, and a few were punished by the court with heavy fines.

The outrage was universal. Warsaw University students responded with a mass petition. An extraordinary meeting of the Warsaw chapter of the Polish Writers' Union was called on February 29. Many angry speeches were given. Despite the efforts of some party members to appease the tone, the meeting's final resolution asserted: "The system of censorship and control of cultural and artistic activity is arbitrary and secret; the jurisdiction of particular authorities has not been defined; and no appeal procedures have been specified."[57]

The 1964 letter of the group of thirty-four eventually found more followers. The authorities responded to protests with more student expulsions. On March 4, 1968, a prominent dissident, Adam Michnik, was expelled from the university by the minister of education. This apparently insignificant event marked the opening of a new chapter in the history of the Polish media.

Notes

1. The press run of the first issue of *Polityka* was twenty-six thousand copies, of which 15,000 came back unsold. The planned financial loss was about 5 million zlotys. In comparison, *Po prostu* sold 150,000 copies, with its circulation limited by censorship. The decision to launch a new weekly was strictly political; it was to become a journalistic Trojan horse. Michał Radowski, *Polityka i jej czasy* [Polityka and Its Times] (Warszawa: Iskry, 1981), pp. 11-16.

2. Jane Leftwich Curry, *Poland's Journalists: Professionalism and Politics* (Cambridge: Cambridge University Press, 1990), p. 60.

3. Flora Lewis, *A Case History of Hope: The Story of Poland's Peaceful Revolutions* (New York: Doubleday, 1958), p. 255.

4. Ibid., p. 99.

5. Jakub Karpiński, *Countdown: Polish Upheavals of 1956, 1968, 1970, 1976, 1980* (New York: Karz-Cohl Publishers, 1982), p. 99.

6. Władysław Gomułka, *Przemówienia* [Speeches] (Warszawa: Książka i Wiedza, 1958), p. 21.

7. *Polityka*, October 28, 1957, p. 3.

8. Henryk Korotyński, "Spotkanie Gomułki z dziennikarzami" [Gomułka's Meeting with Journalists], *Zeszyty Prasoznawcze* 2, 1960, pp. 59-60.

9. The party members on the *Po prostu* team were castigated for writing an open letter to Gomułka, because, as *Trybuna Ludu* explained, "protesting with open letters to party organs against resolutions passed by other party organs is contrary to the principles of democratic centralism." In its justification of the expulsion from the party, the party's daily made the point: "The party members expressed their own political line. That was contrary to the resolution of the Eighth and Ninth Plenums of the Central Committee" (October 17, 1957), p. 1.

10. Censorship granted permits for 239 new papers, most of which never materialized. Seventy-eight applications were rejected, among them many church periodicals. Sylwester Dziki, "Kalendarium prasy polskiej: 1957, Część druga" [Chronology of the Polish Press: 1957, Part 2] *Zeszyty Prasoznawcze* 1, 1989, p. 154.

11. *Mysia* (Mouse Street), where the main censorship office headquarters were located, just across from the party Central Committee building in Warsaw, became a symbol of press censorship.

12. In 1956, dogmatism was the main concern and primary danger for Gomułka and liberal-minded party members. In 1957, Gomułka turned it into revisionism—departure from the party line in search of more democracy and socialism with a "human face." At the Ninth Plenum of the Central Committee, Gomułka personally attacked the views of "party member comrade Leszek

Kołakowski" as a typical revisionist who preached integral democracy ("it is nonsense") and "was praised by the Trockist and bourgeois press." Karpiński, *Countdown*, p. 98.

13. The charge was "distributing and storing" materials that "contained false information which could significantly harm the interests of the Polish state." Ibid., p. 105. *Kultura*, an emigré literary monthly, was founded in Paris in 1947 by Jerzy Giedroyć. His main objective was to be a spokesman for the liberal opposition in Poland. In the first issue, Giedroyć explained that "*Kultura*'s wish was to reach the reader in Poland and boost their faith that the values that they believed were destroyed by the sheer power [of Soviet domination]." *Kultura* advocated the theory that the Communist system could be transformed through evolutionary processes into social democracy. It is little wonder that its sale was forbidden in Poland. See more in Peter Raina, *Political Opposition in Poland: 1954-1977* (London: Poets and Painters Press, 1978), pp. 175-177. Along with Radio Free Europe, *Kultura* was regarded as the most dangerous medium of the opposition. It was more dangerous for at least one reason. Its impact as a durable medium, in contrast to ephemeral broadcast, was indeed stronger, especially on students and young members of the intelligentsia.

14. The book *The Seizure of Political Power* by Feliks Gross was labeled by a prosecutor as an anti-state publication. The expert opinion of Professor Hochfeld, a respected political scientist and long-time socialist, was disregarded by the court. See Raina, *Political Opposition*, p. 69.

15. See "Notatka z posiedzenia Komisji Prasowej w dn. 28.IV.1959" [Memo from the Meeting of the Press Commission], *Archives of the Central Committee*, Archives of the New Acts, AAN, the Press Commission 1959, 1960, 1961; 237/XIX-368, k. 13.

16. Curry, *Poland's Journalists*, p. 61

17. Ibid., 61.

18. "Uwagi o prasie, radio i telewizji" [Remarks on the Press, Radio, and Television], *Archives of the Central Committee*, AAN, 237/XIX-92, k. 34.

19. *Uchwały KC PZPR od III do IV Zjazdu* [Resolutions of the Central Committee of the PZPR from the Third to the Fourth Congress] (Warszawa: Książka i Wiedza, 1964), pp. 407-415.

20. *Archives of the Central Committee*, AAN, 237/XIX-386.

21. "W sprawie pracy radia i telewizji. Uchwała Sekretariatu KC PZPR. Kwiecień 1960" [On the Working of Radio and Television. The Resolution of the Secretariat of the Central Committee of the PZPR. April 1960], *Uchwały KC PZPR od III do IV Zjazdu*, p. 502.

22. Ibid.

23. "Wytyczne w sprawie oświetlania w prasie, radio i telewizji problematyki wymiaru sprawiedliwości i zwalczania przestępczości, 23.VII.1961" [Instructions on the Matter of Interpretation by the Press, Radio, and Television of the Issues of the Judiciary System and Fighting Crime, July 23, 1961], *Archives of the Central Committee*, AAN, collection of the secretariat, 237/II, 448, k. 38.

24. "Spotkanie zespołów redakcyjnych *Przeglądu Kulturalnego* i *Nowej Kultury* z członkami kierownictwa Partii w dn. 5.VI.1963 [The Meeting of the Editorial Boards of *Przegląd Kulturalny* (Cultural Review) and *Nowa Kultura* (New Culture) with the Members of the Party Leadership on June 5, 1963], *Archives of the Central Committee*, AAN, the Press Bureau, 237/V-462, k. 8.

25. See the interview with Marian Grześciak, deputy editor-in-chief of *ITD* in the period 1962-1967, in *ITD* no. 198, 1990, pp. 10-13.

26. Władysław Gomułka, "O aktualnych problemach ideologicznych pracy partii" [On Current Ideological Issues of Party Activities], *Nowe Drogi* 8, 1963, p. 5.

27. Gaston de Cereznay, "Polska Gomułki i `list 34'" [Gomułka's Poland and the 'Letter of the 34'], *Kultura* (Paris) 10, 1964, pp. 13-26.

28. This was the first of many similar protests leaked to Radio Free Europe. Therefore, the contents, which had no chance of being published in Poland, could reach both a Polish and an international audience.

29. W. Żyrowski, "Zenon Kliszko i list 34" [Zenon Kliszko and the Letter of 34], *Kultura* (Paris) 12, 1964, p. 149.

30. "Krytyka i interwencja ważną funkcją prasy" [Criticism and Interventions—the Important Function of the Press], *Prasa Polska* 5, 1964, p. 6.

31. *IV Zjazd PZPR: Stenogram* [Minutes of the Fourth Congress of the PZPR] (Warszawa: Książka i Wiedza, 1964), p. 19.

32. Raina, *Political Opposition*, p. 79-82.

33. Karpiński, *Countdown*, p. 107.

34. Raina, *Political Opposition*, pp. 82-95.

35. Karpiński, *Countdown*, p. 109.

36. Since 1717 the Black Madonna has been popularly called the "Queen of Poland." After October of 1956, the pilgrimages to see and pray to it became the major religious events in Poland. They, too, illustrated the growing strength of the church. Later, in the 1970s and 1980s, the pilgrimages included millions of the faithful, but even in the late 1950s there were enough people to irritate Communist authorities. To counter this, Gomułka did not economize on the annual harvest festival (*Dożynki*), which was attended by hundred of thousands of loyal peasants.

37. Robert Jarocki, *Czterdzieści pięć lat w opozycji* [Forty-Five Years in Opposition] (Kraków: Wydawnictwo Literackie, 1990), p. 208.

38. Adam Szajowski, *Next to God . . . Poland* (New York: St. Martin's Press, 1983), p. 20.

39. Józef Lubiński, *Zasady i cele polityki PZPR w dziedzinie komunikowania w latach 1948-1971* [Doctrine and Political Goals of the Communication Policy of the PZPR in the Period 1948-1971] (unpublished doctoral dissertation, Jagiellonian University, 1988), vol. 1.

40. "Notatka o dotychczasowych publikacjach na temat Orędzia w prasie, radio i telewizji" [Memo on the Publications Concerning the "Letter of Reconciliation"], *Archives of the Central Committee*, AAN, collection of the Press Bureau, 237/XIX-98, k. 47-59.

41. Władysław Gomułka, *Przemówienia: 1964-1966* [Speeches] (Warszawa: Książka i Wiedza, 1967), p. 427.

42. "Notatka z pracy służb sprawozdawczych radia i tv w związku z uroczystościami Tysiąclecia podpisana przez S. Olszowskiego" [Memo Concerning the Work of the Reporting Services of Radio and Television Covering the Millennium Celebration, signed by S. Olszowski], *Archives of the Central Committee*, AAN, the Press Bureau, 237/XIX-99, k. 78). Additional costs to carry the extra radio and television programs were estimated at 6 to 7 million zlotys.

43. "Notka, niepodpisana" [Memo, unsigned], *Archives of the Central Committee*, AAN, the Press Bureau, 237/XIX-99, k. 132-135.

44. "Sprawy Kościoła i kleru w prasie" [The Church and Clergy Affairs in the Press], *Archives of the Central Committee*, the Press Bureau, 237/XIX-99, k. 177-179.

45. Neal Ascherson, *The Polish August: The Self-Limiting Revolution* (London: Allen Lane, 1981), pp. 85-86.

46. "Notatka w sprawie ingerencji GUKPPiW w ostatnim okresie w pismach centralnych, grudzień 1966" [Memo Regarding Censorship Interventions in the Central Papers, December 1966], *Archives of the Central Committee*, AAN, the Press Bureau, 237/XIX-99, k. 226.

47. "Wnioski i postulaty pod adresem prasy, radia i telewizji, wynikające z obrad VIII Plenum KC, maj 1967" [Conclusions and Postulates Concerning the Press, Radio, and Television Stemming from the Eighth Plenum of the Central Committee, May 1967], *Archives of the Central Committee*, AAN, the Press Bureau, 237/XIX-100, k. 74.

48. Zenon Kliszko, "Przemówienie na VIII Plenum" [The Speech on the Eighth Plenum], *Archives of the Central Committee*, AAN, the Plenary Meetings of the Central Committee, 237/II/45, k. 15-16.

49. *Trybuna Ludu*, May 18, 1967, p. 1.

50. Władysław Gomułka, *Przemówienia: 1967* (Warszawa: Książka i Wiedza, 1968), p. 202. The ignoble words about the alleged Israeli Fifth Column in Poland were not printed in the book version.

51. An excellent analysis of the Jewish issue in Polish history can be found in a collection by Chimen Abramsky et al., *The Jews in Poland* (Oxford: Blackwell, 1986). In this book a charter by Łukasz Hirszowicz, "The Jewish Issue in Post-War Communist Politics" (pp. 198-249) deals particularly with anti-Semitism among Communist authorities.

52. "Ocena dotychczasowych realizacji wniosków i postulatów VIII Plenum pod adresem prasy, radia i telewizji" [Assessment of the Conclusions and Postulates of the Eighth Plenum Concerning the Press, Radio, and Television], *Archives of the Central Committee*, AAN, Press Bureau, 237/XIX-100, k. 140.

53. Stefan Olszowski, "Główne zadania Krajowego Zjazdu" [Main Task of the National Convention], *Prasa Polska* 12, 1967, p. 9.

54. General Mieczysław Moczar built a power base within the Veterans' Association. At this time, fewer than thirty thousand Jews lived in Poland. But the Partisans drew attention to the Jewish origin of some of the reforming intellectuals and survivors of the "Muscovite" group who lived in the Soviet Union during World War II. Neal Ascherson, *The Struggles for Poland* (London: Michael Joseph, 1989), pp. 174, 176-177.

55. Under Moczar's protection, a profusion of stories, novels, and films appeared that glorified the Polish military traditions. This pleased and excited many Poles who resented the pro-Russian orientation of the official historiography. Ascherson, *The Polish August*, p. 90.

56. Anti-Semitic feeling was fanned after World War II by perceived close ties between the Communist party and Poland's and the Soviet Union's Jewish communities. In the 1950s many Jews held important jobs in the security apparatus. Afterward a few Jews worked in top positions in the media and censorship. Jane Leftwich Curry, ed., *Dissent in Eastern Europe* (New York: Praeger, 1983), p. 18.

57. Karpiński, *Countdown*, p. 112. See also Raina, *Political Opposition*, p. 120.

9

Marching to Nationalistic Tunes
March 1968 to December 1970

The rhythm of conflict seemed to accelerate in Poland. The year 1968 brought a new wave of student riots and intellectual protests. The Communist party chose to counterattack these with an anti-Semitic campaign calculated to win new social support. While such support never materialized, the campaign revived many ghosts from the past.

—Bronisław Geremek, *Between Hope and Despair*

Since the mid-1960s there had been many signs of emerging reform, opposition, and dissident movements in Eastern Europe, particularly in Poland, Czechoslovakia, and the Soviet Union itself. The survival of the Soviet bloc depended on containing that protest. In Czechoslovakia, to roll back the "Prague spring of 1968," the Warsaw Pact had to use tanks as a last resort. In Poland, Władysław Gomułka tried to find ways to contain the protests by launching an antirevisionist campaign, which in reality was directed against all forms of intellectual opposition. Despite Gomułka's intent, the most striking, and perhaps the worst long-lasting feature of that campaign was its incorporation of anti-Jewish prejudice.[1] The breakthrough was an apparently insignificant event, a public demonstration after a theater performance.

In this chapter I focus especially on the exploitation of the anti-Semitic themes by those who controlled the Polish media in their attempt to overpower opposition to Communist autocracy. It was incidental that General Moczar and his Partisan faction aimed at supreme power—that is, the replacement of Gomułka and his team.[2] More important sociologically was the fact that Moczar transformed the Jewish issue into a powerful instrument for gathering support within the party apparat and among the public at large.[3] Moczar's men gained control of Poland's television and radio and nearly all the newspapers.

The Ides of March

The ill-famed "March events" of 1968 (a typical Communist security police euphemism) began with a student demonstration at Warsaw University on March 8. As was described in Chapter 8, students protested against the curtailment of cultural freedoms, of which the banning of the play *Forefathers' Eve* was treated as an explicit sign. A handbill before the rally recalled article seventy-one of the constitution, which assured the right to free speech at rallies and demonstrations. It was an empty promise, because the rally was attacked by police. It is still unknown to what extent the student action was a spontaneous demonstration and to what extent it was the result of police provocation—the Moczar faction merely jumping on the occasion to "teach students a lesson."

On March 9, in local Warsaw daily papers, a very brief account mentioned the "disturbances in street traffic and public transportation" and implied that the "representatives of the Warsaw workers" felt obliged to discipline the hooligans. Then, two days later, *Trybuna Ludu* and a PAX daily, *Słowo Powszechne*, published similarly worded and unsigned articles on the demonstration. *Słowo Powszechne* used an odd word *Zyonist*, claiming that "the *Zyonists* from Poland are taking political orders from West Germany." The article also hinted at information about the so-called ringleaders—all of those indicated had non-Slavic, apparently Jewish names. The word "Zionist" was a new term in Communist propaganda. The readers, therefore, were puzzled: Who were these Zionists? *Trybuna Ludu* gave an explanation in an article titled "What is Zionism?" It identified Zionists as agents of Israel's government who were enemies of the Polish government and the Polish nation. In fact, it was a fabrication for an internal party struggle.

Occasionally, as in an article in *Trybuna Ludu* on March 13, 1968, party propagandists suggested that the organizers of the student movement were using Nazi paraphernalia, such as swastikas, to prove that they were spreading anti-Semitism. And so, like the famous widow in Gogol's *Governmental Inspector* who allegedly whipped herself, the students of Jewish origins were accused to be in reality the true organizers of the anti-Jewish campaign.

Although the full truth about the causes of the March events and the power struggle is still unknown, it is obvious that Moczar's faction, which earlier had assumed control of the major media, used the student protest as proof of a worldwide Jewish conspiracy.[4] It caught the moment as a chance to gain power through assaults on liberals and imagined traitors. The goal was to return the party to dictatorship.

As could be expected, both the police action and the journalistic accounts added fuel to the fire, provoking widespread indignation among students and faculty. The reports and editorials in the press were so distant from reality that the cry "the press is lying" became very popular at student rallies. Enraged participants usually burned newspapers. What was not yet known or understood was that the press, which was the party's weapon in an internal struggle, did not bother with objective reporting. Its apparent aim was the removal of a few Jewish top party officials and intellectuals.

Joining in the anger, a group of Catholic deputies to the Parliament submitted an interpellation to the prime minister, indirectly and cautiously protesting against the police action. The authorities reacted instantly and harshly scolded these daring parliamentarians.

The reprimand triggered a brutal and long-lasting party media crusade against students, intellectuals, and the Jews. From his secret files Moczar prepared lists of Jews in political, mass communication, propaganda, and managerial positions. The majority of top officials of the Stalinist secret police were Jews; among them was Józef Światło (alias Fleischberg), a fact that was not disclosed during the 1950s.[5]

After the Warsaw student demonstration, protests swept across university centers. Students from Jagiellonian University in Kraków declared solidarity with the students of Warsaw.[6] They also demanded that the constitutional guarantees of freedom of the press be observed. Poznań students demanded the abolition of political censorship, adding "we feel solidarity and send greetings to the courageous students in fraternal Czechoslovakia."[7] Despite the efforts of authorities to break communication between students in different cities, resolutions, sometimes mimeographed or simply photographed, were widely circulated.[8]

The party instantly struck back. On March 12, in *Kurier Polski*, an organ of the Democratic Alliance (SD), an article entitled "The Inspirators" attacked writers and professors. Furthermore, the article singled out students of Jewish origin as trouble-makers.[9] Following its publication the authorities launched a campaign of repression against dissenting students, writers, and scientists. Most, especially those with Jewish names, were expelled from the party, lost their positions and jobs, or were forced to leave the country.[10] But the campaign was not entirely anti-Semitic; it was also anti-intellectual.[11] Thus, it left a scar on the entire generation of 1968.[12]

The Seventh Congress of the Polish Journalists' Association was held March 14-15, 1968. A deep rift appeared between the presidium, which followed the party line, and brave rank-and-file journalists, who tried to defend the students. This gathering also revealed the existence of another group of journalists, who disclosed themselves bluntly as being anti-Semitic and attacked the party leadership (Gomułka and some of his protégés) for "lack of responsibility" and "not defending 'true Communists' against the attacks of Zionists and revisionists." They soon became symbols of the so-called March journalism, which was made up of brutal, nationalistic, racist propaganda.[13]

An assault journalist force was formed under the auspices of the Press Bureau of the Central Committee, directed by the Ministry of Internal Affairs (MSW) with the collaboration of the Warsaw party organization.[14] These journalists directly attacked liberal Communist journalists by emphasizing that the profession was politically divided and that the liberals were on the wrong side. The most hated target was the weekly *Polityka* and its editor, Mieczysław Rakowski; both were portrayed as being too lenient regarding international Zionism.[15] They even dared to criticize *Trybuna Ludu*, because it was under the leadership of an editor of Jewish origin.

Such criticism of the central organ had previously occurred only once, in October 1956; however, at that time, it was the reform-minded intellectuals who attacked, whereas the dogmatists only defended themselves. This time the situation was reversed, which meant permission was given from the top. The proceedings of the congress discussions confirmed that the mass media was being used in an internal struggle for power and was dominated by the Partisan faction.[16]

Afraid of losing control, Gomułka joined the pack. On March 19, 1968, in an attempt to appease the Moczar faction, he attacked the Zionists and his favorite targets, the revisionists.[17] Political conditions deteriorated even further.

On the other side of the political spectrum, the students, as well as Catholic deputies, suddenly found a new supporter. On March 21, the Polish Episcopate, which remained silent on the issue of civil rights, submitted an appeal to the government, stating:

> The problem of freedom of opinion, raised by society, the writers, and the Episcopate, was made especially apparent during the academic manifesta-
> tions. The right to honest information guaranteed by the constitution and by the UN Declaration requires free press and objectivity in information. The most important single cause of student indignation was the obvious lies of the press. The Episcopate, which for many years has suffered just such dishonesty of the press, well understands the indignation of the students.[18]

The bishops also demanded that the press accurately inform the public, or at least stop provoking youth and society with tendentious commentaries and editorials.[19] Nothing became of the church requests. The press continued its anti-intellectual campaign. Therefore, on March 23, Warsaw students drafted a new resolution, demanding: "The creation of an independent student press and the reactivation of a national periodical for students and young intelligentsia."[20]

The response of the authorities was swift and clear: Six Warsaw University professors were immediately expelled, a measure not taken even in the 1950s. The fired academics learned of the decision from morning papers. The move stoked the student protest fires. On the same day, a student meeting adopted a declaration that directly addressed the problem of organization in society and the circulation of information. The declaration demanded "the abolition of censorship" and allowed for "punishing writers in a legally predictable manner only when they publish texts infringing on the interests of citizens of society." In addition, public access to information concerning the activities of the state organs and freedom for the public to evaluate these activities had to be guaranteed.[21]

The events of the Prague spring of 1968 increased the fears of Polish leaders regarding freedom of the press.[22] The screw on the press tightened, particularly after the Warsaw Pact invasion of Czechoslovakia in August 1968. On September 14, the presidium of the Association of Polish Journalists reaffirmed the principles of control of the press by the party, using the Czechoslovakian loss of party monopoly as an alarming example.[23]

In journalism all of 1968 was dominated by the Partisan faction, which took a semi-fascist (or, rather, communo-fascist) stance. Some books on Judaism were excluded from the International Book Fair in Warsaw in May 1968. The performance of Giradoux's *Judith* was stopped because it was "too philosemitic." Even encyclopedias were re-edited to fit needs of the propaganda of the day. When volume eight of the Great Polish Encyclopedia was published in 1966, the entry on the Nazi concentration camps straightforwardly and reliably described the anti-Jewish Nazi policy and the nature of the camps, including the most notorious of them—Auschwitz. Two years later, this entry was severely criticized by the Moczar ideologues. The authors of the entry were castigated, and expulsed from the party and then from the country. The publisher was forced to print an amended description of the camps, which was sent in the form of a four-page leaflet to all the subscribers of the Encyclopedia. The new entry emphasized the martyrdom of the Polish nation, while that of the Jews was played down. The reason for this change, given by the corrected entry, was the falsification of the history of the camps perpetrated by capitalist publications (including encyclopedias) and the "tragic, in its political significance, alliance between Israel and West Germany."[24] It is therefore obvious that it was the question of the change in the foreign policy, not that of truth in historiography. At the Fifth Congress of the party, in June 1968, Gomułka emphasized the role emphasized the role of ideological work among the mass media on the ground that the "ideological front grows to the role of a main front of struggle between two political systems on a worldwide scale."[25]

The authorities acted accordingly to that diagnosis—swiftly and decisively. During 1968, more than 1,600 students were expelled, in part through dissolving some university departments. The purge reached the media, too. The August issue of *Prasa Polska*, the monthly organ of the Association of Polish Journalists, reported that in the past few months around 50 journalists employed in the press, radio, and television had been "transferred" to other posts and that at least 5 chief editors had been dismissed. In the entire period, about 800 employees of the Communist party press chain monopoly, RSW *Prasa*, were fired; among them were 254 people holding management positions. They were accused of being revisionists or Zionists or both and were usually forced to emigrate. All in all, by the end of 1968, two-thirds of Poland's remaining Jews had left. Since that time the Jewish issue has lost any relevance to social reality; nevertheless, as more recent developments have shown, anti-Semitism still haunts Polish politics and politicking.

Divisions Within the Official Press: *Polityka* Versus *Prawo i Życie*

The entire official press apparatus did not comply with the nationalistic faction. In the debate over patriotism, Zionism, and cosmopolitanism, the national paper of importance, the weekly *Polityka*, published a somewhat veiled criticism of the nationalistic faction and its policy.[26] For its stance the weekly was denounced by General Moczar as being "national nihilist."[27] This was a very serious charge at the time. The attitude of the editors of *Polityka* demonstrated, however, that it was possible to retain some journalistic integrity even when working for the party's mass media. When, for example, *Trybuna Ludu* (April 10, 1968) alleged that *Polityka* had become a publication of technocrats and managers as an advocate for "market and profit-oriented socialism," the entire editorial board of the weekly rejected these charges.[28] At the time, this was an act of courage.

Although *Polityka*'s example was followed by only a few other periodicals of lesser importance, it helped to strengthen the position of liberals and neutrals. Therefore, the press reflected an internal struggle for power, or for a post-Gomułka succession. But, in addition, it also helped to create a certain pluralism in the media, although much of it had a very ugly, nationalistic face.

On the other side of the political spectrum, the most notorious publications were *Prawo i Życie*, under the editorship of Kazimierz Kąkol, and the army daily, *Żołnierz Wolności*, both controlled by Moczar. Also, the youth press, contrary to the orientation of its "October 1956" predecessors, took a very nationalistic stance. In particular, a Communist youth organization weekly, *Walka Młodych* (The Struggle of the Youth), viciously attacked so-called nonpatriotic, cosmopolitan elements in the party, academia, culture, and the mass media. Prewar fascist, Bolesław Piasecki, chairman of the proregime Catholic organization PAX, continued to propagate his nationalistic ideology through the daily *Słowo Powszechne.*[29]

The anti-intellectual and anti-Semitic campaign of March 1968 was expressed through a change in the official language of the Communist media. This phenomenon should be viewed against an analysis of the language of typical Communist propaganda. It was always different from the language of the Western press, although many words looked familiar. Words such as democracy, freedom, party, or election meant different things in the Communist press than in the Western press. (A brief description of that language was given in Chapter 2.)

Thus, I turn now to the transformation in the party language after March 1968, which added significant rhetorical fireworks to traditional Communist propaganda. First, it toned up the language of editorials, reviving the style of the early 1950s—the peak era of Stalinism. Second, it resuscitated the language of the Polish right, particularly that of the 1930s. And third, it restored the language of the prewar yellow journalism, which catered to emotions and primitive instincts.[30]

If we focus only on anti-Semitic language, a vast array of tricks was used to convey the nationalistic propaganda. To give but one example, for some reason, Golda Meir, more than any other Israeli politician, became an object of shameful attacks. An editorial in a daily paper in the provincial city Łódź suggested that she should not deal with politics but should cook noodles with "her dirty hands." Although the allusion referred to the "dirty war against Arabs," in fact, it had the connotation of a stereotype of a Jew, who always had dirty hands. Information in *Trybuna Ludu* about a visit to the United States by Prime Minister Meir was entitled "How Many Weapons Will Golda Meir Haggle from the U.S.?" By using the word *haggle* (*targować się*), this indirectly alluded to an age-old stereotype of a Jewish storekeeper or trader.[31]

In the nationalistic segment of the press, Poles were always presented in favorable ways, usually as Catholics. The political opposition was painted as composed mainly of Jews. The problem, however, was with those Poles who were anti-Communist. For instance, of the students who revolted only a small minority were of Jewish origin, and of the dissenting writers many, such as January Grzędziński[32] or Stefan Kisielewski, were 100 percent Polish. The propaganda solution for this alleged anomaly was simple. All rebels were treated as traitors to the nation, although they did not act of their own will. The propaganda hinted at close relationship between such renegades and "circles of international Zionists." For example, in a *report* on the so-called Alpinist trial in 1969 in *Życie Warszawy*, we find: "Roots are reaching faraway, yet to Tel-Aviv. Kozłowski sends letters to notoriously known Zygmunt Bauman, who is there, to ask for advice on how to undermine Poland in the most efficient way. Indeed, he could hardly find a better person."[33] This grotesquely primitive segment suggested that Bauman was a bandit and a foreign agent, when, in fact, he had been a respected Warsaw University professor of sociology until March 1968. The article also suggested that the treacherous Pole, Kozłowski, was acting on orders of Bauman, a Jew. This would have been funny if it were not so shameful.[34]

The Emigré Media and the Alpinist Trial

With no possibility of gaining access to the Communist-controlled mass media, the internal opposition learned very early how to use Polish emigré publications and emigré radio stations to reach the national audience with its messages of protest. The most important vehicles were the Paris-based monthly *Kultura* and the emigré-operated radio station Radio Free Europe.[35] It is no exaggeration to state that the political history of Communist Poland would be incomplete without analyzing the roles of *Kultura* and of the Polish section of Radio Free Europe in political developments. Their roles were understood perfectly by the party leadership. In a televised broadcast in March 1968, Gomułka forcefully accused *Kultura* of indoctrinating the youth of the nation in the spirit of anti-communism. Thereafter, a dogged police action and a mass propaganda campaign were launched against the monthly. This only helped to make *it* more popular in Poland.

After the Warsaw Pact invasion of Czechoslovakia, a group of students, reviving the long-standing tradition of sneaking in independent literature from abroad, set up, along with a similar group in Czechoslovakia, a special network for such purpose. Students carried the books of the Institute Litteraire in Paris, the publisher of *Kultura*, and smuggled them over the Polish-Czechoslovak border in the Tatra Mountains.

After several months, they were caught by Czechoslovak authorities and turned over to Polish security services, who found this an excellent excuse to intimidate students and intellectuals. In subsequent roundup, over fifty people were arrested in 1969. Their trial was conceived by the secret police as a political showtrial, intended to intimidate the opposition. The media labeled them "the Alpinists" (in Polish *Taternicy*)—mountain climbers—because they smuggled illegal literature from the West by way of the Tatra Mountains. The trial, as with many similar trials that took place following the Warsaw Pact invasion of Czechoslovakia, became notorious under this name.

Main defendant Maciej Kozłowski, allegedly the group's leader, admitted that he smuggled publications but explained he did it because the Polish press never told the nation the whole truth. He denied accusations that he did anything wrong and said that, in fact, the impeachment was directed against *Kultura*'s publications.[36] But before the trial had concluded, new political developments made it less convenient for the authorities to aggravate the conflict with the opposition. New, more serious problems arose.

For one, the economic crisis worsened. In December 1968, facing growing social discontent, the Press Bureau of the Central Committee of the Communist party found a solution to it by recommending the promotion of "citizens' and journalists' responsibility." In addition, the Bureau scrutinized the political orientation of journalists; the party controllers were generally satisfied with the journalists' work.[37] Nevertheless, it ordered a tightening of censorship.[38]

In December 1970, the government increased prices for staple foods. This in turn spurred workers' protests and caused riots on the Baltic coast. On December 17, soldiers opened fire on workers going to the shipyards in Gdynia, and at least forty-four people were killed. Then, in a unprecedented move, on the front page of a local daily, *Kurier Szczeciński*, on December 20, 1970, along with the news of sit-in strikes and negotiations, a proclamation was published by the publication's printers. They showed disregard for censorship and published this unusual issue.[39] Surprisingly, the unauthorized action was praised by the paper's editorial board.[40] *Trybuna Ludu*, on the other hand, offered the information-starved national public an article stating that all was normal. Only its last sentence pronounced that "In Szczecin, the tension maintained itself, although no further events occurred."[41]

Despite *Trybuna*'s official denial, the situation was far from normal, which spelled the end of Gomułka's leadership. However, against all odds, instead of choosing the new party leader from the Partisan faction, top members of the Central Committee opted for the more low-key approach of the Silesian faction, headed by Edward Gierek, a party boss in the major mining and industry region of Poland. Gierek's rise to power also anticipated a change in the media policy.

Conclusion

March 1968 marked a turning point in party policy through a reversion to a period of intellectual darkness, which was almost as black as the days of Stalinism. The authorities lost their last points of contact with economic and social realities. The media lost what credibility it had gained, if any, since October 1956. March 1968 began as an open struggle for power within the party, in which the Partisan faction was not victorious. In one sense, it was a final act in the internal party struggle that had begun in 1955-1956 or, arguably, even earlier.[42] In another, it was an open attack on society and its first signs of self-organization. The Polish church perceived the campaign to be merely an internal party affair and maintained, except for the violence against students, a silence. Perhaps it did so because it remembered recent attacks on its hierarchy and felt vulnerable. In 1969 Gomułka leadership slowly retreated from its most drastic measures (such as the anti-Zionist campaign), and some papers and publicists who were very vocal at the time disappeared from the public scene. Nevertheless, many others held their newly acquired positions for many years.

Since 1968 the anti-Jewish theme had become an established, although not especially prevalent component in Communist propaganda. It was used particularly in times of crises—after the workers riot in June 1956; following the establishment of the Workers' Defense Committee (KOR) in 1976; and, later, after the establishment of the military regime in 1982 and 1983.[43] Nationalistic tunes were played frequently: They did not persuade ordinary people to embrace communism, but they did stir the feeling that "there is no smoke without fire." Some ghosts from the past were, therefore, revived. All of this showed that the Communists were adept at playing a nationalist card, and that national motifs made effective headlines.

The anti-Jewish campaign was aimed at sowing confusion and deceiving the public. These two goals were indeed achieved. In addition, for the first time since October 1956, the party was invigorated at the grass roots level. An intimidated society did not react to the new oppressive law against intellectual freedom.[44] The participation of Polish forces in the invasion of Czechoslovakia also passed virtually without protest.

One of the most important consequences of the anti-intellectual campaign was the change in the nature of opposition. Up until 1968, intellectual protest had put its faith in a renewal of the principles of 1956, in the capacity of the party and the system to reform themselves and lead the nation toward democracy. Party propaganda termed this revisionism. Although portrayed by these propagandists as a serious danger, revisionism was later described by its followers as being "a grand illusion."[45] Following March 1968 the revisionist tradition lost most of its supporters. The intellectuals and students found themselves isolated, without active support from either the workers or the majority of the

Catholic population. The mainstream within the opposition had been liberal, in the sense that it sought to find a secular, humanist path between the opposing currents of Catholicism and communism. Nearly ten years later, when the intellectual opposition was revived again, it took a very different form: It was more conservative and more influenced by history, and it looked to the Roman Catholic church for moral guidance and protection.[46]

However traumatic the events of December 1970 may have been, the change in party leadership somehow placed the events of March 1968, and the 1960s in general, in context. The next decade would be marked by Gierek's new policy and, less noticeable at the time, by the Roman Catholic church. In fact, competition and, occasionally, latent cooperation between Gierek and the church characterized the entire decade. This unique relationship created favorable conditions for the birth of Solidarity.

Notes

1. This thesis has been supported by two astute observers of the Eastern European scene, Agnes Heller and Ferenc Feher: "In the case of Moczarism, its social function was, through the mass rehabilitation of the Armia Krajowa [the Home army, non-Communist insurgent army whose members were persecuted in the 1950s and just tolerated afterward] and other measures, to mobilize national masses against rebellious intellectuals and university students with a basically chauvinistic and anti-Semitic `Black Hundred´ Ideology." *From Yalta to Glasnost: The Dismantling of Stalin's Empire* (London: Blackwell, 1990), p. 164.

2. Marek Chęciński, *Poland: Communism, Nationalism, Antisemitism* (New York: Karz-Cohl Publishing, 1982), pp. 160-161.

3. Much was said and written about Polish anti-Semitism, especially in the interwar period 1918-1939. At that time, one-tenth of Poland's population was Jewish, and the proportion was much higher in cities. This issue is too complicated to be discussed at length in a book on media policy. It seems appropriate, however, to show the political dimension of the issue after World War II. In the aftermath of the Holocaust there were about fifty thousand Jews in Poland; that number was halved by the post-October of 1956 emigration to Israel. Regardless of their small number, most of the Jews in Poland were party members. Many came with the Red army or the Polish army as political officers or Communist agitators. They later became engaged in the security apparatus, and some even occupied top positions in the party or the government. Many other were involved in writing, research, or art; prominent among them were leading Communist activists. This, together with the high proportion of Jews in the prewar Polish Communist party, fueled popular animosity— particularly among the peasants—against the Jews. See Łukasz Hirszowicz, "The Jewish Issue in Post-War Communist Politics," in Chimen Abramsky et al., ed., *The Jews in Poland* (Oxford: Blackwell, 1986), pp. 198-248.

4. See notes to Chapter 4. Also see Neal Ascherson, *The Struggles for Poland* (London: Michael Joseph), pp. 174, 176-177.

5. See Lucjan Blit, Anti-Jewish Campaign in Present Day Poland (London: The Institute of Jewish Affairs, 1968), p. 6.

6. Over three thousand Warsaw University students and professors passed a resolution that, under the subheading "We Demand," called for "Immediate rectification of the false picture of events given by the press." Peter Raina, *Political Opposition in Poland: 1954-1977* (London: Poets and Painters Press, 1978), pp. 130-132.

7. Jakub Karpiński, *Countdown. The Polish Upheavals of 1956, 1968, 1976, 1980* (New York: Karz-Cohl Publishers, 1982), p. 124.

8. Ibid., p. 125.

9. Using the age-old stereotype of youth as being rebellious and not observing traditional manners and beliefs, it was also hinted that their parents, who enjoyed high standards of living and frequently traveled abroad, satisfied all of their children's wants. Among other things, they provided them with bananas and other exotic fruits that were very difficult to buy in Poland. Therefore, the epithet "Banana youth" instead of the traditional "Golden Youth" was popularized. Thus, anti-Semitism was hidden or, rather, was mixed with more widespread popular jealousy, making it more acceptable and influential.

10. Needless to say, in many cases it was not the young people but their parents who were punished or fired from jobs and forced to emigrate. They were accused of not bringing up their children properly.

11. I give just one example here. The well-known Polish professor Leszek Kołakowski was also forced to emigrate.

12. At the time, being a young assistant at Jagiellonian University, I felt not only threatened but also insulted by the propaganda campaign.

13. See *Judenheze in Polen. Eine Dokumentation von Simon Wiesenthal* [The Anti-Jewish Campaign in Poland. The Documentation by Simon Wiesenthal] (Bonn, 1969).

14. The proof is to be found in the articles written by those journalists, which include many details that could be known only to persons with access to police files.

15. As Neal Ascherson noted, "Mieczysław Rakowski, editor of the party weekly *Polityka*, gave no space to the anti-Semitic slanders." *Struggles*, p. 177.

16. *Proceedings of the Seventh Congress of the Polish Journalist Association*, in the Archives of the SDP.

17. Józef Lubiński, *Zasady i cele polityki PZPR w dziedzinie komunikowania w latach 1948-1971*, unpublished doctoral dissertation (Kraków: Uniwersytet Jagielloński, 1988).

18. Text in English from Karpiński, *Countdown*, p. 131. Full text Raina, *Political Opposition*, p. 144-145.

19. The undersigned were Cardinal Wyszyński and Cardinal Wojtyła; the latter became Pope John Paul II.

20. Karpiński, *Countdown*, pp. 132-133.

21. Lubiński, *Zasady*, vol. 2, p. 499.

22. The events were interpreted as a simple consequence of the Communist party losing control over the mass media, especially radio and television. "Pelikanization" [Pelikan was the name of director of the Czechoslovak radio and television], that is, autonomy of radio and television, was considered the ultimate reason for the Soviets to intervene.

23. Lubiński, *Zasady*, vol. 2. p. 501.

24. Publisher's insert to vol. 11, *Wielka Encyklopedia Powszechna PWN* (Warszawa: PWN, 1968).

25. Lubiński, *Zasady*, vol. 2. p. 506.

26. Content analysis done by the Press Research Center in 1969. Characteristically during the Solidarity period, polemics in the free press appeared to reject this thesis regarding the Jewish character of Stalinism in Poland. Of the Communist press only *Polityka* shared that position. See M. Mieszczankowski, "Jednostronne spojrzenie" [A One-Sided Point of View], *Polityka*, May 23, 1981, p. 8.

27. Moczar interview in *Trybuna Ludu*, April 13-15, 1968, p. 3.

28. Raina, *Political Opposition*, p. 157.

29. However, Piasecki's PAX association was not supported or recognized by the Roman Catholic church in Poland. Piasecki had a very bad reputation, especially since 1953 when his organization accepted the takeover of the respected Catholic weekly *Tygodnik Powszechny*.

30. An excellent analysis of this language, properly called "March babbling" (*Marcowe gadanie*), was prepared by Michał Głowiński and published in a book under the same title (Warszawa: Nowa, 1991).

31. *Trybuna Ludu*, September 25, 1968, p. 1.

32. One of the less known dissenting Polish intellectuals, Grzędziński, was subjected to harassment and abuse. Jerzy Piechowski, "Zemsta na Januarym Grzędzińskim" [The Vengeance Against January Grzędziński], *Solidarność*, September 22, 1990, p. 9.

33. February 8, 1970, p. 4.

34. It is unnecessary to add that the prolonged press hysteria over purges and emigration and a lack of clear public condemnation of this campaign by the Polish Roman Catholic church tarnished Poland's reputation abroad, especially in the United States.

35. *Kultura* was very influential in Poland, because it printed, under pen names, articles of eminent Polish writers and scholars. It was confined to special shelves in university libraries and a special permit was needed even for professors who wanted to read it.

36. Raina, *Political Opposition*, p. 174.

37. "The recent media history of Poland, Hungary, Czechoslovakia, and the former East Germany confirms that under certain circumstances, nominally nonparty journalists and, among the older generation, former right-wing and erstwhile fascist journalists can prove to be more reliable than some party members who still cling to their ideals rather than letting themselves be guided by the instinct for survival. This was shown during the large-scale 'anti-Zionist'—anti-Semitic and anti-intellectual—campaign in Poland in 1968." Paul Lendvai, *The Bureaucracy of Truth: How Communist Governments Manage the News*

(Boulder: Westview, 1981), p. 40.

38. Lubiński, *Zasady*, p. 536.

39. The issue was unusual because at that time no provincial daily was printed on Sunday.

40. *Kurier Szczeciński*, December 20, 1970, p. 1.

41. *Trybuna Ludu*, December, 20, 1970, p. 1.

42. Ibid., p. 205.

43. Hirszowicz, "The Jewish Issue," pp. 198-208.

44. The new law on the organization of college education was introduced, which further restricted already limited academic autonomy.

45. Bronisław Geremek, "Between Hope and Despair," in *Daedalus* 119 (Winter 1990), p. 100.

46. Adam Michnik, in his influential essay of the mid-1970s entitled "The Church, the Left and the Dialogue," tried to reconciliate the hitherto hostile traditions of the lay left and the Catholic church. His other essay, the famous "New Evolutionism" of 1976, rejected the intellectual traditions of internal opposition to the Communist system, called "revisionism" and "newpositivism" (that is working to improve the system), and proposed gradual change and rejection of the regime through activities independent from the state. This laid ground for the re-birth of the concept of "civil society." More on this in William Echikson, *Lighting the Night: Revolutions in Eastern Europe* (London: Sidgwick and Jackson, 1990), pp. 158-159, and Jacques Rupnik, *The Other Europe* (London: Weidenfeld and Nicolson, 1988), pp. 218-219. H. Gordon Skilling considers Michnik's essays, together with Havel's article "Power of the Powerless" as the most inspiring for development of a new opposition in Eastern Europe. See his *Samizdat and an Independent Society in Central and Eastern Europe* (London: Macmillan, 1989), p. 182.

10

From Gierek's Harmony to Dissidents' Discordance
December 1970 to June 1980

Gierek was responsible for creating the extensive, centralized television system.
— Madeleine Albright, *Poland: The Role of the Press in Political Change*

The samizdat, always confiscated and destroyed but always resurrecting, became the embryonic form of a new public sphere.
— Agnes Heller and Ferenc Feher, *From Yalta to Glasnost*

Edward Gierek was the first top Communist leader who instinctively grasped the significance of the new mass medium, television. In his first nationwide televised address, he used de Gaulle's techniques of persuasion: patriotic substance, big words, and statesman's gestures. Gierek's approach worked.

The Uses of Journalists

To build its power base, Gierek outlined a plan of broad political and economic reforms, in which public support and propaganda was to play a much more important role than it had under Gomułka's party leadership.[1] Gierek, when he was party secretary of the most industrialized region of Poland, dealt cleverly with the local media. He used a blend of stern control, bonuses for journalists' loyalty, and close relations with top media managers.

As a victim of Stalinism, Gomułka condemned the "cult of personality" that was characteristic of national party leaders in the Communist countries.[2] Therefore, he did not seek personal popularity, even when, as was the case in October 1956, he was almost a national hero. Gomułka disdained the press, the journalism profession in general, and certain journalists in particular.[3] Nor did he believe in the power of charismatic leadership or of the media. At best, he simply ignored the media. Gierek, in contrast, was inclined to use the mass media for his own personal promotion. For this he needed to secure cooperation of the journalists. Therefore, his information policy attributed more eminent status to the journalism profession. Journalists who supported him were admitted into the party elite or were at least close to it. Their working conditions were ameliorated, wages were increased, and travels abroad became more frequent. At the same time, the journalist became even more of a party adjunct than had been the case under Gomułka's rule. In short, Gierek carried out a policy that utilized both the carrot and the stick, whereas Gomułka had operated only with the stick.

Initially, information policy became more flexible. On March 10, 1971, a new position was created, that of government spokesperson. Moreover, press conferences were organized with ministries and other senior officials. Gierek himself initiated press conferences and meetings with journalists and editors. A new television program entitled "Citizen's Tribune" was inaugurated to serve as an open forum. However, it did not last long. All of these new measures were taken partially to inform citizens about the new party policy and partially were to show the new leadership's openness and desire for change—novelty that was well received by journalists, intellectuals, and the public at large.

In the Gierek years, the major change in the system of mass media was the return to the Stalinist concept of propaganda linked with technical modernization of the media. The first tactic was evident in Gierek's strategy the "propaganda of success."[4] As described in Chapter 6, this kind of propaganda had its precedents in the early 1950s, when the optimistic picture of the pursuit of happiness by Poles within a framework of "the camp of fraternal socialist countries" was painted continually in the press, in newsreels, and on radio. To that perception Gierek added a new tone: Television, particularly the evening news, became the most important means of building the leader's image.

The new information policy was made party law at the Sixth Congress of the Polish United Workers Party (PZPR) in 1971. For the first time in party history, the highest party forum focused intensively on the mass media.[5] The final resolution stated that "in the functioning of the entire system of the state, the media of mass information and propaganda plays an essential role. It is one of the main instruments for inspiration and mobilization of the nation to precipitate the development of socialism and an improvement in the well-being of working people."[6] The resolution specified that the tasks of the mass media were to procure support for the political and propaganda lines of the party, strengthen the authentic ties of the party to the nation, illuminate the role of party leadership in sociopolitical life, and promote citizen initiatives. The media was directed to upgrade political knowledge, develop Marxist-Leninist thought, and stimulate patriotic and internationalist-proletarian feelings.

To balance this typically propagandistic role of the media with the demands of journalists and expectations of the audience, some paragraphs of the party documents stressed the role of criticism, the importance and relevance of public information, and the function of the press as a platform for dialogue and exchange of ideas. However, in reality the government was only paying lip service to the concept of genuine public dialogue.

The new element in the party's communication policy was a different emphasis on the role of the mass media. It was no longer regarded as an instrument of ideology but was considered to be a mouthpiece for the top leadership, especially for Gierek himself. Therefore, instead of selling just the ideas of Marxism-Leninism, the media was compelled to "gather the nation around the party and its program." In practice that meant it should support Gierek and his policies. Therefore, whereas media contents were de-ideologized, the public relation ingredient was magnified.

The Zenith of Polish Television

Previously a secondary means of mass communication, under Gierek's leadership television became the most important means.[7] Party dogma maintained that those who control television control society. In the 1960s, television served primarily as a cultural and an entertainment medium, and as such it enjoyed relative autonomy. However, in the 1970s, as a political medium, it was put under the most rigorous party control. On the programming side, its control was taken away from regional directors and was placed under the direct rule of the Department of Press, Radio, and Television.

The newly appointed television boss and Gierek's close collaborator, Maciej Szczepański, considerably increased the investment in television, expanded the broadcast range, and provided subsidies to lower the price of television sets. Throughout the 1970s the technical facilities of radio and television were substantially improved. The number of hours of emission of television broadcasting increased about 60 percent during that decade.[8] At the same time, the hours of local broadcasting decreased, and centralization of management increased.

As a reflection of television's growing popularity, the number of television sets increased many times. To further increase its audience, television began to broadcast Western—mainly U.S.—programs, such as "Kojak" and "Charlie's Angels." The evening television news bulletin, then widely and avidly watched, was transmitted simultaneously on both television channels. It lasted an hour or more and was filled with information that tended to underscore all of the so-called achievements of socialism. When such facts were not at hand, the editors usually invented them. Bad news was hidden, if not contradicted. Thus, the news bulletin was jokingly referred to as "An Hour of Prosperity."

Centralization of the Media System

In addition to the centralization of television, the press system became more centralized, largely because of the increased importance placed on the party daily organ, *Trybuna Ludu*. The special party resolution of April 1972 affirmed *Trybuna Ludu*'s leading role in regard to all local party organs. The central daily was again to serve as a compulsory model for all local newspapers. Its leading role was illustrated by the number of citations and references made to it in local papers.

As such an important and valuable daily, *Trybuna Ludu*, had to be even more closely supervised. Logically, the resolution empowered the secretariat of the Central Committee with full control over the contents of programs. The party's resolution also called for an increase in the number of pages, the circulation, and, eventually, the readership of *Trybuna Ludu*. For these new goals to be met, improved technology and distribution, as well as higher pay and other privileges for the editors, were urged. It became the first Polish newspaper to be printed simultaneously in several major cities, it received the best telecommunications equipment, and its journalists received the highest salaries. Gierek and his secretary for propaganda, Jerzy Łukaszewicz, personally controlled *Trybuna Ludu*, which in turn set a model for regional papers. The latter were also controlled by local party bosses and were additionally supervised by an instructor from the press section of the Propaganda Department. The pyramidal model of the press was strengthened as it was highly effective. However, it demanded a considerable increase in the number of propaganda department and censorship offices personnel.

Because Gierek's ascent to power was supported by the regional Silesian media, especially by the daily *Trybuna Robotnicza* (Workers' Tribune), the increased role of the central newspaper was very ironic. However, the decision to exert greater control over *Trybuna Ludu* was influenced by Gierek's experience with controlling local media through the regional party daily.

To strengthen party control over the media, and to centralize within the Propaganda Department of the Central Committee, several other measures were undertaken. The tendency toward centralization was evident in the merging of many magazines and newspapers during the period 1972-1975. For example, the three film periodicals were merged to create one weekly, *Film*. The illustrated youth weekly *Razem* (Together) replaced two similar weeklies. The main party publishing house, RSW *Prasa*, was reorganized and became even bigger. On January 1, 1973, the giant press concern RSW *Prasa-Książka-Ruch* (The Workers' Publishing Cooperative Press-Book-Movement) was established. To its almost monopolistic newspaper and magazine publishing activities, the former RSW *Prasa*, was added *Książka i Wiedza*, the party book publishing house, and, more important, the state-owned distribution agency, *Ruch*, which had a monopoly on distribution of the press. *Ruch* had already brought enormous profits from its nationwide network of newsstands.

The important gain for RSW was also the appropriation of *Ars Polona*, a major foreign trade company that specialized in exporting silver, works of art, and books. This was an interesting development within the Communist media. RSW became not only an ideological, highly centralized concern but also a profit-making machine that supported the party with both Polish and foreign currency.

In July 1975, the local territorial reorganization of the country was announced. Seventeen large voivodships were divided into forty-nine much smaller units. This territorial arrangement placed the regional dailies under the strict control of the Press Department. Therefore, they were renamed "dailies of the PZPR" and lost their status as agents of regional party committees. Special consulting boards, composed of party apparatchiks and chaired by a representative of the Propaganda Department, were set up to merge the editorial policy of regional papers with the policy of the Central Committee.

In the newly established voivodships local party weeklies were created, thereby creating the appearance of real decentralization. However, these weak little papers were totally dependent on local party committees, which were usually even more narrow-minded than the Central Committee.

The Congress of Victors

In 1975 everything seemed to be going well for Gierek. Like Gomułka in 1956 and 1957, he was almost a national hero. The propaganda of "socialist" success was also an apparent success. The general mood of the populace was still quite favorable. Many journalists eagerly joined the party by their own choice. The best example was that of Stefan Bratkowski, a journalist who always had new ideas. He set up a special section, "Life and Modernity," in the popular daily *Życie Warszawy*, which despite some reservations supported and promoted Gierek's push for Polish modernity. It is significant, however, that Bratkowski had an "invisible" party sponsor—namely, Stefan Olszowski, head of the Propaganda Department. When Bratkowski eventually became disillusioned with the party's policies, he lost his section, and his and Olszowski's paths parted entirely.[9] When Bratkowski and Olszowski met again, their views were completely opposed.

In 1975, the Seventh Congress of the PZPR proved to be an excellent occasion for the celebration of the success of Gierek's strategy. Accordingly, the Congress was unofficially and aptly nicknamed "the Congress of Victors." The best example of the prevailing mood is illustrated by the pronouncement of the editor-in-chief of the television news department, Czesław Cześnin. In straight and candid words Cześnin formulated new journalistic duties:

> The journalism profession is still considered by certain people as a so-called free profession. That was long ago and, besides, it was never true. Every journalist, no matter under what geographic longitude, has worked or works for and has to wait on someone. We, Polish journalists, serve the party and its leadership. And both the party and the leadership have no other goal than to serve the nation.[10]

The logical conclusion was obvious: By serving Gierek, the journalist serves the nation—the latter being a sacrosanct obligation of a true Polish intellectual. In establishing such a simple, transitional, logical relationship among the party, its leadership, and the nation, Cześnin expressed the essence of Gierek's new approach: What was good for Gierek was good for the country.

At the congress the general tone of assessment of the performance of the mass media and the journalism profession was enthusiastic. "Never before," said many speakers, "had the mass media and journalists such excellent conditions for work," and, in typical party verbiage, "never before was the status of journalists so high; never before were the trust and confidence of the party leadership so positive. This, however, should not lead to self-satisfaction but, rather, to ever further improvement of our work."[11] Yet, in comparison to former policy pronouncements and the party's practice of propaganda, the Seventh Congress took a step backward. This was evident in Cześnin's explanation of the new responsibilities of journalists:

> A journalist who dispassionately ponders all "fors" and "againsts" takes either a harmful pose or simply does not understand at all what the party's

stance is based upon. We [journalists] are party activists to whom the party granted special responsibility to offensively spreading its arguments, not doubts, and to promote effective propaganda of the general line of the party leadership.[12]

By the mid-1970s, the quasi-Stalinist media policy had been formulated and accepted at the highest party convention. No doubts about its effectiveness were held or allowed to be voiced. Only timid criticism was occasionally allowed in the official media. Kazimierz Koźniewski, a veteran prewar journalist, dared only to note that "the centralization of the press has reached an intensity that—let us be frank— is not beneficial to a creative journalist. Frequently, a journalist must give in, adapt to various demands and censorship, and work in situations and under the system imposed upon him."[13] The effects of propaganda in the first half of the 1970s were clearly visible—they effectively incited people's expectations, bringing about a so-called revolution of rising expectations, a phenomenon well-known from the Third World modernization drive.

However, the contents of the media evolved from pure ideology to include more entertainment. There were more classified announcements and commercials in the party press. This was done to earn money so ever-growing party needs could be satisfied. In addition, the RSW launched profit-oriented magazines that focused on entertainment. Once again, ideology had retreated in the face of the need profit.

Paradoxically, but endemic of Polish history, after the height immediately came the nadir; the Congress of Victors marked an end to Gierek's successes. From that time on, the Polish economic miracle was failing, and the only way to save appearances was to exert more control over the media. Signs of pending doom were beginning to emerge. Despite all pretenses of modernization, the Sunday editions of dailies were canceled in January 1975 on economic grounds. "The Tenth World Economic Power," as Poland was christened in the "propaganda of success," became a country in which the daily press was literally a thing of the past.

In order to tame more investigative journalism, the main office (of censorship) was enlarged and became more centralized. The tightening censorship policy is best demonstrated by conditions and events pertaining to the influential weekly *Polityka*, which in the 1960s and even the early 1970s maintained some editorial independence and published critical articles.[14] Born as a counter-paper to *Po prostu*, the weekly *Polityka* became a respected voice for reform-minded intellectuals, technocrats, managers, and even some party apparatchiks. But during the 1970s, *Polityka* was transformed from being a relatively liberal and restricted critic of the system to being a moderate apologist. At the time of the Radom and Ursus workers' strikes in June 1976, *Polityka* defended Gierek's disintegrating strategy, and its esteem diminished immediately. In the words of Adam Michnik this event meant an end "to the illusion that the system could be reformed from above."[15]

The discovery of the impossibility of reforming communism led many intellectuals to adopt a new strategy called "new evolutionism."[16] Its goal, conceding that there was no hope for reform from inside the party, was to gradually restore civil and political liberties. The issue of freedom of expression, therefore, became very important and was openly discussed. This liberalization in Poland reflected the international political thaw that was taking place at the time. It was in the spirit of the Helsinki agreement of 1975, especially the so-called Third Basket stipulations, that Polish artists began to demand more freedom. The Polish writer Kazimierz Orłoś bluntly expressed this feeling in an article entitled "On Freedom of Speech and Censorship After the Ratification of the Pacts of Human Rights."[17] He accused the authorities of sustaining censorship, in direct contravention of the Declaration of Human Rights and the Human Rights Convention. The Polish state, he claimed, is bound by these documents.[18] The stand taken by Orłoś represented a new and strong tone in the voice of the Polish intelligentsia.

The First Discord: The Debate over the Constitution

After the Seventh Congress of the PZPR, all promises for a more democratic Poland had faded. To appear stronger, and perhaps to please Brezhnev, Gierek brought forward a new draft of the constitution, which included clauses about the "unshakable fraternal bonds with the Soviet Union" and "the leading role of the Communist party."

Gierek's move was too demanding for the church and the intellectuals to accept. A protest against such clauses was lodged to the speaker of Parliament by fifty-five Polish poets, lawyers, priests, and academicians. In the memorandum they demanded that the government observe the right to freedom of expression as guaranteed by the constitution.[19] The memorandum can be regarded as the antecedent of the Charter 77 civil right proclamation, signed by some Czechoslovak intellectuals a year later.[20] Resistance soon swept the country. Students joined the protest, and letters from supporting intellectuals followed. The declaration of "The Democratic Movement" (Warsaw, October 1977) stated that "without freedom of speech there can be no development of culture, resulting in the stagnation of social life . . . public opinion is prevented from emerging."[21]

The outrage was so strong and widespread that it led to a watering down of the proposed amendments. Hence, something dangerous to the regime occurred. The precedent for at least partially successful political protest was set. More important, the church also expressed its displeasure. Cardinal Wyszyński consistently demanded political concessions, including a relaxation of censorship, and this time his words were much more harsh. The pastoral letter, read in every church, blatantly stated, "The media is in the hands of people guided by principles of militant atheism and an ideology hostile to all religion. They are used to carrying on persistent propaganda of a godless ideology and the cult of the robot man, to spreading secular moral attitudes as a human model, and to justifying political violence and class hatred and struggles."[22] The church's clear stand pushed a network of Catholic intelligentsia clubs to openly debate the content of the media and its control.

However, it was a group of hardened dissidents, with rather liberal lay attitudes, that formed the first effective opposition organization in Eastern Europe. What is more important for this study, they created the first truly effective information network.

The Underground Is Reborn

Gierek not only failed to recognize the changing mood of the church and the intelligentsia; he also misread the mood of those on whom his legitimacy was based—namely, the working class in the major industrial plants. Thus, he did not object to a June 1976 increase in meat prices. In response, the workers in two Polish industrial towns, in Radom and Ursus, demonstrated against the increases, as their predecessors had done in 1956 and 1970 in Poznań and Gdańsk, respectively. The authorities withdrew the price increase but severely punished the revolting workers; some were beaten, and many more were fired.

The government repression prompted a small group of intellectuals to organize private help for the victims of the persecution. Known as the Committee for the Defense of Workers (KOR), the group was formed by six young men who had been involved in the student revolt in March 1968; among them were Jacek Kuroń, Adam Michnik, and Antoni Maciarewicz. KOR not only defended prosecuted workers but also began to publish information about the official reprisals. The taboo of silence was broken.

If the foreign radio was the first independent medium of mass communication in the Communist countries, the independent underground publications were the second. In building opposition, they were much more important and effective than foreign radio, which focused on sustaining anti-Communist feelings rather than providing active behavioral responses.

Although Poland has an age-old tradition of underground publishing, it was almost impossible to publish anything illegal in Stalinist Poland.[23] Illegal leaflets only appeared just before October 1956. In party milieus, the Khrushchev "secret speech" was illegally duplicated and widely circulated. But even then no special urge to publish beyond censorship was felt. Dissenting intellectuals preferred to publish their works under a pen name in emigré publications rather than risk publication in Poland.[24]

Ironically, illegal publication did not begin in post-October Poland, with its relatively liberal censorship and party control and its tradition of publishing abroad, but in the Soviet Union.[25] The phenomenon is, therefore, better known in the West under its Russian name *samizdat*.[26] Initially, samizdat was briefly defined as "typewritten copies, transferred by hand" and later and more adequately as "unapproved material reproduced unofficially by hand, typewriter, mimeograph or, occasionally, by Xerography."[27] In the 1970s, samizdat became virtually a second literary system in Eastern Europe, overcoming governmental control over the Gutenberg-type presses. Following the Soviet Union's dissident example,[28] samizdat appeared in Czechoslovakia[29] and eventually in Poland during the mid-1970s.[30] The beginning of the new uncensored press in Poland can be dated to September 29, 1976, when the first issue of *Komunikat KOR* appeared.[31] It was soon followed by hundreds of usually ephemeral periodicals.

The tendency to choose independence instead of compromise (with authorities and their censorship) moved people to establish various periodicals. Usually, this was clearly stated in their inaugural issues. The biweekly *Robotnik* (Worker), which began publishing in September 1977, stressed that its "fundamental task would be to convey the truth, since the official press did not fulfill this role; on the contrary, it was full of lies and slanders."[32] The goal of *Bratniak* (Fraternity), a student periodical, was to "keep the younger generation informed about the events in the student and, more broadly, the youth movement."[33] The literary journal *Puls* (Pulse) was more specific. It justified the grounds for its establishment by pointing to (1) the lack of freedom of speech and criticism, which paralyzes the development of culture and destroys its wealth and variety; and (2) the enforced silence, or the forced expression of ideas contrary to personal conviction, which destroys the sense of personal dignity of people and of the writer.[34] The farmers' monthly *Gospodarz* gave the following reasons for its appearance: "to defend the right to the land, to an honest life, to the faith of our fathers, to freedom. We want it to be both the ally [of the workers movement] and a weapon."[35] Everywhere, the motive to publish was based on the desire to express the opinions, feelings, and attitudes of the group that decided to risk making these feelings public.

Between 1976 and 1980, over one hundred independent periodicals emerged. Some were printed in relatively large runs, considering the facilities at the disposal of underground print shops. *Robotnik* appeared in an offset form and reached a press run of forty thousand copies.[36] Moreover, its readership was well targeted at a vital section of the working class: intelligent, well-educated men and women.

Beginning in 1976, samizdat assumed the proportions of a major industry in Poland. A separate volume is needed to describe these presses. Let us stress only their overall political importance. The independent publisher Tomasz Mianowicz observed: "There was no longer samizdat. A whole network of independent publications was created, a readers' market, and a distribution system for works of literature, journalism, and academic works unhampered by censorship. These uncensored publications were only a part, but the most important part, of a general self-defense of society against the totalitarian apparatus of the state."[37]

Despite the impressive output of the underground presses, the production could not compete with official publications in terms of readership. Not everyone read or was interested in samizdat publications. Nonetheless, as Mianowicz wrote, underground publications broke "the Communist state monopoly of information."[38] Perhaps even more important, the presses created new cadres that were ready to take over power if the occasion ever arose. Paradoxically, then, samizdat supported Lenin's concept of the underground press as a basic tool for organization of the mass movement.[39]

In the spirit of 1970s détente, the regime could no longer control all knowledge, behavior, fashion, and art. Reluctantly, the Communists reconciled themselves to new currents. Whether in Moscow or Leningrad, Budapest or Pecs, Cracow or Warsaw, Berlin or Leipzig, thousands of young converts to various forms of Western experience appeared. They ranged from the old-style hippies to Hare Krishna, punks, and skinheads. Official attitudes were initially reluctant to accept such subcultures, later they became more tolerant, but even those who favored banning them admitted that such censorship had become virtually impossible since the invention of the taperecorder. Thus, the emergence of the counterculture was connected with some forms of information flow—somehow, new ideas, pictures, and habits found their way through the Iron Curtain.

In addition to samizdats, magnizdats appeared, which were illegally produced and distributed audio-video tapes. They had a special impact on the youth. Occasionally, political cassettes were produced, such as Bratkowski's "spoken newspaper," an audiocassette that circulated as a weekly publication.[40] This particular mixture, the youth and the taperecorder, ultimately became very explosive. Plato had wisely foretold that when a style of music changes, a change in a form of government follows. Communists had for years been saying that those who have the youth have the future. When they lost the youth, they held no future.

Ironically, from the mid-1970s on, journalists were trapped in the Gierek system. They lost control over the dissemination of information and criticism, not only because of Gierek's limits on them but also because of his regime's failure to limit the "uncensored" press. Partly because of increasing isolation and partly because of a desire to buy off intellectual disaffection and Western creditors, the regime allowed this press to exist virtually in the open.[41]

The Escape of a Censor

On March 10, 1977, a censor from Cracow, Tomasz Strzyżewski, escaped to the West with a suitcase filled with confidential censorship documents. These were soon published in Polish, then in English, making the Polish censorship system a *cause celèbre*.[42]

The corpus of more than seven hundred pages, named in the West *The Black Book of Polish Censorship*, consisted mainly of guidelines and instructions for censors, which described with pedantic exactitude not only the nature and scope of information and in what manner its use by the mass media was to be prevented but also the type of information that was not to be promoted and supported. These instructions and prohibitions comprised a vast range of subjects from matters of general national concern to the most obscure topics. Particularly detailed were the restrictions concerning religious matters, nationalities, and socioeconomic matters. In these fields access to truthful information by the general public was almost totally inhibited. The guidelines contained additional prohibitions and so-called codes (*zapisy*) that related to specific blacklisted persons, facts, figures, and events.

To illustrate the scope and range of censorship, I quote a few instructions, taken at random from the *Book of Codes and Recommendations* of the Main Office of the Control of the Press, Publications, and Public Performances (GUKPPiW):

1. No personal attacks should be permitted against heads of states with which Poland maintains diplomatic relations . . .
13. All information concerning Archbishop Jan Cieplak, who died in 1925, should be eliminated . . .
33. No information concerning the awarding of a state decoration at the main board of the Polish-Soviet Friendship Society should be permitted . . .
61. No information, reviews, etc. should be permitted concerning Jerzy Stembrowicz's *Structure, Organization and Operation of the*

> *Government of the Polish People's Republic.* This prohibition is intended solely for the information of the censors . . .
>
> 99. Care should be taken that material on the situation in the United States and the policies of the U.S. government that are published during President Ford's visit to Poland be presented in a factual, sedate tone.
>
> 142. Materials on the trials of the participants in the incidents in Radom and Ursus [June 1976] may be permitted only through the intermediary of Polish Press Agency. [43]

The regulations instructed that the treacherous massacre of several thousand Polish prisoners of war in Katyń Forest by the Soviets in 1941 was to be blamed on the Germans; therefore, authors had to follow the line laid down in the *Great Soviet Encyclopedia*.[44] This example reveal in the best way that censorship was never practiced by the Polish authorities alone. The Soviet Embassy in Warsaw was the censor-in-chief, the "custodian of ideological purity" in Poland. A close associate of Gomułka, Władysław Bieńkowski, insisted on this in his *Open Letter*, written in March 1976.[45]

However, it would be preposterous to assume that Polish censorship was the strictest in Eastern Europe. Evidence suggest the contrary. Ceauscescu's Romania officially renounced censorship; so did Honecker's East Germany and Husak's Czechoslovakia. In the Soviet Union, *Glavlit* existed and operated, but its existence was frequently officially negated or its importance minimized. Censorship evidently was a sign of the weakness of a Communist regime, not of its strength. When it existed, the decisions on whether to publish were made by an administrative body and concrete persons. It was, therefore, possible to argue with them or, in a lost case, to explain to fellow journalists faults in one's writing that were caused by censors' alterations or cuts. Paradoxically, under Communist rule, creative writers felt more comfortable with formal censorship than without it. Paraphrasing Hannah Arendt's famous expression of the "banality of evil," censorship was not only banal but also had, literally, a human face. Thus, I end this sad description with an touch of humor: "A Song on Censorship," written by a poet, Adam Zagajewski, who had numerous occasions to meet not-so-anonymous censors when his unacceptable verses were bowdlerized:

> Censorship is not terrible, not at all
> There are no cellars and streams of water
> Dripping down the stony walls
> . . . .
> But there is sun in windows, wooden desks,

And a kettle whistling cheerful

. . . .

To the ripples of laughter of a chubby woman clerk
Who holds normal scissors in her hand.[46]

The Visit that Changed Poland

The end of Gierek's decade was marked by an event of great importance for the Polish nation. This topic can be easily exaggerated by a Pole, so I quote a widely respected observer of the Eastern European scene, Timothy Garton Ash: "If I were to be forced to name a single date for the `beginning of the end' in this inner history of Eastern Europe, it would be June 1979. The Pope's first great pilgrimage to Poland was that turning point. Here, for the first time, we saw that large-scale, sustained, yet supremely peaceful and self-disciplined manifestation of social unity, the gentle crowd against the party state."[47]

Indeed, the crowds were there. The pope spoke to more than 6 million people and delivered around thirty sermons and public addresses. More important for my purposes here, however, is that the pontiff's journey was a television spectacle and media event of an unprecedented scale in Poland.[48] Around 1,200 foreign journalists were accredited to report the visit. In the West, hours of television and radio programming covered this joyful and moving event.

The aim of manipulated media coverage was to minimize the importance of the political aspect of the visit and even to use it as an example of "People's Poland achievements." Therefore, all images of vast crowds were to be eliminated, a task that was impossible to achieve. Once again it was proved that nothing was impossible for the Communist media. Usually, millions of believers attended the masses. Yet, Polish camerapeople focused on small crowds, predominantly composed of old nuns, and groups near the altar. Television cameras would fix on the popemobile or on a helicopter for several minutes to avoid any other shots. The media sought to minimize the impact of the pope's visit and to prevent the dissemination of his pleas for more religious freedom, human rights, and brotherhood.

In Poland, the media coverage was orchestrated to the last detail. Party papers could not publish photographs of the pope, except for *Trybuna Ludu*. Information was provided exclusively through the state news agency, PAP; therefore, dailies carried virtually the same story. In fact, the Propaganda Department acted as a metaphoric "collective journalist." To assist the few Polish journalists in attendance (unlike their Western counterparts, very few were accredited), two special five-man agitprop teams worked around the clock at the Propaganda Department.

On average, television devoted only about fifteen minutes a day to the visit, with extended time for special occasions, such as masses at different locations. Only three events—the arrival, the visit to Auschwitz, and the departure ceremony—were covered nationwide; all others were shown on local television. Moreover, no details of the visit were left to chance. According to a well-established practice, the Propaganda Department issued instructions for the media accredited to handle the event. The contents of the document were foreseen and proscribed long before the pope's visit. The document, however, was leaked to the Western press and was published in *Time* magazine. Once again, as was the case with Strzyżewski's escape, the murky reality of media control was fully exposed to the world. This single event had many direct and indirect repercussions, not the least of which affected Poland's communications system. But the truth was too obvious to be hidden. The church showed its strength, determination, and organization. Courage and confidence returned to millions. The official media lost its credibility entirely. The effects were clearly manifested one year later.

Notes

1. From today's perspective it seems that Gierek, like Tito and Ceauscescu before him, tried to develop a nationalistic and independent version of communism. This supports the thesis of R.V. Burks that all communism tended to become national communism. See J.F. Brown, *Surge to Freedom: The End of Communist Rule in Eastern Europe* (Durham: Duke University Press, 1991), p. 10.

2. Gomułka made these remarks at the party plenum in October 1956, when he explained that the cult of personality was a system that prevailed in the Soviet Union and was grafted onto all Communist parties.

3. Similarly to Khrushchev, Gomułka publicly voiced his critical opinion of writers and journalists that opposed him, such as, for instance, M. Wańkowicz, P. Jasienica, and A. Słonimski.

4. This may have stemmed from the fact that Gierek was educated as a party apparatchik during Stalin's years; his orthodox Stalinist concept of the press was apparent in his report on the unrest in Poznań in June 1956.

5. The section on the mass media consisted of thirteen paragraphs.

6. "Uchwała VI Zjazdu PZPR" [The Resolution of the Sixth Congress of the PZPR], *in VI Zjazd PZPR* (Warszawa: Książka i Wiedza, 1972), pp. 279-283.

7. This does not mean that its significance went unnoticed in other Communist countries. On the contrary, in the 1970s crash programs designed to develop television were undertaken everywhere. The Soviet Union was again a model. See Ellen Mickiewicz, *Split Signals: Television and Politics in the Soviet Union* (Oxford: Oxford University Press, 1989), Chapter 1.

8. It increased from 5,309 hours in 1970 to 8,976 hours in 1980. *Rocznik statystyczny GUS* [Statistical Yearbook, GUS] (Warszawa: GUS, 1989), p. 473.

9. In the late 1970s, Bratkowski founded an informal working group called "Experience and the Future" which prepared several reports that were devastating for the government. This was another reflection of growing discontent among intellectuals.

10. *VII Zjazd PZPR. Stenogram w zespołach problemowych* [The Seventh Congress of the PZPR. Minutes of Topic-Oriented Sections] (Warszawa: Książka i Wiedza, 1976), vol. 3, p. 62.

11. Ibid., pp. 62 ff.

12. Ibid., p. 62.

13. *Polityka*, February 11, 1978, p. 7.

14. Adam Michnik, explaining why the Polish situation differs from that in other Eastern European countries, stressed that it allowed for freedom of expression "not only [for] KOR and the uncensored publications but also for our official ones (not only *Tygodnik Powszechny* or *Więź* but also *Twórczość, Pamiętnik Literacki*, and even *Polityka*)." See "Maggots and Angels" (1979), in *Letters from Prison and Other Essays* (Berkeley: University of California Press, 1985), p. 188.

15. Adam Michnik, "Why Are You Not Signing . . . A Letter from Białołęka Prison" (1982), in ibid., pp. 13-14.

16. Ibid., pp. 135-148.

17. *Zapis* (Warszawa/London) 4, 1977, pp. 70-77.

18. A similar attitude was expressed by a Polish writer, Andrzej Szczypiorski, in the article "Poland—Fiction and Reality," *Index on Censorship*, November-December 1979, p. 3.

19. Peter Raina, *Political Opposition in Poland: 1954-1977* (London: Poets and Painters Press, 1978), p. 212.

20. See *The White Paper of Czechoslovakia* (Paris: International Committee for the Support of Charter 77, 1977).

21. Raina, *Political Opposition*, p. 452.

22. A. Ostoja-Ostaszewski et al., eds., *Dissent in Poland: Reports and Documents. December 1975-July 1977* (London: Association of Polish Students and Graduates in Exile, 1977), pp. 182-186.

23. In the mid-1940s there were some illegal publications of the Home army and of the London government, but they were found and terminated. From the late 1940s only a small number of illegal publications continued to appear, and those in reduced numbers in the form of typescripts or even manuscripts.

24. See Chapter 9 on emigré monthly *Kultura*. Among eminent Polish writers who published extensively abroad for more than twenty years was Stefan Kisielewski.

25. This is the opinion of all Poland watchers. Brown explicitly stated that even under Gomułka, "Polish cultural life remained relatively free and quite dynamic; there was much private freedom of speech, and the Polish media remained the liveliest in Eastern Europe." *Surge to Freedom: The End of Communist Rule in Eastern Europe* (Durham: Duke University Press, 1991), p. 72.

26. At first it represented exactly what the word means: The term *samizdat*, used by a Moscow poet as an ironic parody of such official acronyms as *Gosizdat*, meaning State Publishers (short for *Gosudarstvennoe Izdatelstvo*), was an abbreviation of the description of the bound, typewritten publication of his po-

ems, Samsebyaizdat—Do-It-Yourself Press. In fact, samizdat is nothing more than the revival of the methods used by the opponents of Stalin in the 1920s and the 1930s. After the left opposition was denied the party's and the state's printing facilities, it tried to disseminate its material "from hand to hand." "Illegal" printing and circulation was one of the charges brought against it in the 1930s. See George Sanders, ed., *Samizdat: Voices of the Soviet Opposition* (New York: Monad Press, 1974), pp. 7-8.

27. D. Pospielovsky, "From Gosizdat to Samizdat and Tamizdat," *Canadian Slavonic Papers* 20, March 1978, p. 44.

28. According to estimates, various types of dissent documents were found in the Soviet Union: forty-seven items in 1965, double in 1966 that number, and double the number again in 1968. The grand total over the first decade (1964-1974) was about two thousand. F.J.M. Feldbrugge, *Samizdat and Political Dissent in the Soviet Union* (Leyden: A.W. Sijhoff, 1975), p. 12.

29. Gordon H. Skilling, *Samizdat and an Independent Society in Central and Eastern Europe* (London:Macmillan, 1989), pp. 11-13.

30. According to the statements of the most active KOR members and the founders of the first independent publications, the greatest impetus came from the samizdat movement in the Soviet Union. With the attitude of "if they can do it, so can we," Polish underground publishing took the Soviet example to heart; *Komunikat KOR* clearly followed the editorial methods of the Soviet samizdat publication *Chronicle of Current Events*. M. Kołodziej, "Underground Press in Poland," *Radio Free Europe* 42, 1986, part 1, p. 2.

31. The editor stated that the aim of the bulletin was to "break the state monopoly over information, which is protected by censorship. The information it contains serves the cause of openness in public life" (Special edition, no. 8, February 1977). The readers were asked to: "read it, copy it, and pass it on." Peter Raina, *Independent Social Movement in Poland* (London: LSE/Orbis, 1981), p. 55.

32. *Robotnik*, September 1977, p. 1.

33. Raina, *Political Opposition*, p. 55.

34. Ibid., p. 57.

35. Ibid., p. 58.

36. Lidia Ciolkosz, "The Uncensored Press," *Survey* 24, Autumn 1979, p. 9.

37. Tomasz Mianowicz, "Unofficial Publishing Lives On," *Index on Censorship* 2, 1983, pp. 24-25.

38. Ibid., p. 25.

39. *Lenin About the Press* (Prague: International Organization of Journalists, 1972), pp. 190-199.

40. This occurred after martial law.

41. Jane Leftwich Curry, *Poland's Journalists: Professionalism and Politics* (Cambridge: Cambridge University Press, 1990), p. 67.

42. Therefore giving the impression that control of the media was more severe in Poland than anywhere else in Eastern Europe, which obviously was not the case. Ceauscescu's Romania did not have formal censorship, which illustrates Kołakowski's thesis that censorship was, in fact, an element of weak, rather than strong, Communist rule. See Leszek Kołakowski, "On Total Control and Its

Contradictions," *Encounter* 9, 1988, p. 21.

43. All examples are taken from *The Black Book on Polish Censorship*, edited and translated by Jane Leftwich Curry (New York: Vintage Books, 1984). The book contains hundreds of other regulations, both major and petty.

44. Ibid., p. 340.

45. Bieńkowski wrote: "Apart from our own office of the censor, the office of censor-in-chief is vested in the representative of the Soviet Union in Poland." See Raina, *Political Opposition*, pp. 367-368.

46. The text translated from the samizdat publication *Cenzura* (Warszawa: Nova, 1987), p. 13.

47. "Eastern Europe: The Year of Truth," *New York Review of Books*, February 15, 1990, p. 17.

48. For analysis of this event in the Eastern European context, see Paul Lendvai, *The Bureaucracy of Truth: How Communist Governments Manage the News* (Boulder: Westview, 1981), pp. 93-99.

11

Solidarity Media Improvisation
August 1980 to December 1981

Respect for the freedom of speech, print and publication guaranteed by the constitution of the PRL [Polish People's Republic] and, therefore, no repression of independent publications and access to the mass media for representatives of all denominations.
—a demand of Gdańsk workers, August 1980

Democratic movements can neither come into existence nor remain democratic in the absence of effective lines of internal communication.
—Lawrence Goodwyn, *Breaking the Barrier: The Rise of Solidarity in Poland*

In 1980, the main source of information for most people in Poland was the evening television news, transmitted simultaneously on both of the available channels and watched every day by about 60 percent of the adult population. Newspapers were read by approximately 40 percent of adults; radio news reached a slightly smaller audience—about one-third of the Polish adults. The party-controlled media had, therefore, a real hold on the Polish population. The problem, however, was that the media, although widely read, watched, and listened to, was not evaluated highly. On the contrary, since the mid-1970s, confidence in the mass media had shown a decline and was at a very low level by the end of the decade. The main reason for this was the authorities' inability to stop the deterioration of the economic situation, which provoked widespread discontent.[1]

At the same time, younger and better-educated Poles looked for information in alternative—unofficial—channels. Among these were foreign radio stations, especially those that broadcast in Polish. In addition, thousands of mimeographed bulletins and books printed without asking for censors' permission were gaining a growing readership.

Under these conditions, attempts to control information through censorship were countered with the flow of information from alternative sources. People faced with disinformation and hostile propaganda reacted with revulsion and rejected the messages. Nonetheless, the authorities continued with their propaganda of success, although they faced failure in the economy.

The Road to the Gdańsk Agreement

When the economic outlook darkened, the authorities were compelled to increase food prices, a decision that was announced after the fact on July 2, 1980. This sudden, seemingly arrogant move angered workers and provoked strikes in major industrial centers in eastern Poland. The government kept silent but the Committee for the Defence of Workers (KOR) spread the word around the country. Foreign broadcasts constantly updated the news. In his first televised assessment, Edward Gierek portrayed the industrial unrest as a kind of minor dispute between workers and management. The head of television, Maciej Szczepański, appealed for civic responsibility, but to no avail. The strikes continued, and nothing was stated in the official media.

On July 16, the local media in Lublin first used the term *work stoppages*. A few days later, *Trybuna Ludu*'s editorial "People Want Order—Order Depends on People" served as the first sign that the subject was open to public discussion and marked the onset of a campaign by the party to rationalize the workers' protest. Nonetheless, hostile commentaries were published, especially in local papers. Instead of appeasing emotions, they acted as catalysts for further protests.[2]

The strike wave, therefore, continued and spread. On July 21, newspaper delivery drivers in Warsaw joined the strikes. Apparently afraid, the government tried to appease the industrial unrest. Jerzy Urban's commentary in *Polityka*, obviously a commissioned article, admitted economic mismanagement. Then, on August 12, for the first time since October 1956, the word *strike* was officially used in the media and the party referred to the workers' protests as being justified.

Psychological measures were not, however, sufficient to contain the economic discontent. Workers, influenced by years of propaganda that denoted ever increasing prosperity, felt both deceived and frustrated. On August 14, workers at the Gdańsk shipyard, the heart of Polish heavy industry, joined the protest and staged an all-out strike. This event made the difference. The workers were supported by seasoned dissidents, especially KOR militants and by some of the most brilliant Polish intellectuals. The demand for an independent, free trade union was included in the list of exigencies. The strikes immediately became politicized. In response, the authorities imposed a kind of communication blackout on Gdańsk. The shipyard's director banned the strike committee from the works' public address system. All intercity telephone lines were cut off. Leaflets that expressed hostility to the strike leaders and their demands were dropped from airplanes. The workers were infuriated. In a riposte, they called for immediate publication of all of their conditions in the media. At the shipyard, the first issue of a newspaper *Solidarność* was printed as an independent voice of the strikers.

The prolongation of the strikes increased the criticism of the leadership among the party rank and file. On August 24, Jerzy Łukaszewicz, secretary of propaganda, and Szczepański, head of radio and television, were singled out as the main culprits in the crises, and subsequently lost their positions. Szczepański was even later imprisoned for alleged financial appropriations.

Despite finding scapegoats and receiving appeals from the authorities, television commentators, and even Primate Wyszyński, the workers' strikes continued and spread, thus encouraging other professions to demand their rights. On August 25, a group of journalists sent a resolution to the Association of Polish Journalists (SDP), complaining about the party directives to write false reports about the shipyard and the events on the Baltic coast. They deplored censorship and demanded legal control of its decisions.

By the end of August, the party had reluctantly decided to sign an agreement with the strike committee. Communications with Gdańsk were restored. The youth daily, *Sztandar Młodych*, published the full list of the Gdańsk strikers' demands. On the next day, however, the party propaganda resumed its harsh language about the strikers. This about-face was an obvious sign of internal party disputes on how to manage the crisis. Eventually, a final agreement was signed on August 31. The media were allowed to report the event, and the dailies published a full text of accords. The closing ceremony was shown on Polish and Western television, which made Lech Wałęsa a national hero. The most propaganda-loaded broadcasts, such as the infamous program "Here Speaks the Number One [radio channel]," were suspended or changed their style. Joining the enthusiasm, *Słowo Powszechne*, the PAX Catholic daily, reprinted the previously censored letter from Pope John Paul II to Primate Wyszyński.

The Agreements on Censorship and Access to the Media

Among the most surprising demands made by the workers were the calls for truth, openness, and freedom of the media. This demand was very high on their agenda, second only to the demand for pay raises.[3] Indeed, in the bargaining sessions with the authorities, the Gdańsk workers secured several provisions addressing the mass media.[4] Thus, the strikers included in point three of their provisions the demand for freedom of speech, print, and publication. In point five they insisted on "publication in the mass media of the formation of the Interfactory Strike Committee and its demands." Point six pressed for "providing full public information on the socioeconomic situation" and more specifically demanded "giving all social groups and strata the possibility of participating in discussions on the reform program."

Even more surprising was the fact that the demands were eventually accepted by the government and the party. The signed agreement promised that state radio would broadcast a Catholic service to the nation every Sunday. Censorship would be restricted to protecting state and economic secrets, and a bill on censorship would be sent to Parliament within three months.

Each of these demands and promises was revolutionary in terms of Communist doctrine and practice; they meant de jure a curtailment of the party monopoly over the press and, to a lesser extent, over broadcasting. Even the veteran British journalist Neal Ascherson was caught up in the excitement: "These were stupefying documents. Not since the revolutions of the nineteenth century had a European people forced such a treaty on its own rulers. In a Communist system the agreements were almost unimaginable."[5] However, one may be reminded here that as early as February 1921, in Soviet Russia, the rebel marines in Kronstadt had demanded freedom of speech and the press, as well as freedoms for associations, political parties, and trade unions. This confirms that the call for civil liberties is so essential that is impossible to suppress over the long run.

Journalists' Mutiny

The workers' victory encouraged Polish intellectuals, even those who were party members, to reclaim their professional rights. The climate of widespread criticism increased. The Communists in the Warsaw branch of the Union of Polish Writers demanded "exemption of certain publications from censorship and abolition of the black list of forbidden books and authors." The lawyers' weekly *Prawo i Życie* initiated discussion on the future of censorship law. Journalists in the proregime Catholic PAX organization issued an appeal to all Polish journalists, calling for scrupulous adherence to the professional code of ethics. The executive board of the SDP discussed information policy, the limits of censorship, and propaganda. Always outspoken, Stefan Bratkowski went the furthest and denounced the party as bearing total responsibility for the crisis. Journalists began to prove that he was right.

The press began to print sensational information on Communist corruption. Investigative reporting on falsified statistics and political affairs was presented daily to the public, as had been the case in October 1956. The traditional roles of the daily and weekly press changed. Dailies began to utilize in-depth reporting and lengthy essays, whereas weeklies kept abreast of ongoing political developments, informing people about events of the day. The weekly *Kulisy* revealed details about the identity of censors and their work conditions.[6] Editorial discussions of formerly forbidden topics were organized and published. On September 21, for the first time in the history of the Polish People's Republic, Catholic mass was broadcast on radio.

The party announced changes in the propaganda sector of the Central Committee. Józef Klasa, who had earned a reputation for being a party liberal, was named head of the department. The Polish Parliament engaged in criticism, and the press reported its proceedings in full.[7] The journalistic hit was *Gazeta Krakowska* (Cracow Gazette). The editor-in-chief and a party member, Maciej Szumowski, made it a masterpiece of "objective journalism." On the front page, he placed the party declarations and Solidarity answers side by side, which made the orthodox party media controllers furious.[8] But Szumowski had a highly placed sponsor—Józef Klasa, who was the former party boss in Cracow. Much like the situation in October 1956, people again lined up for copies of daily papers.

But there was still a kind of communication blackout on Wałęsa—when he met with a vice-premier no film coverage was given, although the television crew was on hand. When exiled Polish author Czesław Miłosz was awarded the Nobel Prize for Literature, it took four hours for the media to announce the news. These examples illustrate an ambiguous, hesitant official policy toward compromise with the emerging Solidarity, partly because the party was in the midst of a personal and conceptual crisis. Accordingly, the confrontation between liberals and dogmatists led to an indecisive policy.

On October 15, top party officials held a meeting with representatives of the major media from all over the country. All of the speakers strongly criticized the state of information policy. Miłosz's Nobel Prize made the Communist propaganda, which for years had blacklisted him, look ridiculous. A party commentator, Jerzy Putrament, revealed that five years ago some Communist writers had demanded that Miłosz's work be published, but the party leadership ruled otherwise.[9]

In the fall, the major event proved to be the extraordinary congress of the SDP. The atmosphere was characterized by violent debate. Censorship was condemned, together with excessive party control. The SDP dignitaries and other proregime journalists were refused their moral right to speak in the name of the journalistic community. A new executive board was elected. The new president, Stefan Bratkowski, demanded that censorship should stop protecting the interests of various pressure groups and should instead confine itself to matters that related to Poland's vital geopolitical interests. In plain words this meant avoid aggravating the Soviet Union. All of this criticism amounted to nothing less than a journalists' revolution. Still, the party hardliners were temporarily forced to tolerate such defiance. After months of politicking, Bratkowski was eventually expelled from the party—an apparent sign of an upcoming party blow to the profession and Solidarity in general.

The Law on Censorship

One of the main demands of the striking workers was that censorship, which was seen as one of the main instruments in suppressing information on the true situation in the country, be limited.[10] Their aim was to replace the secretive administrative means of controlling the press—the decree of 1946—with a law. This amounted to a legal revolution, because censors' decisions could be disputed in the courts. As Karl Marx knew, the only way to make censorship a law-abiding institution was to abolish it.[11] The law, however, had to prolong the life of the agency and enlarge the freedom of expression—no small task. Although the preparation of a new law on censorship was to be completed within three months, it took almost one year to develop and pass the new legislation through Parliament.[12]

The law was enacted on October 1, 1981, and survived in its initial formulation for only two months, until the imposition of martial law. Nevertheless, during that short time censorship lost both court cases brought against censors' decisions. This shows that even such "permissive" party control was incompatible with the judicial protection of free expression and social standards for its restrictions.

Paragraph one of article 1 of this law reminded everyone that the Polish People's Republic ensures the freedom of speech and print in publications and public performances, but it then stressed that it was the duty of state bodies to ensure and preserve that freedom. The concluding paragraph stated that the use of this freedom was regulated by the present law. In essence it was a breathtaking legal construction. The obvious intention of which was to square the circle.

The second article of the law outlined the restrictions regarding the use of press freedom, although still in a rather vague and broad way.

Particularly significant among these restrictions, and the most frequently marked points were the following:

1. An attack on the independence or the territorial integrity of Polish Poeple's Republic [PRL]
2. A call for overthrowing, insulting, ridiculing, or demeaning the constitutional system of the PRL
3. An attack on the constitutional principles of the foreign policy and alliances of the PRL . . .
6. A call for criminal activities or praise of them.

The public knowledge of this law was important because it gave authors and editors the right to mark a censor's intervention by including in the text or in a separate note a special announcement specifying the legal basis of the decision—title of the act and the number of point in article 2 that was allegedly violated. This was a meaningful amendment, because it made the operation of censorship visible and occasionally even amusing.[13]

More imaginative readers quickly learned how to decipher the possible meaning of a cut from a censor's mark. For instance, point number three suggested that the author had probably written something unpleasant about the Soviet Union (for example, mentioning the murder of Polish officers in Katyń Forest in 1941) or criticized Fidel Castro or the leadership of North Korea. Point number six was the most tricky—it did not mean the author was really calling for criminal activity, which was rare, but that, for instance, he or she may have referred to Lech Wałęsa as the Solidarity chairman. To the authorities the banned Solidarity was still illegal and, therefore, could not have a legal chairperson.

Despite its essentially voluntary implementation, the new law led to many changes in the practice of censorship, principally by making it responsible to the administrative courts. Speeches made by parliamentarians, court decisions, scholarly journals, all other publications whose circulation did not exceed one hundred, church publications on religious matters, and, perhaps most important, house publications— bulletins, newsletters with mastheads "for internal use," that is, with restricted circulation to members of trade unions and political organizations—were all excluded from censorship control. In practice, this qualification put all Solidarity bulletins beyond censorship.

The most astonishing thing about Solidarity was the pace of its growth. From three members of the founding committee of the free trade unions of the Baltic coast in August of 1980, Solidarity grew to approximately 10 million members by early November that same year. And this occurred when the party still controlled all mass media, imposing a kind of media silence on Solidarity news. Because no organization can do without communication, the Solidarity phenomenon also must be explained in communication terms.

Solidarity Media Network

In its initial phase, Solidarity was a movement of the spoken word—spoken at thousands of strike meetings and organizational gatherings.[14] After the strike began on August 14, the next day the authorities cut off all telephone and telex lines between Gdańsk and the rest of Poland. When the telephones went dead, they were replaced by human carriers: "They smuggled messages from the shipyard and delivered them to other striking plants. The authorities responded with the roadblocks that were thrown up around the Gdańsk region. The courier or in reality information war against the party-controlled news environment had begun. The workers' preconditions for talks focused on the courier war and the telephone blockade."[15]

Despite initial difficulties, the movement ingeniously used all of the new communication vehicles that were within the workers' reach. Thus, in a move to get more support, the strike committee took control of the shipyard public-address system. Consequently, negotiations with the authorities were made public. Moreover, delegates would record what was said on tape; later, the cassettes were replayed over loudspeakers. The plant information boards, vestiges of Stalinist-type propaganda, were used as billboards for posting workers' demands, commentaries, and political humor. In addition, the union organization benefitted from daily news bulletins and other programs in Polish on foreign radio stations, particularly Radio Free Europe and the BBC World Service.[16]

As Lawrence Goodwyn remarks, KOR's spokesperson, Jacek Kuroń, provided alternative information to individual Western correspondents in his press releases and on the telephone. Radio Free Europe, which had access to Western news dispatches, was able to summarize Gdańsk demands, reporting that "strict observation of freedom of speech and the press is demanded, including ending censorship and reprisals against independent publications, as well as providing access to the media to representatives of all religious denominations."[17]

However, Goodwyn points out that "A central KOR claim, implicit in many works [on Solidarity, by Timothy Garton Ash, Jerzy Holzer, and Jan Józef Lipski], takes the following explicit form: `Jacek Kuroń directed the strike by long distance through Borusewicz on the coast.'"[18] This was not so simple. Goodwyn rightly stresses that "despite the importance of international news coverage, provided by KOR, Western correspondents, and foreign radio stations, they were too distant from the region to provide information necessary for the incipient movement."[19] Thus, Solidarity used telex machines. In the first three months after its inception, it had practically no access to mass media, especially daily papers, radio, and television. Photocopiers were rare and were strictly controlled by management. Telephone lines could be cut off, and they were usually tapped. Only telex machines operated in every plant as an essential part of the network of bureaucratic telecommunication, which was so well developed under Gierek's program of modernization.[20] They could provide indispensable links in interfactory communication. Telex lines linked the Gdańsk headquarters with the entire country and therefore served as a substitute for an information and propaganda network. Some resourceful Solidarity operators inserted carbons under a single teletype paper to obtain multiple copies, which were then posted on bulletin boards.

Solidarity's own communication network was supplemented by the union's so-called "windows" (columns) in the official party papers. Later, the union began to print several regular, high-circulation newspapers and weeklies. By the end of 1980, the government agreed to allow Solidarity to publish a weekly newspaper, *Solidarność*, with a press run of half a million copies. In addition, Solidarity could retrieve free of duty donated printing equipment that was seized by the authorities at customs. The government even gave Solidarity some air time on radio and television. The success of these broadcasts was so enormous that it did not repeat the offer.

After Solidarity's formal registration, the number of bulletins rose to nearly fifteen hundred.[21] All legally published Solidarity publications, although editorially independent from the party and the government, had to be submitted to censorship. But the union was strong, so censorship had to be cautious and liberal. Thus, vast parameters were created for an independent, free word. The official union publications were supplemented by hundreds of small, uncensored independent bulletins that were based on strike bulletins issued during the summer of 1980. The most daring of these were various underground publications; some were continuations from the proceeding decade, and many more were new.

Therefore, despite Solidarity's lack of access to television, radio, and the daily press, the union was in touch with millions of members. However, despite this impressive network, access to the national media was still vital and necessary to ensure Solidarity's survival.

The Openness Before Glasnost

Solidarity was not disinterested and passive toward hostile

propaganda it could not counter directly.[22] The movement also knew it would need its own media to sustain its membership and their ardor. Solidarity also wanted the media to report on the fulfillment of the government's pledges. During the negotiation of the Gdańsk agreement, Solidarity's intellectual advisers were well aware that the monopoly over information was an important element of political and social control. Logically, one of the major Gdańsk demands was for social control and access to mass communications.

Later, this demand was pressed for more than purely theoretical reasons. Victimized by vicious attacks from the party media, in October 1980 Solidarity demanded thirty minutes of television time to respond to allegations, and it insisted on fair coverage of its activities by the official media. It also wanted access to the media in the form of independent publications and television programs.

All of its demands were ignored. The party refused to grant television and media rights to an adversary that had 10 million strong membership. It felt Solidarity also had control over most means of public communication. Moreover, it was supported from the church's pulpits. In turn, the state radio had powerful competitors in Western Polish-language stations such as Radio Free Europe, the Voice of America, and the BBC. Therefore, television was the only medium the party could fully control and more important, to spread its message throughout the country. As the party's last mass weapon, television could not simply be handed to the adversary.

Although the church made no secret its full support, the negotiations went slowly, and for a long time no progress was achieved. The Polish Bishops' Conference stated that the "people's labor representatives should be given access to the media."[23] In addition, the bishops wrote a pastoral letter in mid-September: "The mass media are important instruments given to humans by its creator so that they could exert a positive influence on the development of the family."[24]

Eventually, on May 26, 1981, Solidarity and government negotiators reached a tentative agreement. Yet, the settlement was never implemented. The issue of access was not resolved and continued to increase tension between Solidarity and the party. As the self-appointed spokesman for Solidarity and the SDP chairman, Bratkowski issued a letter of protest against the "campaign of misinformation" being waged in the media against Solidarity. In response, the Polish Press Agency released a commentary denying that Solidarity lacked access to the media. As proof it enumerated that Solidarity published six weeklies, and a biweekly, had a "flood" of house bulletins, and printed an "avalanche" of flysheets and posters. Moreover, the commentary continued, both the party dailies and general magazines devoted much space to Solidarity activities. It concluded that "never in the history of trade unionism has there been a union with such broad access to the mass media."[25]

On August 9, the government took an unprecedented step and offered Wałęsa television time. He was permitted to make an address, followed by a public debate with the reform-minded Deputy Prime Minister Rakowski. Suspecting bad intentions, Wałęsa declined the offer. By the end of August, printers had staged two days of a national strike action called "Days Without News" an event without precedence in the history of the Communist media. The iron rule was that propaganda is more important than butter—although the shops may not have had butter, the newspapers still had to be sold on a daily basis. The move brought a reproach from the Soviet government newspaper *Izvestiia* when it was reported that Solidarity was driving toward a seizure of state power. At the time this was a very serious accusation.

Prior to Solidarity's first national congress, an ad hoc agreement was reached for independent programs to be produced on radio and television. However, as occurred previously, negotiated promises were later broken. The congress opened on September 5 with no live television coverage, but access to which was of the utmost importance for Solidarity. During the two-month-long assemblage, access to mass media was discussed by several working sections. Draft theses demanded strongly a voice in the media. Despite their somewhat repetitive nature and use of language that unintentionally imitated that of the party resolutions, the Solidarity theses still deserve to be recalled at length.

The union will fight against hypocrisy and lies in all spheres of life because our society wants to live in truth and has the right to live to.[26]

Speaking and printing the truth is essential for the development of public awareness and for maintaining national identity. We must know the truth of our times so we can build a better future.

Stating the general principles for free expression, Solidarity specified its stand:

1. We regard censorship in the mass media as an evil we tolerate only for the time being and out of necessity. We reject censorship in science and art. Nor can censorship deny the nation's right to know history and literature. Censorship's abuses will in each case be opposed by Solidarity.
2. The propaganda language, which damages our desired way of expressing thoughts and feelings, is a dangerous pack of lies. Solidarity will seek to give back to society the Polish language that makes it

possible for people truly to understand each other.

3. Solidarity will support the development of independent publishing agencies because their activities are some of the ways to speak the truth and to overcome the trammels of censorship.

The following points called for "live-in truth" and ridding national history and culture of lies. The next theses addressed the issue of access directly.

The means of social communication is public property. It must serve all our society and be subjected to its control.

Solidarity's struggle for access to the mass media is a struggle in the interest of all communities and for the whole of society's rights.

Solidarity demands that the constitutional principles of freedom of speech and exchange of views be observed. Therefore:

1. Solidarity deems it unacceptable to interfere with the reception of information by jamming radio broadcasts, confiscating publications, tearing down posters, and so on.

2. Solidarity will participate in preparing the draft law on publications, which should include all the means of public communication. The congress instructs Solidarity's authorities to support decisively the socially accepted draft law.

3. Solidarity will consistently seek to have the authorities recognize and implement the right of citizens and their organizations to have agencies and access to radio and television. In the case of organizations, the share in question should match their size and true social significance. We need public control over the allocation of paper, printing facilities, radio and television time, and access to radio and television technical facilities.

4. Solidarity is against all forms of information monopoly. Solidarity demands the abolition of the state administration's monopoly in running radio and television because it is contrary to the constitution of the Polish People's Republic. This means Solidarity demands that the 1960 law regarding the Committee for Radio and Television be changed. Solidarity will take action to institute genuine public control over radio and television by appointing a managing and executive body representing government, political parties, trade unions, religious associations, social organizations, professional artists' unions, and self-management groups of the employees who produce and beam the program.

5. The union's activities to date concerning Solidarity's ongoing participation in the means of public communication have not been adequate. It is necessary to implement as soon as possible the decisions on the means of public communication ratified by the Solidarity

National Coordinating Commission. At the same time, we demand the establishment of an independent Solidarity editorial board within the central and local units of radio and television.

6. Solidarity will defend its members who are employed in institutions of public communication and journalists who observe principles of professional credibility and honesty. We recognize the right of editorial boards to share in decisions on the appointment and dismissal of editors-in-chief. The Association of Polish Journalists deals with issues of the honesty and professional ability of all journalists and with the self-governing character of editorial boards. Solidarity will support the association's efforts in this field.

7. Solidarity will set its own information, photographic, videotape, film, and recording agencies and press publications. Solidarity's authorities should take action to set up on general principles the union's general press and information agency.

8. It is necessary to appoint within the National Commission a council for dealing with the means of public communications.

9. In line with article eighty-three, enactment two, of the constitution of the Polish People's Republic, Solidarity demands that it be enabled to set up its own radio stations and to beam its own programs.

10. In the struggle for access to radio and television and for reform of the means of public communication, Solidarity will use all the resources provided by the charter. [These included the general strike.]

The Solidarity program can be briefly summarized as constituting glasnost before the time of glasnost. Interestingly, many Polish journalists interviewed at the time were not completely supportive of Solidarity's demands with respect to total editorial control over their own programs.[27]

Undoing March 1968 and Other Doctored Campaigns

The media at the time was interesting for the Polish audience, not only for its political considerations but above all for its type of pre-glasnost historical and political revelations. On television, on the radio, in magazines, and in daily newspapers one could read about events from the past, and learn unknown aspects and facts—explore "blank spots." Polish history had been rewritten, at least partially, because of still-valid censorship taboos on Polish-Soviet relations. However, what could not be published officially poured out of underground presses.

In 1981 anti-Semitism was characteristically met with widespread public indignation. Very significant were a letter signed by over one hundred eminent Polish intellectuals, printed in the official paper *Życie Warszawy*,[28] and the exceptionally large number of supporting letters received by the paper.[29] But in this period of a partially free press, polemics rejecting the thesis of the Jewish character of Stalinism in Poland were still rare and usually appeared only in Solidarity papers.[30] As far as the Communist party press was concerned, only *Polityka* opposed the anti-Semitic version of Poland's recent history, which presented the Jews as coming from the Soviet Union to mastermind and implement a brutal and criminal suppression of the anti-Communist opposition.[31] The PAX Catholic press showed no disposition to reject this falsification of the process. Such a restricted attitude might perhaps support the thesis that although intellectuals engaged in the pursuit of liberal values, Polish anti-Semitism was not only a politically degenerated strategy but also had historical roots.[32]

The Solidarity period brought radical changes in the contents of the mass media. The new common perceptions of the social and political structures revealed themselves in the latent and overt contents of different papers. An analysis of the press of the time shows this clearly.[33]

The weekly *Solidarność* stressed the sharp dichotomy between the authorities (*władza*) and society (*społeczeństwo*), or, in more popular terms, "them" and "us." "They" were always wrong, "we" were always right. A Catholic weekly, *Tygodnik Powszechny*, saw two conflicting forces in society in a slightly different way—on the one side Solidarity, which expressed demands of working people, and on the other the state authorities, or the "new class," or "*nomenklatura.*" In turn, Solidarity's newsletter *Serwis informacyjny* stressed the conflict between the people (*lud*) and the "tri-lords elite"— masters of the political, economic, and ideological domains.

In the party-sponsored weekly *Polityka*, a more complex image was promoted in which society was portrayed as a multistrata structure and the main conflict was seen as being between Solidarity and the party apparatus. The latter was more privileged but hardly the richest or the most unified or uniform. The weekly saw the small-business private sector as the most prosperous group, and it emphasized the differences between workers and the intelligentsia; both images went against common Solidarity wisdom.

On the other side of the political spectrum, a unique Marxist-Leninist weekly, *Rzeczywistość,* catered to the needs of the most orthodox, hard-line faction of the party apparatus. According to this publication, the fundamental societal conflict existed between the working class (*klasa robotnicza*) and the possessing class, which included some party apparatchiks who had too much money and power. The weekly claimed that in the Polish People's Republic there still existed the propertied classes of peasantry and the middle bourgeoisie. It recommended the simple solution to economic and political problems—a permanent revolution, that is the elimination of small businesses and private property in agriculture.

As this brief analysis shows, the mainstream media perspective was that of a simple dichotomous structure and, with the exception of *Polityka*, a simple resolution of ongoing conflict—one side should win and should eliminate the other.

By the end of 1981 one could still discuss the dominant position of the Communist party in the media, but it was no longer possible to claim that the party still had an information monopoly. This situation was new and very embarrassing for the Communist authorities, who were not used to such conditions. This loss of control over the media pushed part of the party apparatus to demand and later to support Wojciech Jaruzelski's solution to Solidarity's growing power by imposing martial law.

Notes

1. "Komunikowanie masowe w Polsce. Próba bilansu lat siedemdziesiątych" [Mass Communication in Poland: Report on the 1970s], *Zeszyty Prasoznawcze* 1, 1981, p. 74.

2. Tomasz Goban-Klas, "Information at the Time of Sociopolitical Crisis: Poland in the Summer of 1980," in Ellen Wartella and D. Charles Whitney, eds., *Mass Communication Review Yearbook* (Beverly Hills: Sage Publications, 1983), pp. 490-493.

3. Calculation made by Ireneusz Krzemiński, *Czego chcieli, o czym myśleli? Analizy postulatów robotników Wybrzeża z 1970 i 1980 roku* [What Did They Want and What Did They Think? The Analysis of the Baltic Coast Workers' Stipulations] (Warszawa: Wydawnictwa Universytetu Warszawskiego, 1987), pp. 26-29.

4. Timothy Garton Ash, *The Polish Revolution: Solidarity* (New York: Vintage, 1985), p. 43.

5. Neal Ascherson, *The Struggles for Poland* (London: Michael Joseph, 1989), p. 207.

6. About four hundred persons were employed, either as censors or in an administrative capacity in central and local offices of censorship. See *Radio Free Europe RAD Report* 92, p. 98.

7. For instance, the issues of the Warsaw daily *Życie Warszawy* that contained details of the Sejm debate were seized by officials at the East Berlin airport.

8. Madeleine K. Albright gives an excellent description of *Gazeta Krakowska* in her study *Poland: The Role of the Press in Political Change* (New York: Praeger, 1983), pp. 73-78.

9. *Radio Free Europe Report*, November 2, 1980, p. 3.

10. I should explain here why the strikers did not simply demand the abolition of censorship. Madeleine Albright recalls in her book that during the feverish debate on the night of August 16, a dissident civil rights fundamentalist proposed

that they insist on a total retraction of censorship. In response, a more seasoned dissident intellectual asked, `You know what happened when they abolished censorship in Czechoslovakia in 1968?´ That ended the dispute." See Albright, *Poland*, p. 44.

11. Karl Marx and Frederick Engels, *Dzieła* [Works] (Warszawa: Książka i Wiedza, 1961), vol. 1, p. 71.

12. *Dziennik Ustaw* no. 20, item 99, August 12, 1981.

13. It sometimes happened that the censors mark, which was three lines long, was much longer than a suppressed item, which could consist of only one or two words.

14. Roman Laba, *The Roots of Solidarity: A Political History of Poland's Working Class Democratization* (Princeton: Princeton University Press, 1991), p. 129.

15. Lawrence Goodwyn, *Breaking the Barrier: The Rise of Solidarity in Poland* (New York: Oxford University Press, 1991), pp. 213 and 364.

16. Laba, *The Roots*, p. 129.

17. Ibid., p. 210.

18. Goodwyn, p. 364.

19. He also gives a remarkable example: "A Silesian courier who came to the shipyard on August 22 said: `I was sent here by my factory to find out what was going on. Someone [that is, Radio Free Europe] tells us that fifteen factories are on strike, then the [government] radio news says a similar number have gone back to work. So I am here to observe first hand what is happening on the coast.´" Ibid, p. 365.

20. A slogan of the day read "A telex in every village."

21. M. Kołodziej, "Underground Press in Poland," *Radio Free Europe* 42, part 1, 1986, p. 3.

22. Albright describes a conversation in February 1981 between a Belgian journalist and a Solidarity spokesperson on the importance of the union having direct access to television, an all-important medium: "But didn't members of Solidarity appear on television from time to time?" the Belgian asked. "That's true," was the answer, "but it's almost always at times of low listenership, very late at night or during the day." Albright, *Poland*, p. 110.

23. "Poland: A Chronology of Events: July-November 1980," complied by Anna Sabbat and Roman Stefanowski, *Radio Free Europe RAD Background Report* 92 (Poland), March 31, 1981, p. 80.

24. Associated Press dispatch, September 20, 1980.

25. *Poland: A Chronology of Events—August-December 1981*, Radio Free Europe Report, July 16, 1982, p. 10.

26. Program of the Independent, Self-Governing Trade Union Solidarity, adopted by the First National Congress, Gdańsk, October 7, 1991, translation in *Radio Free Europe RAD Background Report*, 1982, pp. 128-129.

27. Albright, *Poland*, pp. 115-116.

28. March 20, 1981, p. 3.

29. From Łukasz Hirszowicz, "The Jewish Issue in Post-War Communist Politics," in Chimen Abramsky, ed., *The Jews in Poland* (Oxford: Blackwell, 1986), pp. 246-247.

30. M. Mieszczankowski, "Jednostronne spojrzenie" [A One-Sided Point of View], *Polityka*, May 23, 1981, pp. 8-9.

31. Hirszowicz, "The Jewish Issue," pp. 198-248.

32. A similar opinion was voiced by Sławomir Wiatr, formerly a Communist party secretary, in his book (with Hans-Georg Heinrich) *Political Culture in Vienna and Warsaw* (Boulder: Westview, 1990), p. 84.

33. I refer here to a content analysis of the Polish press done by Krzysztof Podemski in his study "The Nature of Society and Social Conflict as Depicted in the Polish Press in 1981," in Zbigniew Rau, ed., *The Re-Emergence of Civil Society in Eastern Europe and the Soviet Union* (Boulder: Westview, 1991), pp. 51-75.

12

A General in Search of a New Key
December 13, 1981, to February 1989

By capturing with an outflanking movement Polish radio and television-building, not to mention telephone exchanges, General Jaruzelski has covered the Polish armed forces with glory.
        —Adam Michnik, *The Polish War of 1981*

The means of communication improved by years in the second half of the twentieth century and made impossible total control of every source of information.
        —Z.A.B. Zeman, *The Making and Breaking of Communist Europe*

At midnight on December 13, 1981, General Jaruzelski struck first and proclaimed martial law. The weather that year was very cold and snowy; "General Winter" helped General Jaruzelski. Among other measures, including the imprisonment of thousands of Solidarity militants, the special decree suspended article 8 of the constitution of the Polish People's Republic on freedom of speech and the press and introduced special legal regulations regarding all forms of communications.

Communication Blackout

All telephone and cable links with the outside world were cut on that night; the entire civilian telephone network and the telex network were disconnected. Private and public telephone lines went dead; the authorities, however, could use their own special lines.

All theatrical performances, public gatherings, conferences, lectures, and art exhibitions were forbidden. In the cities a general curfew was imposed. Military sentries patrolled the deserted streets. Travel between cities required special permission. Thus, special militia-military checkpoints were set up at city limits and on main roads. All newspapers were curtailed and many were banned, with the exception of two central dailies (the party's *Trybuna Ludu* and the Army's *Żołnierz Wolności*) and sixteen remodeled regional newspapers.[1]

These sixteen provincial papers were publications of a special type—joint ventures in which regional urban dailies were temporarily merged into one newspaper. Following the direct instructions issued by the Propaganda Department, they were edited by teams of party apparatchiks, who selected loyal and trusted journalists. Their editions did not even bear the usual information specifying where and by whom they were edited and printed; those that did simply stated "by the editorial team," with no names.[2] In the first issues they mainly reprinted martial law decrees and regulations, and their propaganda line presented the workers' protests against martial law not as serious strikes but as minor disturbances that had arisen out of the people's state of shock and confusion, which some Solidarity "extremists" had tried to exploit.[3] Lists of the regional Solidarity activists who were arrested after December 13 on charges of violating the new military order were also published in the local press. Subsequently, details of the charges and summaries of trial proceedings against martial law violators became a regular feature.

By the weekend of December 19 and 20, these newspapers seemingly returned to the normal form of the regional newspaper, with familiar style and layout, and regular columns and features. However, a striking phenomenon of these "war papers" was the concentration on local events and oblivion to everything that was happening outside their own area. The local press was the first to bring news about the dismissals of many high-ranking officials throughout the country—including university rectors, directors of state agencies, managers of enterprises, and local government officials—accused of being soft on Solidarity.

The press had been turned into a voice for military and party hardliners. This was even more true of television and radio, which had immediately become militarized—to demonstrate this, anchors appeared on screen in green soldier uniforms. To make control more effective, only a single, shortened television program was broadcast, instead of the former two. Similarly, only one radio program, out of the previous four, received air play. The radio constantly played military and classical music; television changed its programming to include more propaganda broadcasts and war movies.

The only independent and uncontrolled means of communication left was private conversation, except on telephone lines. During telephone connections, a voice could be heard announcing: "This talk is monitored."[4] In short, a full communication blackout was imposed on all citizens. Without any doubt, the communication segment of martial law was executed perfectly, and it was effective in suppressing the almost 10 million members of Solidarity, with little resistance and bloodshed.

"Normalization" of the Media System

The state of total blackout lasted one month. Gradually and slowly the former state of communication was restored, with the obvious exception of the Solidarity media. By the end of December, the temporarily banned dailies of the two allied parties, the Democratic Alliance (SD) and the United Peasant party (ZSL) were allowed to reappear. On January 17, 1982, a second radio channel resumed broadcasting. In February, two other radio programs reappeared, and on April 5, a second television channel again went on the air. In the summer of 1983, one radio and one television program were temporarily suspended, although this time the decision was based purely on economic grounds.

The attempts to wholly "normalize" radio and television were, however, challenged by the resistance of the thespian community. Actors and theater directors reacted against militarization of radio and television in the most unexpected and unique way—they proclaimed a boycott of all radio and television performances.[5] For more than a year the best actors worked against their own vital professional interests, and chose not to perform on television, losing not only money, but also public recognition. Those who did perform were chastised by over-applause from the theater audience—an act of solidarity between the boycotting actors and the theater public.

The boycott was harmful not only to the image of Jaruzelski's martial rule, but also to radio and television programming. Over the long term it destroyed tradition of television theater, which had been regularly programmed on Polish television and, in the BBC-style, popularized the best national and international plays. Television viewers lost their taste for Monday and Thursday spectacles; in turn they received Brazilian miniseries and soap operas, which the militarized television used to stuff its programming time.[6] However, the boycott also added prestige to the histrionic profession; it revived the tradition of creative artists as preserves of national identity.[7]

Initially, the Solidarity underground called for mass boycotts of television news bulletins, especially the main evening edition, by asking people to turn off their sets during the emission of such news. People also lit candles in windows to show solidarity and resistance to official propaganda. In some regions, calls were issued for people not to read party newspapers or at least not to buy them. Both types of calls, however, received very weak responses. The demand for information, even distorted information, was greater than moral dismay.

In contrast to the actors, journalists were not in position to openly resist while maintaining their jobs. In an operation named "verification," or, in simple words, a purge of journalists, all obstinate, unreliable, or disobedient journalists were simply expelled from their papers. Many editors-in-chief lost their managerial positions or were simply fired. In the newspaper chain RSW alone, approximately two hundred newspeople were fired, and many editorial positions were replaced. For example, of the fifty staff members of the SD paper *Kurier Polski*, thirty were dismissed and twelve others were asked to reconsider their positions. It took more than a month to restore the staff of the popular Warsaw daily *Życie Warszawy*. In central and regional radio and television headquarters hundreds of journalists were dismissed. The purge continued into a second month, but that was the result of personnel conflicts. Nevertheless, in the process more journalists lost their jobs, either through dismissals or forced resignations, when they refused to work for martial law propaganda.[8] As in Gomułka's time, they had a choice: either to support the party or stand against it. If they chose the latter, they had to change their profession—some did leave it, at least temporarily. Jacek Maziarski, a well-known columnist for the weekly *Polityka*, set up his own antiquarian bookstore. Another popular journalist, Maciej Wierzbicki, chose a career as a taxidriver.

Nevertheless, the majority of newspeople opted to stay in the profession. Thus, the Communist press experienced few problems with staffing and by the end of the first quarter of 1983 resumed its former scope. More than 2,600 periodicals were officially on the market. Of that number new publications comprised around 15 percent of the market share; they were mainly party local newsletters and bulletins. The changes in the RSW were also not that striking; of RSW's 271 titles, only 36 disappeared, 22 new publications were launched, and the rest continued. Despite the ineffectiveness of the call for a direct press boycott, the decrease in readership was drastic. Circulation of newspapers per capita, which reached 109 copies in 1976, fell to 97 copies in 1983. However, the reason was mainly economic—impoverishment of the populace and perhaps, to a lesser extent, a loss of interest in politics.

Rebuilding the Underground Media

Martial law stopped the operation of all official and unofficial Solidarity publications. In December 1981, more than 1 million leaflets and 4 million posters were confiscated. Eleven radio transmitters were silenced; 380 underground printing shops were discovered and closed. The termination of all nongovernmental communications created an enormous demand for news. As they had during World War II, Poles turned to foreign radio stations; this time, however, they could listen without fearing for their lives. In the first months of martial law, most political information was provided by foreign broadcasts in Polish, particularly by Radio Free Europe and Voice of America. In fact, all foreign radio services augmented their hours of emission, revised the schedules, and added new programs.

Nevertheless, this was not enough for the Solidarity activists and supporters. The official press was tightly censored, but people continued to say what they thought. Despite severe jail terms, some of the most courageous individuals began to publish illegally. Their main task was to rebuild the broken nervous system of Solidarity—its impressive communication system.

Thus, although the communication blackout and police searches effectively banned most Solidarity media, verbal opposition to the military junta was launched almost immediately.[9] Flyers with patriotic slogans and appeals for peaceful resistance appeared the day after martial law was imposed. Soon thereafter, information bulletins and newsletters appeared, followed by the regular illegal press.[10] Publications often carried the appeal to "read, copy, and pass on." The first newspapers published were *Tygodnik Wojenny* (War Weekly) and *KOS* (abbreviation for the Committee for Social Defense). The most important weekly became *Tygodnik Mazowsze* (Mazowsze Weekly), published in the Warsaw region.

The main problem for underground publishers was the lack of resources. Copiers, printing machines, and occasionally even typewriters in factories and institutions were kept under lock and key. The supply of paper and ink was also controlled by the state. Yet, all of these resources could be purchased on the black market, which was thriving. Printing was occasionally done in someone's cellar, but usually it took place in a garage, a craftsperson's workshop, a farmer's shed, or a workers' hostel. Editors remained anonymous, and the mastheads sometimes carried humorous captions, such as "editorial address know only to the editorial team."[11]

Later, several publishing houses were established; some were the continuations of the same clandestine institutions that had operated since the late 1970s, such as NOWA, Głos (The Voice), and the May 3 Constitution Press. Many others also appeared, such as CDN (the Polish acronym for "to be continued") and Sisyphus Press. They published newspapers, such as regular weekly *CDN—Głos Wolnego Robotnika* (CDN—The Voice of the Free Worker), and hundreds of books yearly. More than eighteen illegal publishing houses printed hundreds of thousands of books and literary periodicals. It was not by chance that the most frequently published books were Orwell's *Animal Farm*, with fifteen editions, and Solzhenitsyn's *The Gulag Archipelago*, with seven editions. Although the quality of printing and art of typography was usually poor, some illegal books were true works of art.

Despite all of the difficulties and the severe punishment for illegal printing, the underground press flourished. By the end of April 1982, there were approximately 140 different papers, and by the end of the year the list had expanded to at least 700 separate titles.[12] One surprising phenomenon was the appearance of illegal newsletters in the internment camps for the Solidarity activists. These included *Nasza Krata* (Our Bars), *Kurier Wiezienny* (Prison Courier), and *Kipisz Codzienny* (Daily Inspection).[13]

In addition to newspapers and books, clandestine publishing included hundreds of specialized periodicals that addressed different professional and social groups. Teachers and doctors were the best served. Even soldiers had an illegal paper entitled *Reduta* (Redoubt).

Interestingly, the martial law period was a fruitful one for the printing of poetry, fiction, and literary criticism. Poems, short stories, and diaries appeared in many underground publications. In addition, several literary reviews were devoted solely to such genres. This also held for humor and satire: They were indispensable ingredients of most of the free publications, and several were devoted entirely to satire. The titles were meaningful: *Scarecrow, Crow, Vulture, Wasp, Mole,* and *Hornet.* They all referred to insects, rodents, and other reptile animals, reflecting the attitude of underground humorists toward "the crow" (a pun on the Polish acronym for the military regime).

Yet, despite harassment and, initially, very severe persecution, underground printing during the 1980s assumed the proportions of a major industry. It later became the first industry to catch up with new technology and to use desktop software and laser printers to improve and increase its output.

For obvious reasons, attempts to create alternative broadcast media were not successful. However, underground Solidarity challenged the government even on this ground for purely symbolic reasons: Any break in the monopoly of the airwaves demonstrated the determination and strength of the banned movement. Thus, four months after the declaration of martial law, on Easter Monday, April 12, 1982, the official monopoly of the Polish airwaves was broken for eight and a half minutes when Radio Solidarity transmitted on the FM band in the Warsaw area. The broadcast was preceded by a call sign, the first eight bars of a popular underground wartime song, "Axe, Shovel, Moonshine, and Glass"—a clear reminder of the unbeatable spirit of the Polish nation.

Next, a man and a woman alternately read an editorial critical of martial law. This was the first of nine broadcasts by the Mazowsze branch of Solidarity. The second transmission took place on April 30, on the same frequency and at precisely the same time. This time, however, the broadcast lasted only four minutes before it was silenced by the police.[14] The next broadcasts Radio Solidarity transmitted were immediately jammed with pop music. Although overall the broadcasts did not have a great impact, the Solidarity transmissions represented a tactical victory over the government in the field of telecommunications.[15]

The alternative media system also included some other, albeit less popular, means of communication. Apparently influenced by Iman Chomeini, Stefan Bratkowski, the chairperson of the then-dissolved Association of the Polish Journalists (SDP), began to produce a "spoken newspaper,"—oppositional political audiocassettes. These cassettes offered a regular review of the news of the week with appropriate commentaries, jokes, and music. Cassettes were individually copied free of charge and then circulated by the thousands. Their influence, however, was very limited—they served more as a demonstration of independence and obstinacy.

More politically important was the Roman Catholic church's support of independent communication. In the 1980s, the church supplied its parish centers with video recorders. It also allowed independent moviemakers to use its camcorders and video equipment to record Solidarity protest demonstrations, register brutal behavior of riot police, and make documentaries on repression. In addition, parish screening rooms showed both religious and "forbidden" political movies to large audiences.

Although martial law finally ended after the second papal visit to Poland in July 1983, it was subsequently replaced by almost equally severe emergency laws. Nevertheless, a balanced picture should be drawn: Polish martial law was probably less rigid than the normal situation in Romania or Czechoslovakia at that time. Neal Ascherson noted that martial law did not really destroy the pluralism of Polish society. Over a hundred years ago the poet Cyprian Kamil Norwid wondered why so many "vast armies and valiant generals" gathered against Poland to suppress "only a few ideas: none of them new."[16] Jaruzelski was no more successful. Despite his initial efforts, the alternative media survived the blackout and "normalization" and later began to flourish in the shadow of Gorbachev's glasnost.

Taming the Journalists

Initially, the authorities clamped down severely on intellectuals. Many.

eminent writers, academicians, and theater and movie directors were jailed during martial law. Although this was soon considered a "mistaken action," performed by zealous die-hards in the security apparatus, the damage was nevertheless done—the crème de la crème of the Polish intelligentsia was punished for its support of Solidarity.

The journalists were hit in a different way. There was no need to imprison prominent journalists. The authorities knew that the profession as a whole would be easy to subjugate. They perhaps did not fear the leaders of the profession enough to take the precaution of isolating them. Bratkowski was left free, and, according to some rumors, he deeply resented this lack of recognition on the part of the security apparatus.

Perhaps second only to Solidarity itself, the SDP was the organization most hated by the Communist die-hards, and in particularly the secretary for propaganda, Stefan Olszowski. He could not stand the open defiance of Bratkowski and his colleagues and their new doctrine of professionalism and editorial independence.

However, it should be noted that since 1951, the SDP had stood as a Stalinist-type transmission belt organization and had been served as a loyal supporter of Communist media policy. Only in rare times of political unrest had some of its members raised the issues of professional integrity, censorship, and freedom of the press. It was only after the emergence of Solidarity that the role of the association changed radically. Beginning in October 1980, the activities of the association and of Bratkowski were persistently directed at stretching the autonomy of the press and protecting the professional rights of its members. Yet the SDP did not attack the very foundations of the political system; to its credit, it demanded a curtailing of censorship and worked hard to enhance the prestige and sovereignty of journalistic work.

Therefore, it was not surprising that the SDP was the first professional organization to be formally dissolved under martial law. The decision was made public on March 20, 1982, by the mayor of Warsaw. Acting as a front for the ideological party apparatus, he claimed that the SDP had "failed to fulfill its statutory obligations as well as to follow the prescribed scope and methods of activity."[17] In general, the dissident journalists proved to be a hard nut to crack. Significantly, immediately a new professional organization, the Association of Journalists of the Polish People's Republic (SDPRL), was instituted by a group of journalists who vocally supported Jaruzelski's policies.[18] It was obvious that the formation of the new association was an action orchestrated by the Propaganda Department. It is little wonder that the new organization met with no difficulties when it applied to be registered in court.

A strong statement of protest against the banning of the SDP was issued immediately by its leading activists. They criticized the dissolution as "the crowning blow in a series of unjustified and illegal repressive actions directed at our profession."[19] They also appealed to all journalists to reflect upon journalistic ethics before deciding "whether it is appropriate to join a new journalists' organization."

The disbanding of the SDP was the culmination of an intense campaign of criticism and vilification of the association. The party enlisted certain journalists in that cause. On March 16, a group of loyal journalists wrote a letter to Jaruzelski arguing that "the continued existence of the SDP with its previous structure and authorities, especially at the central level, is both undesirable and totally impossible because such an organization would be incapable of fulfilling the political tasks facing the journalistic community."[20]

This enunciation was apparently doctored by the Propaganda Department to suggest "spontaneous" anger among reasonable journalists and to contrast them with "unreasonable" leaders of the SDP. The letter was also a pretext for a massive purge of editorial boards. On March 12, four days before the publication of this letter, Stefan Olszowski announced at a party meeting that the leadership was about to start an important process of reshaping the socialist organization of Polish journalists.[21] A new journalists' association was created immediately following his pronouncement.

The Rise of Jerzy Urban

In the summer of 1981, when tensions between the government and Solidarity reached their heights, General Jaruzelski designated Jerzy Urban as a governmental spokesperson. He was a well-known and well-liked journalist, formerly a columnist for the famous weekly *Po prostu*,[22] and a nonconformist staff journalist for the party weekly *Polityka* (in 1962 and 1963, and again in the period 1969-1981). Although not a member of the Polish United Workers' Party (PZPR), and usually at odds with the propaganda line, Urban occasionally served the Propaganda Department as a ghost writer. This occurred only during the most difficult times for the party, when, for instance, he would write editorials on food price increases or workers' strikes. Now, however, his task was more serious and prolonged—to argue aggressively with Solidarity and launch attacks of his own. He performed that mission spectacularly.

During the next nine years, until the end of his governmental position in 1989, Urban became the most hated person in Poland. He was sometimes even compared to Goebbels.[23] This was, of course, not only an insult, but an obvious exaggeration. Urban was never fascinated with propaganda, especially its methods and means. Being remarkably intelligent, cynical, sarcastic, and iconoclastic, he was a strange figure among the members of the military establishment, who liked secrets and were not used to engaging in public relations. Urban's task was to disclose specific facts and data, and in the process he became the most outspoken Polish spokesperson to hold this position. He did his job in a most professional way. His main task was to use symbolic violence to intimidate his audience, thereby rendering the use of real power and military might unnecessary. Fully utilizing his position within the media, he slandered, insulted, sullied, and bullied Solidarity leadership.

However, his new vocation began after the imposition of martial law, after all other sources of dissident information had been destroyed, and when the government was enjoying a full monopoly of the official media. He initiated the practice of holding weekly conferences for the domestic and foreign press, and in so doing, he broke an aura of secrecy surrounding the official scene and governmental business. He never refused to answer a question, no matter how sensitive the subject. Urban invented a new approach to dealing with the foreign press: His conferences were dynamic, provocative, and pugnacious. He was a master of insinuation, distortion, and misrepresentation. Sometimes he revealed information that could not be obtained in other ways and at other times corrected rumors. Surprised that they had not been expelled by the junta, foreign correspondents attended the hearings, knowing that they too played a propaganda game. Urban was the main source of official information for foreign journalists about martial law and the plans of the authorities. Excerpts from the conferences were shown on Polish television. Although he was widely hated, he laughed openly at public opinion, and his performances always aroused much interest.[24] Everybody, it seemed, loved to hate Urban.

The Rewriting of the Censorship and the Press Laws

During the 1980s, the Polish law machinery had been more productive than ever before. This also holds true for the area of mass communications. Prior to the 1980s, several decades had passed with no significant changes in the legal base of media activities. In contrast, after the 1980s, the legal framework of the media was noticeably altered several times. For the first time in Poland's postwar history, a law on censorship was adopted by Parliament in 1981, thereby replacing the "temporary" decree of 1946.

The new law on censorship became binding on October 31, 1981. Only two months later, martial law suspended all its hardfought provisions. It was officially explained that the law was adopted "at a time of great emotion and tension, [and it] contains internal contradictions"; therefore, it was too liberal for the times.[25] Nevertheless, General Jaruzelski promised that all laws and regulations would remain valid; they were only temporarily suspended and would soon be adapted to new circumstances. This new situation would emerge when the martial law regulations expired.

In 1983, the government prepared a revised version of the legislation. The governmental bill represented an apparent return to the state monopoly over the freedom of expression. But it was the post-Solidarity period, and even in Jaruzelski's Parliament some representatives dared to speak against the proposed amendments. An eminent sociologist, Professor Szczepański, warned that "censorship, which is repressive by its nature, accelerates a social explosion and becomes self-destructive." He reminded the parliamentarians that rigorous censorship did not help former Communist leaderships, especially in 1956 and 1970, to deal with their respective political crises. Karol Małcużyński, a popular anchor of the late 1960s, emphasized that the new bill was "ill-timed and would hinder public dialogue and reconciliation."[26] Nonetheless, opposed by only a few negative votes and some abstentions, the censorship law amendments were eventually approved on July 28, 1983.[27]

The changes in the law were considerable. Therefore, the altered piece of legislation could again serve as a tool for administrative and discretionary control of the press. Only a last-minute concession to the church's demands excluded all works with fewer than one hundred copies, scientific research publications, and bibliographies from censors' control. Anything that fell under the blanket term "a threat to state security or defense" or whose content "obviously constitutes a crime" was forbidden. Photographs and exhibitions were also subject to censorship. Reprints of publications, which had already been passed by the censors and in 1981 were exempted from censorship, were again subjected to it.

This was not enough for the legalistic orientation of Jaruzelski's rule. The 1981 law on censorship was accompanied by a resolution that obliged the Council of Ministers to prepare a draft press bill and submit it for public discussion by April 1982. A special Codification Commission on the Press Law was set up, but it had to interrupt its work because of the imposition of martial law. Work was resumed six months later. The government draft was presented to the Sejm on July 14, 1983. It was eventually adopted on January 26, 1984, with only one negative vote and five abstentions. At that time, only two other Soviet-bloc countries, Czechoslovakia and Romania, had such a comprehensive legal act regarding the mass media. Yet, in contrast to those countries, the Polish law was intended to introduce a more liberal system.[28]

The press law became binding on July 1, 1984.[29] It, therefore, took

Communist Poland nearly forty years to produce its first comprehensive act defining the legal framework for the functioning of the mass media. Prior to this time, various media regulations referred to a decree that was issued in 1919 and amended nineteen years later by the presidential decree of 1938. These facts demonstrate how irrelevant it was for the Communist system to have legal regulation of the media. Spoken rules and administrative decisions were sufficient to control all means of public communication.

The new press law was a major act. It fell into nine parts, including a detailed list of journalists' rights and duties, the establishment of a press council, the organization of journalistic activity, responses to press criticism, the regulation of advertisements, the right to reply, and legal newspaper responsibility.

The initial part, called "General Remarks," broadly defined the media's tasks in Poland. It saw them not as information or entertainment, but, rather, as "strengthening the country's political system." The media had to serve the "progress of socialist relations." In a strange, original formulation, the moral duty of the press was stated as follows: "The press tends toward truthful description of displayed phenomena."[30]

Another important point concerned journalists' access to information. From then on, all institutions were obliged to provide upon request any information (state and economic secrets excluded) journalists needed for their reports. No one could be punished or discriminated against for having supplied such information to the press.

Articles dealing with the status of journalism stressed the demand that journalists "serve society and the state" and show loyalty to the "program line" of their editorial boards. A maverick attitude would be regarded as insubordination and could cost a journalist his or her job. However, to improve their poor image, journalists were granted the right to "professional secrets."

The law regulated in detail how printing and publishing permits would be awarded to private persons, a major renouncement from Communist policy. However, in order to make conditions less favorable, the government established an obligation to obtain a prior permit from censorship for "conducting publishing activity" and "for the actual publication of a given paper." If a private citizen applied for such a permit, he or she had to provide a statement from local authorities that there was a need to set up a private publishing venture in the area.

A separate section of the law imposed on the editor a duty to publish readers' explanations of or corrections to a published article. Another section listed the editor-in-chief's duties regarding the publication (free of charge) of official communiqués issued by central and local administrative offices. The law also stipulated that advertisements had to be in line with the paper's policy and had to conform to the standards of social conduct.

Among the undisputed, positive points of this act were the journalists' right to "professional secrets" and the legal assurances that no informant could be punished for supplying required information to the press. To oversee press matters, a special body, known as the Press Council, was established. As Articles 17 and 18 of the Press Law stipulated, the Press Council's primary tasks were the following: presenting its opinions and proposals regarding the observance of freedom of speech; preparing guidelines for the development of the mass media, publishing houses, printing works, and the distribution and utilization of newsprint and similar materials; preparing studies on the satisfaction of the public demand for information; shaping and monitoring journalists' ethics; coordinating studies on the press; and drawing up training programs for the mass media.[31]

The Press Council did not convene until one year after the bill had come into effect, on June 19, 1985. Two-thirds of the members were chosen by General Jaruzelski from a list of candidates put forward by journalists' organizations and publishers. The remaining third were selected directly by the prime minister from "representatives of the state administration and scientific and artistic circles."

A singular feature of the composition of the Press Council was the inclusion of seven editors from Catholic publications, including three papers that were very close to the Roman Catholic church: Jerzy Turowicz, the highly regarded editor-in-chief of the Cracow-based weekly *Tygodnik Powszechny*; Father Maciłka, director of St. Adalbert Publishing House in Poznań; and Sławomir Siwek, a member of the editorial board of the monthly magazine *Królowa Apostołów* (The Queen of Apostles).

Although the Press Council's activity did not bring tangible achievements, it represented the legal body that recognized a limited plurality within the press system; further, it was certainly an important novelty in a Communist media system. However, press law largely remained a dead letter; it was too vague and ran contrary to the pattern of party control.

Signs of Change

Despite all restrictions imposed by the legal framework, the media quickly seized new opportunities and changed rapidly. Throughout the 1980s, numerous periodicals changed their profiles, and various new titles appeared. Although the number of dailies remained stable, new weeklies and monthlies materialized and old ones underwent profound transformations. Because publications had to be more profit-oriented, they began to cater more to popular tastes and interests than to party ideological requirements. Even in a Communist country, the changes meant more sex, more crime, more human-interest stories. Some party papers even dared to print color photos of nude women.

The new titles were usually hobbyist in nature, such as personal computer magazines, and ski and tennis monthlies. Advertisements and shopping newspapers appeared, and a pale copy of a soft-porno, male magazine, called *Pan* (Mister) was introduced by the RSW to earn more money for the party.

The Catholic press, meanwhile, not only survived martial law but actually enlarged its press run and readership. In 1983 the global circulation of the religious press reached over 2 million copies. Of sixty-one papers, only one was a daily, and a few others were mass-circulation weeklies. All others were small publications, usually monthlies and quarterlies. In addition, there were twenty-three periodicals published by non-Roman Catholic denominations.

Television was firmly under government control. Nevertheless an alternative form of viewing appeared. The video and the camcorder are examples of so-called new communication technologies, or new media. In comparison with the slow pace of implementation by official structures, their adaptation by dissidents and then by people at large was extraordinarily fast, especially by the end of the decade. Camcorders were sometimes used to produce visual documentaries of events government television could not or would not cover, such as videos of the life and murder of the Catholic priest Jerzy Popiełuszko. Cassette videorecorders became an instant hit in Poland. One can explain the phenomenon by stressing that whereas government propaganda was dull, video brought a colorful and rich Hollywood world into Polish homes. By the end of the 1980s the number of videorecorders passed 1 million, which was more than 10 percent of the number of households.

They were supplemented by the fast-growing number of satellite dish antennae directly delivering Western images to Polish homes. In 1986 the government, evidently concerned about transborder satellite television, issued regulations that made installation of dish antennas possible. Three years later, there were approximately twenty thousand such installations in the country, and the number was growing rapidly. More than forty businesses sold and installed these dishes for a few hundred dollars apiece. Satellite television and video rendered the Communist monopoly over the airwaves illusory. Hence, as occurred in the West, the crushing of the Berlin Wall was watched live in thousands of Polish homes.

Gorbachev, Glasnost, and the Polish Follow-Up

The changes in the official Polish media system in the second half of the 1980s cannot be explained without taking into consideration the so-called Gorbachev factor. Of course, there was glasnost in Poland, as in Hungary, before Gorbachev. Martial law without certain openness might have been unbearably oppressive and may have led to violent public outbursts. Official Polish tolerance within the public sphere served as a safety valve and as part of the authorities' camouflage. What was more, official glasnost in Poland had to vie with a formidable freedom of expression in independent, uncensored, and therefore illegal publishing (samizdat) and with the ecclesiastical communication circuit, including the Catholic press. This did coincide with Gorbachev's new approach in Eastern Europe. A hardliner on the surface, Jaruzelski kept his nerve. He was the only East European Communist leader to develop a proper, even cordial relationship with Gorbachev. Openly friendly during Gorbachev's visit to Poland in 1988, Jaruzelski, along with the Polish public, was hoping for further Soviet reforms that would facilitate a Polish transformation.

General Jaruzelski carefully observed Gorbachev's reforms and adapted his policy accordingly. To give but one example, soon after the Soviet party congress widened glasnost in 1987, the new chairperson of the Polish Radio and Television Committee pledged more openness in radio and television programs, the key vehicles of political communication. He announced that there would be "no taboo topics" in journalism, meaning an easing of censorship and control.[32] And surprisingly, this promise was at least partially kept. Despite growing opposition, Jaruzelski's administration could not tighten the screw: On the contrary, it had to loosen it.

It was time for a radical change in government policy, because signs of a new discontent, already obvious in 1986, became even more apparent in 1987. A wave of spring and autumn strikes in 1988 showed the determination of a younger generation, which sheer power could no longer contain. This determination also took inventive, amusing forms.

In 1988 the inhabitants of Wrocław, especially the police, were dumbstruck by a sit-in at a telephone booth. The cubicle was stuffed with as many people as it could contain. They were equipped with sleeping bags, a clear sign of their determination to stay there as long as possible. The sit-in did not last long. Soon, all of the participants found themselves in the local police precinct.[33]

Contrary to initial perception, the protest was not against the poor conditions within the Polish telephone network but was an artistic performance by the Orange Alternative, a student group at Wrocław Fine

Arts College. They announced the Socialist Surrealism (SS) Manifesto, which jokingly "updated" the official art and propaganda doctrine of the Stalinist system—socialist realism—and proclaimed a new concept of SS. The students viewed political and social life as a special reality that could be understood only through surrealism. At the zenith of Solidarity's popularity, in 1981, the Orange Alternative installed at Wrocław University a new department called "Fort No. 1," whose principal theoretician and organizer was Waldemar "the Major" Frydrych. According to him, "Happenings should demonstrate that art and life are one."[34]

Frydrych was not content with words only; he loved to organize public happenings. Even martial law did not silence the Orange Alternative. Beginning in 1982, dwarfish faces began to appear on public buildings, at a time when painting anything unapproved by authorities was strictly forbidden and feverishly painted over. The enigma was solved in 1987 on International Children's Day when a dozen people in little red caps appeared on the streets of Wrocław singing children's songs. They were carrying a huge push bear and handing out sweets. Innocent play, one might observe; it was not so for the authorities. For the first time in the history of Poland, illegal dwarfs emerged from underground. The dwarfs sang innocent songs, but their music had the same rhythmic intonation as chants of the banned Solidarity, and they wore the same dark glasses as General Jaruzelski. As they were packed into police vans, sympathetic onlookers shouted "Lock up Winnie the Pooh!"

This event epitomized the general strategy of the Orange Alternative. The street theater was based on humor and the desire to create warm feelings and a sense of community among an atomized mass of Wrocław's inhabitants. "Do not fear; do comment of the situation; do laugh; do organize"—was the message. Thus, the group organized such happenings in the streets as Who's Afraid of Toilet Paper?, International Secret Policeman's Day, October Revolution's Eve, and Independent Celebration of Police Day. All events were very popular and successful.

These happenings, did not, of course, influence or inspire General Jaruzelski to propose the roundtable discussions. However, they symbolized the changed mood of most students and young intellectuals. The Poles, despite the hardships of everyday life, began to laugh, the most dangerous moment for a semitotalitarian regime.

The TV Debate that Shook Poland

After the waves of strikes in the spring of 1988, it became obvious that a form of deal must be made with the still banned Solidarity movement. Without such a deal, neither social peace nor economic reforms could be accomplished. This was perhaps the reason Alfred Miodowicz, president of the state trade unions, envisaged a project of reintroducing Lech Wałęsa—still the head of underground Solidarity—into political life as a minor partner in the labor movement. In order to do this, he proposed a live television debate on the most pressing Polish problems.[35]

Miodowicz was a member of the Politburo of the Communist party, which did not make a good impression on Polish workers. Nevertheless, the position gave him a clear advantage over Wałęsa. He gained much experience in arguing his points. Thus, at the onset, he was the clear winner of a such one-on-one televised debate. However, some of his colleagues had doubts, not about his abilities, but because of the publicity such a broadcast could give Wałęsa.

Created mainly by the mass media, Wałęsa was already a kind of hero in 1980. His famous burst onto the international political scene lasted only two weeks in the summer of 1980, but it involved three basic elements: (1) his own talents and personality, (2) calculated efforts by Poland's intellectual opposition to promote his image as a worker to the heights of national leadership, and (3) Wałęsa's attractiveness to the Western mass media.[36] The rebel worker and commander of a strong protest movement made for excellent magazine covers and front-page stories. Western television teams were pleased to have found such an excellent personification of the complex social process. More important was the effect of Western promotion on the Polish audience. The image of Wałęsa as an internationally recognized leader was projected back to Poland. Those images increased Wałęsa's charisma and helped to convince many skeptics of his talents and position at a time when the official Polish media was not believable.[37]

After the imposition of martial law, Wałęsa became the preferred target of malicious propaganda that was carried out by an intelligent, clever, and unscrupulous Jerzy Urban. However, the 1983 Nobel Peace Prize increased Wałęsa's prestige. The banned Solidarity movement needed a leader. Consequently, Wałęsa again began to serve as a national symbol. Nevertheless, after so many years, nobody was certain how strong his reputation was in the eyes of the masses and, more important, how brilliant he really was. At his press conferences, Urban described Wałęsa as a "private citizen," stressing that at best the electrician from the Gdańsk shipyard was nothing without his intellectual advisers, such as Professor Geremek or Tadeusz Mazowiecki. Urban believed eight years of spiteful propaganda would leave its imprint on the attitudes of Polish intellectuals and workers.[38] There were some doubts even in Wałęsa's camp. He was seen as Everyman—a good worker, a good Catholic, a pater familias, and, at best, a smart negotiator.[39] A live television debate might have been too much for his wit and intelligence. On the other side,

Miodowicz considered himself—and, indeed, was considered by his Politburo colleagues—a clever, intelligent, telegenic tribune of the trade-union movement with its 7 million membership.

After a few stressful days of negotiations and the rejection of certain proposals of the Wałęsa team, the debate was finally organized and broadcast live.[40] This occurred on November 30, 1988, just after the main evening news bulletin at the height of prime time. A big clock was placed in the center of the stage—to prove that the broadcast was really live. The stage had an almost spartan decor—a gray background, the big clock, and two modern armchairs. It was arranged by the official television staff, and Wałęsa's team had nothing to say about the set. The entire debate was prepared in a great hurry, with much improvisation, many suspicions, and many last-minute changes.[41]

Despite some petty obstacles directed toward Wałęsa before the broadcast probably intended to increase his nervousness, both participants received an equal chance and equal time. Miodowicz appeared at ease. He wore his usual black shirt, which made him look a bit like a gangster. Wałęsa seemed to be nervous, and he looked like a worker in his Sunday-best suit. It was Wałęsa's first appearance on Polish television in eight years as other than a target of Urban's malevolent attacks.

A television representative appeared for only a moment, announced that the debate would last exactly forty-five minutes,[42] introduced the participants, and gave the floor to Miodowicz.[43] He looked nervous and talked for too long. In his turn, Wałęsa made it clear that he was not speaking as a private individual but as someone who had been chosen to represent Polish workers. Turning to the invisible audience, he thanked the public for its continued confidence in Solidarity. Then, he attacked the official trade union for doing nothing to improve the situation of workers.[44] He made many intelligent comments. The last ten minutes belonged entirely to Wałęsa, who was verbally much stronger and more argumentative.

The debate shocked and shook Poland. Public reaction was overwhelmingly enthusiastic and in support of Wałęsa: "It was like a breath of freedom," said a housewife. "He showed the true class of the Polish worker," remarked a shipyard worker. "Wałęsa stole the show," commented a journalist. "It was a smashing victory for Wałęsa; I would give him an 8 to 2 victory," a governmental official had to admit.[45] Wałęsa's advisers and independent personalities from various circles also praised his performance. "It was a great moment for all of us," declared Bronisław Geremek, the Solidarity's mastermind.[46]

Wałęsa's manifest victory put the authorities on the defensive. Instead of dying from overexposure, Wałęsa emerged from the television debate as a strong national leader. Without this television opportunity, he probably could not have returned so quickly and smoothly to the Polish political scene as a popular, undisputed leader with whom the majority of Poles could identify.

The Same Institutions, the Modified Practices of Control

As the single most important political event of 1988, the Wałęsa-Miodowicz debate was an unthinkable phenomenon in all other Communist countries. To give the floor to a declared and forceful opponent was totally against Leninist principles. It was not one case of a Polish departures from the logic of the Communist political system. Since the mid-1980s, Poland had been a land of inconsistencies, if not contradictions. According to the 1986 party program, the political system was still at the stage of dictatorship of the proletariat—the Communist party. The party claimed the leading role in society and in the country, stressing that the goal was still Polish socialism, with the people rallying around the party. Its propaganda was still compulsory for all, with Poland tied to the "Socialist camp," in particular to the Soviet Union.[47] Thus, on the surface, it was a country in which the Communist party still maintained total control over society. In practice, however, conditions were very different.

Underground publications were not only published in great numbers but were sold openly in the streets. Foreign broadcasts in Polish were no longer jammed; moreover, the politically offensive Radio Free Europe freely and regularly broadcast live telephone conversations with Polish oppositionists. There was censorship, but it lent more credibility to the Catholic press, which used its right to mark censors' interventions, than to the Communist press, which, although also censored, did not. There was a critical shortage of paper, but dozens of new papers appeared each year, and only a few disappeared. The main television news bulletin had the lowest credibility of any of the mass media, but more than 60 percent of television viewers watched it each evening.

The party elite was fully aware that the time for the old-style propaganda and communication monopoly was over. It, therefore, commissioned reports and analyses of adapting the media system to the "new philosophy of propaganda." One of these went so far as to propose:

1. Remove the doctrinal shackles on propaganda
2. Use objective information well combined with interpretation so as to suggest skillfully the desired attitude to the news . . .
5. Adapt the message to the audience—promote specialization and

decentralization of the media . . .

7. Rely on the agenda-setting, agenda-building, and cultivation functions of the media rather than on direct persuasion.[48]

This was obviously a manipulative approach to improving party propaganda, but, nevertheless, it was a break with the ideologization of the media. In a paper delivered to the same party caucus, I demanded the media reorientation: toward development of its information function and reduction of propaganda load.[49] My paper also demanded the abolishment of supervision of new information technologies, commercialization of information, and admission of pluralism in the information and communication systems. This was of course possible because the party in a panic was looking for new, more acceptable policy.

On the legal level, the Communist party still had a monopoly of power, but in practice and with reluctant tolerance, many spheres of life were beyond its control. But when eventually the party was ready to accept the reforms, it was too late. All of Solidarity's apparently suppressed ideas had reemerged by the end of the decade.

Notes

1. The regional dailies of the Polish United Workers' Party published special editions totaling 4.7 million copies nationwide, reproducing the proclamation of the Military Council of National Salvation and other official communiqués. All of the other local papers were suspended, with the exception of the Gdańsk and Cracow papers, which were temporarily amalgamated with the party press. Anna Sabbat-Swidlicka, "Poland's Underground Press," *Radio Free Europe Reports* 30, July 29, 1983, part 1, p. 1.

2. Ibid., p. 2.

3. Ibid., pp. 3-5.

4. It was mainly propaganda measure, devised to make people afraid of the ubiquitous government control.

5. Such a boycott had, however, a precedent in Polish history. During the Nazi occupation, Polish actors preferred to work as waiters and waitresses rather than perform in German-sponsored spectacles.

6. The most spectacular television success during these years was a Brazilian tele-novela, *Isaura*. This long and complicated love story about a slave woman and a handsome, but cruel landlord created a frenzy in Poland. When the duo came to Poland, they received a royal welcome and red-carpet treatment from both the enthusiastic viewers and the Communist authorities, who were eager to achieve some legitimization.

7. Not all, however, directors and actors were convinced that the boycott was a right decision. One of them, the reputed theater director Kazimierz Dejmek made a public outcry when in 1994 as the minister of culture he publicly called that boycott "a stupidity."

8. The party secretary in charge of propaganda, Stefan Olszowski, had reportedly said that of the estimated seven thousand journalists employed in the Polish press and radio and television networks, no more than fifteen hundred were fit to keep their jobs. Dan Fisher's report in the *Los Angeles Times* (January 11, 1982), p. A9.

9. Jadwiga Czachowska and Beata Dorosz, *Literatura and krytyka poza cenzura 1977-1989* [Literature and Criticism "Beyond Censorship"] (Wrocław: Ossolineum, 1992), p. 124.

10. Sabbat-Swidlicka, "Poland's Underground Press," p. 2.

11. Ibid., p. 3.

12. According to estimates made by *Tygodnik Mazowsze*, March 10, 1983, p. 7.

13. Sabbat-Swidlicka, "Underground Press," p. 4.

14. Ibid., p. 2

15. Andrzej Michajłowicz, "Solidarity Goes on the Air," *Radio Free Europe Reports* 31, June, 6, 1982, Part 2, p. 1.

16. Neal Ascherson, *The Struggles for Poland* (London: Michael Joseph, 1989), p. 229.

17. Radio Warsaw, March 20, 1982.

18. Jan B. de Weydenthal, "The Normalization of Polish Journalists," *Radio Free Europe Reports* 7, April 2, 1982, Part 1 of 2, pp. 1-10.

19. Dariusz Fikus, *Foksal 80* (Warszawa: Czytelnik, 1989).

20. *Trybuna Ludu* March, 17, 1982, p. 1.

21. *Trybuna Ludu*, March 13-14, 1982, p. 3.

22. The weekly is described in Chapter 9.

23. In 1992 Urban filed a suit against a former PAX leader for calling him the "Polish Goebbels."

24. Anna Sabbat-Swidlicka, "Urban's New Information Order," *RFE Reports* 22, June 2, 1989, Part 5, pp. 19-21.

25. Jerzy Bafia, *Prawo o cenzurze* [The Law on Censorship] (Warszawa: Książka i Wiedza, 1983), p. 35.

26. Ibid., pp. 13-14.

27. B. Margaritte, *Figaro*, July 29, 1983, p. 1.

28. Ewa Celt, "Poland Adopts Its First Press Law," *Radio Free Europe Reports* 11, March 12, 1984, Part 1, p. 10.

29. Full text in *Dziennik Ustaw* 5, 1984, item no. 24.

30. Ibid.

31. From the Press Law.

32. Interview with *Przegląd Tygodniowy*, December 7, 1987, pp. 6-7.

33. See Tomasz Jerz, "The Telephone Booth Strike," *Studium Papers* 4, October 1988, pp. 114-115.

34. Ibid., p. 115.

35. Miodowicz officially made his offer in an interview with the party daily *Trybuna Ludu* on November 15, 1988, p. 3.

36. Voytek Zubek, "Wałęsa's Leadership and Poland's Transition," *Problems of Communism*, January-April 1981, p. 69.

37. More about unknown Wałęsa in Jarosław Kurski, *Wałęsa : Democrat or Dictator* (Boulder: Westview, 1993)

38. Communist propagandists still believed that a lie repeated a thousand times becomes truth.

39. Roman Laba, *The Roots of Solidarity: A Political History of Poland's Working Class Democratization* (Princeton: Princeton University Press, 1991).

40. After a number of apparently deliberate misunderstandings and attempts to discredit Wałęsa as someone who had engaged in foul play (the official press agency accused him of insulting his opponent and using aggressive language before the debate, but it was later forced to retract its allegations), the debate was finally run.

41. The Wałęsa team was certain that some eavesdropping devices were used.

42. The original idea was that each of the two speakers would speak for ten minutes, and then each would have five minutes in which to respond to what the other had said. In fact, the debate lasted a few minutes less then allowed, because both speakers agreed to end it early.

43. The two speakers were introduced simply by their names, in keeping with Miodowicz's convention that they would merely be "a steel worker talking to an electrician."

44. See Anna Sabbat-Swidlicka, "Wałęsa Victorious in Television Debate," *Radio Free Europe Reports* 50, December, 16, 1988, Part 3, p. 3.

45. Also, an instant poll conducted by the state television Public Opinion Research Center showed that 97 percent of those who had seen the debate (the sample consisted of three hundred residents of Warsaw above age of fifteen) thought it was a positive event. Of these, 18 percent believed it was a breakthrough on the road to agreement between the authorities and the opposition, 61 percent felt it was a small step but one that held a promise of hope, and 17 percent saw it as proof that no agreement between the two sides was possible. Radio Warsaw, November 30, 1988, at 10:00 p.m.

46. From telephone interviews with Radio Free Europe; Sabbat-Swidlicka, "Wałęsa," p. 6.

47. Hans-Georg Heinrich and Sławomir Wiatr, *Political Culture in Vienna and Warsaw* (Boulder: Westview, 1991), p. 99.

48. Wiesław Rosiecki, "Warunki wzrostu efektywności pracy propagandowej," paper presented at the Third National Theoretical and Ideological Conference of the Polish United Workers' Party, January 1989, p. 7.

49. Tomasz Goban-Klas, "The Problems of the Making of a New Information Policy," paper presented at the Third National Theoretical and Ideological Conference of the Polish United Workers' Party, January 1989.

13

The Kapellmeister Vacates the Pulpit
February 1989 to April 1990

The photograph of a huge, bagel-shaped, round table, seen from above, went as, they say, 'round the world. More to the point, it went 'round Eastern Europe.
—Timothy Garton Ash, *The Magic Lantern*

The role of the media in the upheavals of 1989 will find its historians. The media supported the Communist regimes and helped to defeat them.
—Z.A.B. Zeman, *The Making and Breaking of Communist Europe*

Despite all of the changes in the late 1980s, the basic structure, philosophy, and rules of the Polish political system were still monopolistic by nature; thus, new social forces could not find a place within the system. They could effectively challenge the system, rather than play a constructive part in it. The inconsistencies and contradictions between the monopolistic ideology and one-party domination and de facto sociopolitical pluralism created ever-growing social tensions.

The so-called Solidarity period, 1980 and 1981, proved that it was impossible for a large, independent trade union to operate within the confines of a rigid political structure without a resultant full-scale head-on confrontation with the authorities. Martial law, then, reinstated the logical Communist order, even though it could not suppress all manifestations of resistance to the system. Although Solidarity was made illegal, its publications went underground. The taste for freedom of information and access to the mass media was not entirely forgotten.[1] In the face of growing discontent and hatred of the youth—intensified by the deepening economic crisis—and only after the wave of strikes of 1988, the leadership eventually decided to initiate profound political reforms. The essence of the remodeling was to self-limit Communist party domination and involve other orientations in political power. It was obvious that some legalization of opposition, especially of the banned Solidarity, was a prerequisite to any reform or social agreement. This meant a reintroduction of freedom of association.

The Roundtable Breakthrough

Judging from the experience gained during the last months of Solidarity in 1981, a radical change in the organization of the mass media was a necessary part of such legalization. Everyone understood that freedom of association meant nothing if it was not supplemented by freedom of speech and mass communication. In preliminary informal negotiations the opposition forcefully demanded the right to talk with its own voice and to have access to the mass media.

The authorities agreed, and the roundtable talks began in Warsaw on February 6, 1989. Although their antecedent was the historic Gdańsk negotiations of August 1980, there were meaningful differences. This was not an ad hoc self-selected workers' striking committee led by an electrician, Lech Wałęsa, but a deliberately selected group of seasoned, hardened, and long-term political oppositionists. They faced an equally canny government team, composed of the best reform-minded party intellectuals. Surprisingly, the atmosphere was not one of confrontation, but, rather, of serene cooperation. The issue this time was to share the power, not to outwit the adversary. Of course, no one could predict the final, almost immediate revolutionary aftermath of the agreement that was reached.

The talks were conducted in three major working groups (called "little tables"), which in turn, were divided into smaller groups. The groups the opposition considered to be central were those on trade-union pluralism, on reform of the judicial system, and, significantly, on the mass media. At the table on mass media, as at the others, two "sides" met: the "coalition side," the party-government negotiation group, and the "opposition side," the Solidarity negotiators.[2] The composition of both teams clearly reflected the nature of the negotiations. The issue was control of the media; therefore, it was essential that important representatives of party controllers were involved in the bargaining. The opposition side included mostly journalists who had lengthy and bitter experiences as dissident writers and publishers.

The government group consisted of the delegates from the party and the government. These included heads of the Propaganda Department of the Polish United Workers' party (PZPR) and two of its allied parties (the United Peasant party [ZSL] and the Democratic Alliance [SD]); the spokesperson for the Polish government, Jerzy Urban; and the deputy president of Polish Radio and Television. In addition, a few journalists were included in the government delegation, including the president of the Association of Journalists of the People's Republic of Poland (SDPRL) and some party columnists. The chair of this team was Bogdan Jachacz, former head of the party Department of Propaganda and later president of the Polish Press Agency.

On the other side of the table sat the most important personalities from the intellectual opposition, including Adam Michnik, the leading Polish dissident since 1968, and the former editor-in-chief of the weekly *Solidarność*, Tadeusz Mazowiecki. Representatives of the dissolved Association of Polish Journalists, editors-in-chief of the leading underground publishing houses, representatives of the Roman Catholic lay and bishops' organizations, and some other eminent intellectuals were also included in the oppositionist team. The chair for that side was Krzysztof Kozłowski, deputy editor-in-chief of the prestigious Cracow weekly *Tygodnik Powszechny*. This working group totaled forty-five persons representing both sides.[3] The intellectual weight and fame of the participants was a clear sign of the significance of media reform.

At the inaugural session of the working group on mass media, the opposition declared that without progress at this table, no other major agreement would be possible.[4] The Solidarity team came to the talks with a set of well-defined demands. They sought to enfranchise the entire Polish society in the field of the mass media, which Krzysztof Kozłowski stressed in his opening address.

> It is not only a question of legalization of Solidarity, which is, as commonly known, a crucial element of the agreement, but also the provision of a politically and socially rich context in which Solidarity will operate. Existence of different political associations and, in the future, also political parties would have no real meaning if there are no guaranteed opportunities for free use of the mass media. We need a new information order in Poland. We want, of course, for the state controlled mass media to serve the whole society and be placed under the control of the society, but we also demand the fundamental right to express our views and opinions in our own newspapers and in independent radio and television broadcasts.[5]

All members on the Solidarity side reiterated that without the right to its own media, and without access to communications resources—including newsprint and state television—Polish society felt expropriated. They called for the participation (not simply access) of all political, economic, and social orientations in shaping the media system. The new system should serve free articulation of all shades of public opinion. The media should function as an instrument of public control over political and social bodies. Its role would be to expose government wrongdoings and to direct conflicting group interests into constructive channels.[6]

"We came here to regain our rights," the opposition said, to sum up the general sense of the Solidarity demands. The specific issues were:

- Access of opposition to radio and television
- Fair distribution of newsprint
- Authorization and allotment of a quota of newsprint for new Solidarity publications, both national and regional
- Legalization of underground publications
- Legal liberalization of censorship
- Termination of the licenses for publishing activity
- Reinstatement of the journalists dismissed after martial law and condemnation and rejection of the practice of firing journalists for political reason
- An end to seizures of foreign publications by customs offices

These demands did not carry equal weight in the roundtable negotiations. In getting permission to open a Solidarity media, the most important demand for the opposition was to gain access to newsprint and to television.[7] This was a consequence of the bitter experiences of 1980 and 1981. When the roundtable negotiations began, Solidarity initially reiterated its eight-year-old demands in more decisive and concrete wording. The opposition insisted on controlling one of the two channels operating on Polish television and one radio channel out of the four in existence. Obviously, this was unrealistic and it was made in order to raise the stakes. After a short discussion, the demand was dropped. Solidarity then asked for "windows" in the program schedule—its own broadcasts lasting half an hour. However, even that was too much for the party, which still considered television its last bastion for propaganda. Finally, it was agreed that Solidarity would have the right to broadcast a thirty-minute program on television and a sixty-minute radio program once a week,[8] although these programs would be subject to censorship. This was seemingly not a big gain, but, nevertheless, it broke total party monopoly over the national broadcast media.

The issue of censorship was a very delicate one. The main reason it existed in Poland was not ideological but geopolitical. Given the traditional Polish defiance of Russians, some reasonable intellectuals and journalists treated censorship, especially in regard to foreign affairs, as a lesser evil than self-censorship or a complete lack of both censorship and self-restraint. Nonetheless, in 1980 Solidarity had demanded liberalization and legal control of censorship by replacing the decree of 1946 with a law that would allow censors' decisions to be appealed in court. This law had been passed, although only two months before martial law, and then it was amended in a constrictive way. Thus, when the roundtable began, Solidarity simply demanded a return to the 1981 law—a reinstatement of the legislation approved before martial law. With few trivial exceptions, that point was easily agreed upon.

A more politically contentious issue proved to be the allocation of newsprint. In Communist Poland, as in all of Eastern Europe, newsprint was always scarce. This scarcity was used as a reason to license the press and to keep the circulation of newspapers and magazines under strict party control. Thus, the demand to change the system of newsprint distribution under which the lion's share of all production of newsprint had been given to the RSW, the Communist party publishing house,[9] was reasonable. Without this change, formal permission to publish a periodical would remain an empty promise. The issue turned out to be one of the most difficult, because it threatened the position of the RSW.[10] Ultimately, a compromise was reached through which newsprint could be sold on the free market. Therefore, anyone who could afford it could print anything he or she wanted, providing it did not break the law.

Another delicate and difficult issue to resolve was the legalization of underground publications. By 1989, there were more than five hundred regular illegal periodicals, in addition to thousands of ephemeral papers. Ten major underground publishing houses printed books and journals in great numbers. These ranged from Solzhenitsyn to Popper, from political pamphlets to high-brow magazines. Solidarity wanted all of those publications to be printed legally. The government agreed to allow their regular operation without confiscation and arrests.

The concluding document, signed by all working groups on April 5, 1989, spelled out the new political system based on (1) political pluralism; (2) freedom of speech, implying the possibility for the various political forces to gain access to all media; (3) formation of all representative state organs; (4) independence of courts; and (5) an upgrading of the jurisdiction and free election of the organs of local self-government.[11]

Soon thereafter, the political organization of society was turned upside down. Only one month later, Solidarity election programs began to be broadcast on radio. Then, a new Solidarity daily appeared, appropriately called *Gazeta Wyborcza* (Election Gazette). The paper's aim was to promote Solidarity candidates in the upcoming election. A few days later, the weekly *Solidarność* reappeared under the direction of its former editor-in-chief, Tadeusz Mazowiecki. Amendments to the laws on the press and on censorship were hastily approved by Parliament in June. Although this was only one step in the direction of freedom of the press, the changes in the media were real and significant.

The most fundamental victory was not the legal measures, which were, in fact, mainly legalization of an existing situation, but the break in the philosophy of party-government monopoly in the field of communications. For the first time in postwar Poland, the Communist party renounced the idea that full control over the media was necessary to ensure its leading role in society and its basis for political power. The government was still too timid to reject censorship, but the Solidarity accomplishment amounted to a breakdown of the official monopoly over the media that had been a traditional feature of Communist regimes.

Although indirect, the most important immediate result of these roundtable talks was the many photo opportunities television coverage gave members of the opposition. Previously, even the most prominent opposition leaders were known to most of the Polish audience only because their names were abused by hostile party propaganda.[12] Then, suddenly, they appeared on national television and performed surprisingly well—as intelligent, serious-looking members of the Solidarity team, with large union signs on their lapels and on their proudly exposed file folders.

A much more important effect was the indirect influence of the talks on public opinion and the leadership in Eastern Europe. News about the roundtable was not confined to Poland. It spread rapidly in the region, reaching other Communist leaders through their confidential channels and other opposition leaders through their underground network. In turn, the Eastern European public was also informed by direct or indirect Western media reports. All of this justifies the opinion of many political observers that throughout 1989 opposition movements were aided greatly by the media in imitating each other's success.[13]

The Fall of Jerzy Urban

In order to contain potential damage and ensure their continued predominance in the fields of information and propaganda, the authorities devised a "new information order" that was to be implemented by government spokesperson Jerzy Urban. On April 17, 1989, he was appointed head of the Radio and Television Committee and was given ministerial rank. In a letter to the presidium of the Parliament, Prime Minister Rakowski wrote that the roundtable agreements and his government's reform program made it necessary

to unite the efforts of the state-run media and the state's administrative agencies in presenting to the public and interpreting the government's polices [and] in gaining public approval for the measures it is undertaking and implementing. This task should be entrusted to a member of the government with ministerial rank. He should preside over a team of directors of governmental information agencies that would include the

Polish Press Agency (PAP), the daily paper *Rzeczpospolita*, the government's spokesman and press office, and the Radio and Television Committee. Such a team would be attached to the government. Its task would be to analyze relations between the government and the public and to develop current information policy and the means of presenting the work of the government.[14]

Rakowski's decision came as a surprise to those parties allied with the PZPR. They simply did not like to be associate with Urban. Thus, many of their deputies voted against Urban's nomination: 97 against, with 44 abstentions. He won by a small margin, only 153 deputies voted for him.

From one point of view, this decision represented a major retreat from party dominance over the media. It was the first step in the process of separating state media policy from that of the party, although at the expense of the latter. Urban was not even a party member, but he became responsible for coordinating the operations of the government-controlled media to ensure it maintained a uniform political line in news reporting and commentaries.

Urban explained his new information order as "creating possibilities for people to voice their views by defining certain rules and freedoms."[15] He also claimed that the media should reflect the multitude and diversity of opinions. However, he maintained that the state authorities still had to control television, because this was their fundamental tool for getting in touch with the public. Moreover, he declared that radio and television would not share air time with the opposition, because the work of radio and television "must be ruled by one programmatic concept."[16]

The agreement of May 28, 1989, on relations between the Polish Episcopate and the state gave the church the right to have access to television for the first time. Another agreement, this one between the church and the Radio and Television Committee in June, allowed the church to set up its own independent programming section inside the state radio and television organization.[17] Paradoxically, by signing this act, Urban, a declared atheist, opened the gate for the clergy to enter the Communist television fortress.

Urban's career as information minister and chairperson of the state radio and television organization did not last long. In August, the new non-Communist government fired him immediately, and with visible pleasure. He was again unemployed, but not for long.

Farewell to Censorship and the RSW

By 1989, the censors had self-restricted their control over the press. Of

3,701 registered titles, the office exempted from preventive control 929 periodicals.[18] The number of interventions substantially decreased, from 2,528 in 1988 to 1,506 in 1989.[19] With the naming of a non-Communist prime minister (Mazowiecki) in August 1989, censorship practically ceased. However, the inertia of bureaucracy was such that the budget for fiscal year 1990 still provided the substantial sum of 5 billion zlotys to sustain this useless institution. Only when a group of indignant deputies revolted in April 1990 was the law on censorship revoked by the same Parliament act that had changed some provisions in the Press Law. But even then, in a last-minute amendment the new government tried to save some of censorship's prerogatives by requesting that all publications be presented to the public prosecutor's office.[20] Countermeasure bill, however, was submitted by a group of deputies and approved on April 11, 1990, bringing about the true end of censorship.[21]

The Press Law of 1984 also had to be adapted to new circumstances. Although the basic structure of the act remained intact, amendments had changed it substantially. Of sixty-one articles in the original law twenty-two had been discarded or altered, and six articles had been added. The most important adjustment was that to the system for authorizing periodical publications. The old form of control through the censorship office was replaced by a simple system of registration of new titles in court. A petition for such registration had only to contain (1) the title of publication and the address of the editorial board; (2) personal data on the managing editor; (3) the name, headquarters, and address of the publisher; and (4) the frequency of publication.[22]

The major new media legislation was the law of March 22, 1990, for the privatization of RSW *Prasa-Książka-Ruch*, an almost monopolistic organization over printing and distributing the daily press and a semimonopolistic one over the weeklies. This move destroyed the information control of what until January 1990 had been the Communist party.[23]

Attempts to pluralize radio and television were also started. In 1988, a draft version of a new bill for state radio and television had been prepared.[24] It had not gone so far as to suggest the elimination of the state monopoly; instead, it proposed some cosmetic modifications. It was not until October 1989, after the change in the political system, that the new chairperson of the Radio and Television Committee, Andrzej Drawicz, designated a new commission to reform state broadcasting and broadcasting in general. The commission amended the 1988 draft version of the bill and proposed rejecting any state monopoly over television. This draft became the basis for all subsequent government bills on the broadcast media.[25] A subcommittee of the parliamentary Cultural and Media Committee had began discussing a new media bill in February

1990. It was expected that the bill would soon be ready and approved and that it would regulate both state radio and television and commercial broadcasting. However, it took almost three years for the bill to pass.

Nevertheless, in 1989 and 1990, the change in the media system in the direction of pluralism, independence, and democracy was indisputable. The monopolistic system of media control withered away with the Communist party, and the media began to breathe freely. Unfortunately, after such good beginnings, further transformations proved to be more difficult and less obvious.

Tadeusz Mazowiecki, who had been editor-in-chief of *Solidarność* in 1981, was nominated by Lech Wałęsa to reassume this position on the reborn weekly in May 1989. However, from its start the new version was less popular than it had been in the past. Times were different; former taboos looked pale after a decade of underground publishing. The paper's journalistic style was very serious and mostly anemic. Mazowiecki was not able to repeat the success of the original.

Moreover, the seeds of discord among the Solidarity leaders were sown very early. Mazowiecki's selection as the new prime minister opened his editorial post in August. Surprisingly, Wałęsa moved to put the weekly under his direct control. In his memoirs, Waldemar Kuczyński, a close adviser of the new prime minister, mentioned that Wałęsa bluntly told Mazowiecki "I gave you the government, therefore I take back the weekly. It must be mine."[26] Without consulting the editorial board, Wałęsa nominated Jarosław Kaczyński as the new editor. His move caused half of the staff to resign. When a farewell issue was published, the first conflict within the ranks of the victorious Solidarity was made public; more serious rifts within the movement's leadership soon emerged.

Notes

1. The beginning of the alternative network goes back to the late 1970s when from the humble underground newspaper *Robotnik* (Worker) formed in 1976, a wide range of publications "beyond censorship" had developed.

2. Exact names were slightly different, but that is irrelevant.

3. I was one of the members of this group.

4. The analysis of the negotiation is based on unpublished "Minutes of the Proceedings at the Mass Media Table," distributed among the participants.

5. Krzysztof Kozłowski, "Minutes of the Proceedings," February 12, 1989, typescript.

6. See Jan Skórzyski's interview with Maciej Iłowiecki in *Przegląd Katolicki*, March 19, 1989, p. 4.

7. But this was not a topic for negotiation, because it was treated as part of an agreement on the legalization of Solidarity.

8. Interestingly, in 1981 not all journalists were enthusiastic about the direct access of Solidarity to airwaves. They feared it would impose its own censorship—informal, but equally chilling.

9. RSW *Prasa-Książka-Ruch* was the biggest publisher in the country. It published almost all of the dailies, a majority of the weeklies, and half of the monthlies; it employed about one hundred thousand persons, had a monopoly over distribution of newspapers, and had an impressive network of newsstands. See Tadeusz Kowalski, "Evolution After Revolution," *Media, Culture, and Society* 2, 1987, pp. 184-188.

10. It was called the expropriation of the RSW *Prasa-Książka-Ruch*.

11. Quote in Hans-Georg Heinrich and Sławomir Wiatr, *Political Culture in Vienna and Warsaw* (Boulder: Westview, 1991), pp. 102-103.

12. Western audiences probably had better "face recognition" of leading oppositionists than did Polish citizens. The reason was simple: The opposition leaders were kept away from television; their names could be mentioned, although only in a negative way, however their faces were not to be shown.

13. Z.A.B. Zeman, *The Making and Breaking of Communist Europe* (Cambridge: Blackwell, 1991), p. 311. The well-known Eastern Europe specialist J.F. Brown explained that when martial law banned the Western media in December 1981, no means were available to mobilize public opinion. In 1989, the Western media at large played a very prominent role. Brown recognized a strong correlation between the presence of the Western media and the incidence of unrest in Eastern Europe. He went even further, stating: "Western television, certainly, became a vital factor in the East European struggle for liberty in the late 1980s. The swelling rank of the opposition, especially their leaders, knew that they were now actors on the world stage, and played their roles accordingly." J.F. Brown, *Surge to Freedom: The End of Communist Rule in Eastern Europe* (Durham: Duke University Press, 1991), p. 12.

14. *Rzeczpospolita*, April 28, 1989, p. 1.

15. *Rzeczpospolita*, May 19, 1989, p. 1.

16. *Trybuna Ludu*, May 28, 1989, p. 3.

17. "The Agreement Between the Committee of Polish Radio and Television and the Secretariat of the Conference of the Polish Episcopate, June 28, 1989," *Przekazy i Opinie* 3-4, 1990, pp. 23-25.

18. From an interview with the spokesperson for censorship in *Życie Warszawy*, November 16, 1989, p. 4.

19. Anna Bikont, "Zabijają ludzkie myśli jak zwierzęta," (They Kill Human Thoughts Like Animals), *Gazeta Wyborcza*, January 1, 1990, p. 3.

20. Anna Bikont, "Cenzura jest likwidowana!. Rząd jest reformowalny," (Censorship Is Being Eliminated, the Government Can Be Reformed), *Gazeta Wyborcza*, April 5, 1990, p. 1.

21. The Law on the Abolition of Censorship, April 11, 1990, *Dziennik Ustaw*, 1990.

22. Those who published periodicals without registration were penalized with a levy. Registration could be refused or revoked if a publication committed three press offenses in a year. The authorities had the right to confiscate offending material upon court orders. "The Law Changing Certain Articles in the Law on

the Press, April 11, 1990," *Dziennik Ustaw*, 1990.

23. "The Law of March 22, 1990 on the Liquidation of RSW *Prasa-Książka-Ruch*," *Zeszyty Prasoznawcze* 1-2, 1991, pp. 197-198. There are other published legal documents on this process of liquidation; see ibid., pp. 199-200.

24. "Project of the Reform of Radio and Television, August 1988, by the Committee of Polish Radio and Television," *Przekazy i Opinie* 3-4, 1990, pp. 12-19.

25. "Project of the New Law on Radio and Television, February 1990," *Przekazy i Opinie* 3-4, 1990, pp. 21-26.

26. Waldemar Kuczyński, "Wyznania zausznika: 1989-1990," *Polityka*, February 22, 1992, p. 8.

PART THREE

Media by Request:
Beyond Solidarity

The big European wall has been broken through, and the barbed wire barriers have been cut. And it turns out that was the easiest part.

—Jan Urban, Czechoslovak dissident, May 1990

They set the slave free, striking off his chains; then he was as much of a slave as ever. He was still chained to servility. His slavery was not in his chains, but in himself.

—James Oppenheim, "the Slave," from *Songs for the New Age*

14

Emerging Polyphonic Media

After April 1990

After the government changed in August 1989, the Polish media began to undergo profound structural transformations that affected their legal and economic status. This process can be called "changing the skin" of the formerly Communist media.

The New Media Landscape

The groundwork for the transformation of the Polish media was initiated in mid-1989 when the procedure of licensing newspapers was replaced by the simple system of registration. Before this time, only those organizations recognized by the state could apply to the censorship office for a license to publish periodicals. The only private periodical granted such a privilege during the entire history of Communist Poland was the monthly *Res Publica*, and this did not occur until 1987. After the roundtable agreement, any individual or institution that wanted to start a paper merely needed to notify the authorities.

The chance was eagerly exploited. In the next few months nearly two thousand applications were sent to the Main Office for the Control of the Press; of that number, however, only half actually became publications. In addition, most of the new papers were ephemeral publications that survived for only a few issues. In 1990, the U.S.-based IDEE Fund appropriated nearly one hundred thousand dollars to various publications in Poland. The money went to some publishing houses, such as PEN, Pomost, and Volumen; a few high-brow cultural magazines, such as *Almanach Akademicki*, *Ex Libris*, and *Czas Kultury*; and local Solidarity publications throughout Poland. In the latter category, small-town newspapers, such as *Pismo Wołomina, Ziemia Garwolińska, Głos Wieliczki,* and *Głos Łukowa,* were favored.

By mid-1991, there were over two hundred new microlocal weeklies and biweeklies, particularly in small towns, in the countryside of the western Wielkopolska region, and in the northeastern part of Poland. The main proponents of these publications were the citizen's committees, the Solidarity-originated local election organizations. Other local periodicals were also attached to emerging political parties. A few were founded by ethnic minorities, such as for example, *Rrom po Drom* (Gypsy on the Road).

From this new legal and political situation, the new local press developed rapidly. In a few months hundreds of new titles appeared, almost no town, no matter how small, lacked such publications. The growth, though, was not without difficulties, which were caused primarily by a lack of stable financing from sales and advertisements. Despite these financial difficulties, local papers survived, and many communities, have had their own voices.

The changes in the national daily press came much later. The number of dailies in Communist Poland had been fixed for many years as the result of a deliberate policy, which considered dailies the "sharpest weapon" in the party's propaganda arsenal. Although in this role dailies were eventually replaced by television news bulletins, they were still kept under a rigorous Communist monopoly. Even in the turbulent years of Solidarity (1980 and 1981), when the party had to allow the 10 million member trade union the right to its own publications, it agreed to only one national weekly, although it had the largest circulation of half a million copies.

Immediately after the 1989 roundtable agreements, the censors' office issued a permit and allocated newsprint to the Solidarity daily, *Gazeta Wyborcza* (Election Gazette). A real novelty in the media system, it was an instant hit. One month after its first issue, *Gazeta* circulation reached half a million, and the number of its pages had doubled. Within two years, its circulation rose to close to 1 million on weekends, making it the most widely read and influential newspaper in the country.

The quasimonopolistic situation in the press market pushed the government and the Parliament to move to break up the highly criticized RSW *Prasa-Książka-Ruch* in April 1990. RSW (the workers' publishing cooperative) was not a "cooperative," nor did it belong to "workers." It was merely the Communist party monopoly publishing organization. By the late 1980s, it controlled 87 percent of the total circulation of dailies and 76 percent of weeklies. In terms of titles, RSW had complete editorial control over 47 percent of all press titles.[1] It also held monopoly over the distribution of newspapers, both national and foreign. It owned a majority of the printing plants and consumed more than half of all newsprint, which, at the time, was allocated by the government.

Against the background of the strength of RSW, the editorial resources of the other political organizations were very poor. Only four dailies were published by publishers other than RSW. Even the political parties that, in the past, had been closely aligned with the Communist party (United Party Alliance [ZSL] and Democratic Alliance [SD]) respectively controlled only 1.3 and 1.6 percent of all titles, and 2.3 and 2.5 percent of total circulation. Solidarity had only one daily and a single weekly.

The decision to break RSW was made during the politically euphoric time following Solidarity's electoral victory. A few months later the decision might have been different—RSW might have been nationalized instead of destroyed. If this had been the case, the new government would have had a powerful instrument for shaping public opinion. The process of remodeling the media system in Poland was, therefore, characterized by the dismantling of this huge newspaper chain and not by the process of concentration of ownership.

For many months, *Gazeta Wyborcza* remained the only new daily on the national market. In autumn of 1990, a new journal named *Tesa News*, which called itself a daily for businesspeople, appeared. It was a flop. The following year, the first Polish color daily, *Glob 24*, commenced publication in Warsaw. It was also a flop. In the same year, two new national dailies were started: a conservative daily *Nowy Świat* (New World), which was an organ of the Centrum Alliance party, and an independent, high-quality paper, *Nowa Europa* (New Europe). Although both papers survived, their circulation has not been impressive, and both have deficits. These experiences show how difficult it has been to enter into fixed press structure that is dominated by well-established newspapers and old-fashioned reading habits. In 1992, however, a new political tabloid, *Super Express*, began to threaten the status quo, at least on the Warsaw market.

Major Newspapers and Their New Owners

Before May 1989, there were fifteen dailies with national distribution: of this group, only one (*Dziennik Ludowy*) scaled down to a weekly. Two others changed their titles (the former Communist party organ, *Trybuna Ludu*, became simply *Trybuna*; the former army organ, *Żołnierz Wolności*, was renamed *Polska Zbrojna*). Three years later, nineteen national dailies were in print. Of this number, ten were targeted to the public at large, three were sports dailies, two were rural papers, and two were financial dailies. One was for children, and the army had one central daily.

Initially, *Gazeta Wyborcza* was the unofficial organ of Solidarity. The paper proudly carried Solidarity's logo and a masthead that proclaimed, "There Is No Freedom Without Solidarity." From its inception, *Gazeta Wyborcza* was owned by Agora, a limited liability company established in April 1989 by the famous movie director, Andrzej Wajda and two Solidarity leaders, Aleksander Paszyński and Zbigniew Bujak. Lech Wałęsa nominated the well-known dissident Adam Michnik to be editor-in-chief. The company grew quickly, using the old press *Le Monde* had donated when it modernized its facilities. In 1991, *Gazeta Wyborcza* supported Mazowiecki's party, the Democratic Union, which did not like Wałęsa. As a rebuttal, Wałęsa took back the Solidarity logo—surprisingly without hurting the paper. A prominent journalist connected with the Wałęsa faction later accused the paper of using Solidarity money and preferential credits to push its circulation, an allegation that resulted in a lawsuit which he lost.[2]

After *Gazeta*, *Rzeczpospolita* was the second most-important daily. Formerly a government organ, after privatization *Rzeczpospolita* changed to a limited liability company—a joint venture of the daily, the Polish government, and the French company Socpress, owned by the press baron Robert Hersant. Foreign investments helped to make *Rzeczpospolita* an almost independent, information-based paper. However, in 1992, the government began to regret its decision to sell shares and attempted to regain editorial control over the daily. Obviously, it was too late to make the daily again the mouthpiece for the government.

Established in 1944, *Życie Warszawy* is the oldest of the existing dailies in Poland. In 1991, the paper became the property of a newly established company of Societe Televisiana Italiana, some Polish companies, and Varsovia Press—whose shareholders are *Życie Warszawy*'s editor-in-chief and forty-five staff journalists. The second Warsaw daily, *Express Wieczorny*, for many years the most widely read Warsaw evening paper, was bought by the Solidarity Press Foundation to promote its cause and to earn money.

Trybuna, the former Communist daily, is a limited ability company with five shareholders, all private individuals linked to Social Democracy of the Republic of Poland (SdRP). *Sztandar Młodych*, a former Communist youth daily, is published by the Economic Education Foundation, the Polish Culture Foundation, and Polskie Nagrania, a record company.

The owners of local and national newspapers are often journalists, but rarely can they carry the entire cost. Instead they work with wealthier partners, especially commercial banks and foreign firms. A handful of papers have a Western-style ownership structure. Cracow's conservative daily, *Czas*, was founded with seed money from a French aristocrat Frederick Decazes. *Gazeta Gdańska* was financed by a prosperous cucumber exporter. A building company, Exbud, owns the regional paper *Słowo*

Ludu. Gazeta Wspołczesna's owner is a local branch of Solidarity. A local company, Drogowiec (Roadworker) Ltd., has acquired three local papers.

The Polish press became pluralistic but not really independent. Most Poles continue to see the press as political. It has widely been believed that each party or faction must have a newspaper as its mouthpiece and that every newspaper must have some affiliation with a party or a faction.

Because of the liquidation of RSW, foreign investors have had a chance to buy into the Polish media system. The same process caused the former Communist-controlled press to become not an independent press but, rather, a press controlled by new political parties. Initially, most of the papers were supported mainly by the party associated with Prime Minister Mazowiecki. Later, some were taken by the conservative party, the Center Alliance. The Liquidation Commission of RSW freely conceded that it chose winning bids that were based not on price alone but on other factors as well.[3] Its declared intention was to promote a "pluralistic" press. Therefore some papers were left in the hands of journalist teams, whereas many others were transferred to new political parties for a fraction of their real values. For instance, the popular youth weekly *Razem* was sold to the Confederation of Independent Poland for practically nothing. Nevertheless, some conservative politicians criticized the process as not "de-communizing" the press, because too many papers were left in the hands of the former staff. In reality, this criticism has been directed at papers that have not promoted a conservative program.

The main focus of concern for publishers and journalists has been the economic obstacles that at present constitute a barrier to a free and independent press. Printing and newsprint are extremely expensive in Poland, and their prices skyrocketed after the economic reform program in 1990. Because zloty became so expensive, it is actually cheaper to print color magazines abroad, in Austria or Finland.

The distribution system remains controlled by the state. The state-owned *Ruch* chain of kiosks, part of the largest RSW conglomerate, is the primary distributor of newspapers. About 99 percent of newspaper distribution is still handled by *Ruch;* therefore, its inefficiency makes national distribution particularly difficult.

The economic depression has badly hurt newspaper readership. Many people have abandoned the daily papers and only buy weekend editions. Many papers have found it difficult to survive, with rising costs and sinking readerships. The Cracow daily *Czas* lost thirteen thousand dollars in 1990. Many other papers are on minimal budgets. Big-city newspapers rely on advertising for a surprisingly high percentage of their revenue. *Życie Warszawy* draws 70 percent of its revenue from ads, and *Gazeta*

Wyborcza receives about 60 percent of revenue from that source. For the small local dailies, however, it is much more difficult to rely on advertising for any great amount of revenue.

Readers' Likes and Dislikes

There are significant changes in the press market.[4] In the early 1990s, there was an increase in the circulation and sales of the following types of magazines:

- So-called light papers, especially magazines providing sensational criminal stories (*Detektyw, Skandale, Sensacje, Kobra*); those with mixed content (sensationalism, politics, and sex), such as *Raport*; and erotic magazines (in particular *Cats, Polish edition of Playboy*)
- Shoppers' and ad magazines (such as *Top, Kontakt*, and many other local free papers)
- Pop music papers and fan magazines (such as *Magazyn Muzyczny, Rock'n Roll*, and others), and "audiovisual" magazines that deal with the new media (*Audio-Video, TV-Sat Guide*, Polish edition of *PC World*)
- Horoscopes and "semiscientific" papers, as *Nie z tej ziemi* (Incredible), *Nieznany Świat* (Unknown World), *Szaman*, and *Sfinks*)
- News magazines, such as *Wprost* (Direct).

The readership of certain magazines remained stable, in particular women's magazines, mainly because new, glamorous titles have appeared, as *Twój Styl* (Your Style), youth periodicals (illustrated magazines and a young girls' magazine, *Filipinka*), and certain high brow magazines, such as *Nowa Res Publica* and *Puls*.

Even more papers, though, lost readers. These included:

- Religious, especially Catholic papers. The free-market economy has not helped the Catholic press to flourish. With the exception of a few periodicals, overall circulation has not increased. Moreover, the abolishment of censorship has not helped, either. The Catholic weekly *Tygodnik Powszechny* has faced ever increasing competition in the publication of new, diverse ideas; thus, its circulation has plummeted. The paper used to sell 70,000 copies and at its height reached a circulation of 140,000. At present, and with much difficulty, it sells 40,000 copies.[5]
- Rural press and papers targeted to a rural audience, mainly because of the collapse of the mail subscription system.
- Sociopolitical, traditional newspapers and magazines, such as

Przegląd Tygodniowy and *Prawo i Życie*, except for popular news-magazines such as Poznań's *Wprost*.
- "House organs" targeted to employees of major enterprises or to special professional groups—for example teachers.
- General interest magazines, among them the oldest such Polish magazine, *Przekrój*.

Some journals have beat the bad market. The most spectacular emergence has been the blasphemous weekly run by Jerzy Urban, former martial government spokesperson. He launched the satirical weekly *Nie* (No) in October 1990. In six months' time, he was selling a staggering half a million copies a week by printing humor about Poland's new rulers and the Roman Catholic church, ribald drawings and photos, and anything that smacked of scandal.[6]

Dailies, with the exception of *Gazeta Wyborcza*, have not done so well. In 1980, the average circulation of all newspapers was slightly above 10 million copies. In the following years, circulation fell slowly but steadily. According to 1990 estimates, total circulation had fallen to 5.1 million copies—almost half of what it had been at the beginning of the decade. In 1991, there was an increase in total circulation of newspapers to 5.3 million copies. However, this number was reached by seven-five dailies, whereas in 1980 there were only fifty-three dailies. There was a sharp decline in the press run of all national dailies. In 1986, the average run was about 3.6 million copies; in 1991, it fell to about 2.1 million.[7] In 1991, the press run of all "old"—formerly Communist—papers was only 30 percent of their 1986 circulation. Many new publications simply died.[8]

The Roman Catholic church has a large network of publications—approximately two hundred newspapers and weeklies. Of these, only six have any real influence: *Tygodnik Powszechny*, *Przegląd Powszechny* (Jesuits' Monthly), *Rycerz Niepokalanej*, *Królowa Apostołów*, *Gość Niedzielny*, and *Niedziela*. The latter is the most conservative of the Catholic publications. Its circulation remains the most limited. The church, which did not want to invest in a new daily, made a deal in 1993 with the formerly pseudo-Catholic PAX organization to change the status of its daily *Słowo Powszechne* into the organ of the Episcopate. This was highly ironic, because, in Cardinal Wyszyński's times, PAX had been supported by the Communists to sabotage church actions. Presently, the circulation of this daily is very limited, at approximately twenty thousand copies.

All together, including the Roman Catholic publications, the religious segment of the press market is quite small; it does not exceed 3 to 4 percent of the total Polish press run. In absolute numbers, it equals about 2 million copies. The number of titles is above three hundred, of which number, the lion's share are Roman Catholic publications. Other denominations are marginal. For example, the Mormons have only about a hundred faithful, the Buddhists have only a few hundred more, and the Raya Yoga denomination has an even smaller membership. Yet, non-Roman Catholic denominations seem to be growing. There are some low-circulation non-Catholic Christian periodicals. Among the forty-two legally acknowledged denominations, nineteen publish their own periodicals. A service for non-Catholics is broadcast on the radio every Sunday.

Pirates on Satellite

The changes in radio and television have been much less spectacular. From a legal point of view, in the early 1990s radio and television continued to be regulated by a law adopted in 1960 under Communist rule. This law made the Committee for Radio and Television an exclusive organization with the exclusive right to produce and broadcast radio and television programs.

In the aftermath of the roundtable agreement in 1989 and 1990, only one local independent television station appeared and was allowed to operate. However, the change in the political system caused a spontaneous radio boom. People with idealistic convictions began to work without any subsidies but soon turned to commercial goals to acquire the few available frequencies. Several local radio stations were then legalized for a trial period.

Thus, the French-supported Radio Fun was born in Cracow. In Warsaw Radio Solidarity and Radio Zet began to broadcast. Though presently there are many other smaller radio outlets, of these three, Radio RMF (Fun changed its name to RMF) and Radio Zet are the best known and have the largest audiences. All are serious competitors against state radio in their respective cities. On the national scale, these three stations reach only 7 percent of the total audience, but in the regions they cover that number grows to about 34 percent. Their new, more dynamic, independent style makes them popular, especially with the younger set.

I give one example from the history of underground radio in Poland. Radio *Solidarność* was born in 1982 under martial law. It operated clandestinely and largely symbolically for seven years. Each broadcast lasted only a few minutes. The rise to power of the Solidarity government in August 1989 meant the radio station could soon emerge into the open. Despite the absence of a new telecommunication law, a temporary permit was issued and a frequency on the FM band was allocated. Radio *Solidarność* went on the air legally in September 1990. Station officials began to look for ways to finance regular radio service. Sponsors were eventually found in the United Kingdom, where Radiotrust Plc., an investment trust that invests in commercial radio stations, was seeking to expand abroad. A financial package was created in February 1990. A total investment equivalent to 240,000 pounds from Radio Trust and Abtrust New European Investment Trust Plc. was meant to cover the first two years of Radio Solidarity's operation, based on the assumption that there would be no advertising.[9] However, quite unexpectedly, the station became self-sustaining. Programming was a mixture of 25 percent talk and 75 percent music, with the musical emphasis being on pop. Reaching up to 1.5 million listeners in the Warsaw region, Radio *Solidarność* succeeded in attracting over forty advertisers—including insurers, airlines, travel agencies, shops, hotels, and manufacturers—from Western Europe, the United States, and Poland.

Radio *Solidarność* has had a serious competitor in Radio Zet. Sponsored by Radio France Internationale and the Polish daily *Gazeta Wyborcza*, Radio Zet started broadcasting in 1990. In its first four months, it became the most widely listened to and the most popular radio station in the Polish capital. The company is owned by its president, with only 12 percent of the shares being held by *Gazeta Wyborcza*. Radio Zet is considered to be a supporter of the Democratic Union, although it is careful about being openly involved in politics. The station is financially very sound and receives all of its income from advertisements.

Radio Fun, now known as RMF (Radio, Muzyka, Fakty), began in 1989 as a French outlet in Cracow. The station was launched by the newly established Foundation for Social Communication, a brainchild of the roundtable agreement, which called for more pluralism in the media. The foundation was supported financially by a group of French Polish emigrés and politically by a Polish senator, who had been the chairperson of media talks at the roundtable and later became minister for internal affairs. With such influential supporters, the station easily received a temporary permit to operate, although initially it could only broadcast in French. The program was initially a satellite retransmission of the Paris-based network Radio Fun. After a year, it was allowed to broadcast in Polish.

Like Radio Zet in Warsaw, RMF became an instant success in the Cracow region. Pop music dominates the programming; there is also a regular news bulletin on the hour. In addition, there are five news bulletins in English plus retransmissions of the BBC World Service and Voice of America twice a day. In the evening the format is largely talk shows, whereas during the day it is mainly music and commercials. The radio station is financially self-sufficient and is constantly enlarging its operation. As the first Polish radio station, it went on satellite (Astra), and now covers all of Europe. In January 1994, it began to broadcast to the Chicago region, using satellite relays. In Poland, RMF broadcasts on

FM twenty-four hours a day; now it covers an area inhabited by about 6 million people and reaches about 3 million of them. It is owned by the company called RMF (60 percent of shares) and a bank (40 percent).

There have also been dozens of other independent radio stations in Poland. For example, Radio Alex began to broadcast in Zakopane in March 1990 as a private, one-man-station. Soon, it was followed by many other similar small, independent stations, operating without permit. They were, therefore, called "pirate" stations, although they called themselves "pioneer" broadcasters.[10]

In October 1991, the Ministry of Telecommunications ordered the closing down of all "illegal" radio and television stations in Poland. Radio Wawa was closed for a time; then, other stations such as Radio Fiat in Czestochowa, the Catholic station, that received a temporary permit to operate during the pope's visit in the summer of 1991. The main reason for the closing given was that the station interfered with radio reception in the city. The radio station Delta in Bielsko-Biala and Radio Plus in Dąbrowa Górnicza were also ordered to shut down. They did not. The Poznań station Radio "S" and the student radio station Afera, owned by the Poznań Technical University, were closed, as was the television station Morze in Szczecin. The only stations in Poland that could legally operate were Radio RMF, Radio Zet, *Solidarność*, and the television station Echo in Wrocław. However, the commercial radio station AS in Szczecin was allowed to operate, because it rented a frequency from the local Roman Catholic church, which had a legal right to access to Polish airwaves without license or permit.

The overall situation did not lack problems. The Ministry of Telecommunications had the right to allocate frequencies, but it could not allow a station to operate. That job was to be given to a new body, which was nominated after the law was passed. The ambiguous legal situation helped one of the "illegal" stations, Radio Delta in Bielsko-Biala, to get support from the Office of Interventions of the Senate. It argued that the Polish Agency for Radiocommunication had no legal right to close the station. It justified its support by indicating that the technical requirements for the station to operate had been fulfilled, and, moreover, oral consent had been given by the Ministry of Telecommunications.

Difficulties in fighting red tape at the Ministry of Telecommunications pushed some of the more determined prospective broadcasters to create the Association of Regional Radio, with about sixty members. In addition, a new organization, Foundation for the Support of Private Radio and TV Stations, has been set up. It is affiliated with more than ten stations that broadcast to a combined audience of about 5 million.

Eventually, in the beginning of 1994, the legal situation of the airwaves began to clarify. The newly established National Council of Radio and

Television granted one license for a national television network (to the private company Polsat, owned by one person), and two licenses for national radio networks (Radio Zet in Warsaw and Radio RMF in Cracow). In addition, church radio Maryja, run by the redemptorist order, was allowed to broadcast on the national scale using 38 low-power radio emitters. Strangely enough, the fathers were not happy with this decision; they expected one of the two national licenses. In the provoked crisis, one of the members of the broadcasting council (KRRiT) resigned, two others strongly objected.

Private radio stations are not the only stations that come into conflict with the legal monopoly held by the state radio. Poles still have a choice of foreign radio stations broadcasting on short and medium wavebands. Media freedom did not bring an end to these stations. Although the apex of their popularity was reached in the early 1980s when they were the main sources of uncensored information about martial law in Poland, foreign stations are still widely used. They are no longer jammed and they are permitted to rent frequencies on the Polish radio airwaves. Radio Free Europe (RFE) broadcasts in the morning and in evening on the medium and FM waves used by Polish Radio Channel Two. Ironically, Poles still feel that these stations are much needed. Research commissioned by RFE has stressed that because of weaknesses and biases in the Polish media, Radio Free Europe still has an important role to play in Poland and should continue its broadcasts to Poland over the next years.[11] Nevertheless, the U.S. administration decided to close this station by the end of 1994.

Notes

1. Tadeusz Kowalski, "Evolution After Revolution: The Polish Press System in Transition," *Media, Culture, and Society* 2, 1988, p. 187.

2. "Jacek Maziarski musi przeprosić *Gazetę*" [Jacek Maziarski Has to Ask Pardon from *Gazeta*], *Gazeta Wyborcza*, March 11, 1992, p. 1.

3. See *Więź*, November 1992, p. 34.

4. Z. Bajka, *Polska prasa codzienna 1991* [The Polish Daily Press] (Kraków: Materiały OBP, 1991).

5. Ewa Szemplinska, "Ex Cathedra," *Wprost*, February 28, 1992, p. 27.

6. "We are in tune with social attitudes," the editor explained. Quote from an article about the Polish press, "Free at Last," *Newsweek*, 10 June, 1991, p. 21.

7. Bajka, *Polska prasa*, p. 7.

8. Barbara W. Olszewska, "Prasowi bankruci," in *Polityka*, February 29, 1992, p. 6.

9. "Radio Solidarity," *Doing Business in Poland* (London: British Telecom, Kogan Page, 1991), pp. 205-209.

10. This analysis is based on my report "The Mass Media in Contemporary Poland" to the World Association of Christian Communication (typescript, Cracow, 1992).

11. "RFE in Eastern Europe: Monitor Observations from Focus Groups in Czechoslovakia, Hungary and Poland," typescript, Munich: RFE-RL Research Institute, Media and Opinion Research, December 1991.

15

Under Friendly Fire:
Media and Politics
After the Change in the System

The media systems in Eastern Europe have been both the victors and the victims of the end of Communist rule.
—from a speech by Jane Curry, November 1992

Poland has always been a land of paradoxes, and this did not change after the electoral victory of Solidarity in June 1989. The party got what was decided before election, as 65 percent of all seats in the lower chamber were reserved for the communist coalition. On its turn, Solidarity won all of the seats in the Senate, where the election was totally free, and 99 percent of the seats in the lower chamber to which it was allowed.

Solidarity Loses Its Glamour

However, shortly after such a landslide victory and the capture of the government, Solidarity began to lose its appeal to society. It failed to rebuild the media network it had developed so well under martial law. Of course, underground papers lost their raison d'etre following the demise of censorship. But even the reborn weekly *Solidarność* was a pale shadow of its 1981 predecessor. All other Solidarity publications, except *Gazeta Wyborcza*—including local papers and bulletins—have had low circulation and restricted readership and have constantly lost money since their inception.

Nonetheless, in years past Solidarity has been the major protagonist on

231

the Polish media scene. Ever since its beginnings in 1980, it considered the mass media to be a key element in its struggle for political power and in the realization of its concept of civil society. Democratic communication was seen as being equal to communicative democracy—that is, mass communication was conceived as an instrument of articulation and control in a democratic society. This is why Solidarity always exerted maximum effort toward the development and preservation of both its legal and illegal media and always considered the right to communication as an irrevocable human right.

At the same time, the Solidarity leadership thoroughly controlled its media. Spokespersons for the movement were entrusted with control of its press and the right to intervene whenever Solidarity journalists deviated from the prescribed course. These limits on media freedom within Solidarity had serious consequences. When the movement succeeded in obtaining power in the state and society, its pattern of media management was based on mixed and contradictory doctrines: one that promoted pluralism and freedom of the media and a second that judged media performance on whether it served or hindered the interests of the power structure.[1]

This explains why President Wałęsa's pronouncements on media control have been ambiguous, to say the least. He sometimes has supported freedom of the media and spoken for editorial independence and pluralism. On other, more frequent occasions, Wałęsa has demanded control of television and radio and called for lawsuits against journalists. Perhaps the best example of the latter is the case of his withdrawing Solidarity support for *Gazeta Wyborcza* by banning the use of the Solidarity logo on the front page of the popular daily. This was done in response to what were seen by the Solidarity leadership as articles critical of the union and of Wałęsa.[2]

However, Solidarity's influence on the media today is obviously a remnant of the past, a consequence of its once popular appeal and glamour. It never had any legal basis. The Communist party fall from power, so evident in the first half of 1989, brought about the separation of the party and the state communication policy and made the government the major controller of the mass media. This was manifested in the last months of Rakowski's administration, which exercised more direct control over the media than any previous Communist government. The state not the party had much of effective control. Thus, when the Communists handed over the reins of power in August 1989, they ironically left all the legal levers of media control in the hands of the non-Communist successor government. This left Wałęsa and his organization, Solidarity, without any legal basis for control and without any property within the media. In practice, however, Wałęsa personally retained much of control over state television and radio by influencing the nominations of senior management positions. When, he became eventually the president of Poland, a new law on broadcasting gave him a right to nominate three members (of nine), including chairperson, of the National Council of Radio and Television (KRRiT).

Is the Best Policy No Policy?

The Mazowiecki government, whose associates at the roundtable demanded radical reforms in the mass media, showed no special eagerness to transform the media system according to a democratic plan. Rather, it believed in an invisible hand of the market. Information and communication policy was based on a declaration that there would not be such policy, at all. The spokesperson for the government, Małgorzata Niezabitowska, announced during her first press conference that there was no need for any information policy; there was only a need for the truth.[3] She was seconded by Mazowiecki's closest advisers. Although governmental restraint might be and, indeed, was justified as a rebuttal to the repudiated Communist orchestration of the media, it had disastrous consequences for the government itself.

Yet, despite its laissez-faire attitude, the government did not free television and radio from its control, perhaps for fear that it might lose hold over the transformation process. The government did not nominate a new Press Council as it was legally obliged to do. New bills for the establishment of an independent and private broadcasting were submitted after long delays. To make matters worse, personnel policy was not based on professionalism but on presumed loyalty. The new head of the Radio and Television Committee, Andrzej Drawicz, a tall and trim Kojak look-alike with rapier eyes and a Ph.D. in Russian studies, a close friend of the prime minister, became the new chief of Poland's 12,000-employee state TV and radio networks.[4] He went so far as to announce that he "never watched television, considering it the biggest evil."[5] Although he also proclaimed that there would be no "witch hunt," or purge of staff, in 1990 many former editors and prominent journalists were compelled to leave the institution against their will. The justification given was that "they lost faces telling lies under martial law; they had to leave." The commitment made at the roundtable that a political verification of journalists would never take place was, therefore, broken.[6]

Furthermore, the new administration, which was initially so popular, showed an aversion to engaging in any sort of public relations and communication activities, even in explaining the new economic rules. Therefore, it seemed distant and indifferent to the hardships its shock economic therapy had imposed on the people. This was perhaps the principal cause of both Mazowiecki's defeat in the presidential election and the fall of his government at the end of 1990.

Media policy did not improve under the next non-Communist government, that of Bielecki of the Liberal Congress party, which came to power in January 1991. When Jan Bielecki was a representative to the Polish Parliament, he participated in the drafting of a new, liberal television bill. But his government did not show any overwhelming desire to push the bill through the legislature. Journalists' criticism of the government was met with contempt and indignation. Immediately after his resignation, Bielecki surprised the media by filing a lawsuit against some newspapers and television broadcasts, accusing them of defamation of his person and his administration. Although supported by a few members of his cabinet, the charges were eventually dropped by a public prosecutor, who referred to Bielecki's oversensitivity.[7] Nonetheless, the damage had been done to the image of the Liberal party, whose leader had demonstrated that he did not understand the role of a free press.

From Indifference to Assaults on Media

Jan Olszewski, elected prime minister in December 1991, did no better than his predecessors. Like them, he found neither time nor energy to organize public relations campaigns. A lawyer and former columnist, in his first address to the Parliament, he impertinently attacked journalists, accusing them of lying about the economic situation and hiding the gloomy reality from readers and viewers. Soon afterward, the spokesperson Marcin Gugulski blamed the press for exhibiting bias against the government and announced that only journalists who were considered reliable would be invited to his news conferences.[8] Immediately, a political campaign was begun to regain government control of the media. This strategy was prompted and supported by Olszewski's constituency, a loosely organized citizens' group called the Central Alliance, a Solidarity faction that had supported Wałęsa in the 1990 presidential election.

First, the government recaptured the Polish Press Agency by ousting its president who had been nominated by former Mazowiecki's administration. Through the appointments of loyal top personnel, other state-owned media, such as the Polish Information Agency (PAI) and the Committee for Radio and Television, were subsequently brought into line. The press in general was beyond the administration's control, so only the editors-in-chief of a few government papers were replaced. Olszewski tried also to regain command over the major daily, *Rzeczpospolita*, the former government paper, but he was unable to do so because the paper had sold a majority of its shares to a foreign press chain. Consequently, a new daily, *Nowy Świat*, was made an unofficial organ of the new administration. The state distribution company, *Ruch*, then issued a confidential directive to promote sales of the newspaper.[9] This is ironic, because it was a carbon copy of the 1974 Politburo directive concerning the leading party organ, *Trybuna Ludu*.

Using a pretext of "cleaning" the government of undercover Communist agents and informers, Olszewski's administration launched a major attack on many of his former colleagues from Solidarity, including Wałęsa himself. The prime minister made an emotional speech on all radio and television channels. The change in regular scheduling was made on a direct order from the newly appointed head of Polish radio and television, Senator Romaszewski.[10] However, once again it was documented that control over television does not result in control of people's minds. Olszewski's dramatic address to the Polish nation was met with total indifference. In June 1992, the Parliament immediately voted him out of office under Wałęsa's pressure.

The new prime minister, Waldemar Pawlak, hastily replaced three senior officials: the minister of defense, the minister of internal affairs, and, very significantly, the head of state radio and television. This revealed that, even three years after the end of Communist rule, the army, the police, and the media were still political pillars of the Polish political system. Pawlak, however, could not form an administration and in one month time was replaced by Hanna Suchocka. In the first months of her administration, Suchocka introduced no substantial changes in the public media, exception for creating the office of a personal press secretary who solely represented her views and opinions. She in turn replaced all of Olszewski's nominees in the media with old-guard members of Mazowiecki's team.

Not only non-Communist government officials had difficulty with liberal media policy. Political parties also had problems with formulating opinions on freedom of the media and decentralization of state broadcasting. It is difficult to briefly describe their views because the political scene in Poland had been so fragmented. The so-called major parties were weak in all respects, particularly in terms of electoral support and, accordingly, seats in Parliament. The largest parties had popular support of about 20 percent of citizens.

The main political party in the early 1990s, the Democratic Union, favored a liberal, pluralistic political system based on universal human values, and legal and ethical responsibility of the media. However, this policy was formulated solely in interviews by its leaders; it was never conceived as an elaborated doctrine and, more important, was not implemented when the Democratic Union was the ruling party.

The Center Alliance, formerly a pro-Walęsa Solidarity faction and later an official pillar of Olszowski's government, generally stressed freedom of expression but advocated an antiliberal, authoritarian media policy. During the meeting of the Center Alliance in January 1992, the media was blamed for being antigovernment, and voices were raised saying "something must be done about this."[11] The general secretary of the Center Alliance and a former journalist, Jacek Maziarski, called for firm and decisive government action against broadcasting and the press: "The government must have a direct influence on the mass media. A strong will and iron hand are necessary. It is time for making order in radio and television, in the news agency, and in the press."[12]

The rightist parties have also been outspoken. The chairperson of the parliamentary club of the small but influential Christian-National Union, the Christian fundamentalist Stefan Niesiołowski, said in an interview:

> I consider the astonishing irresponsibility of the mass media to be very serious danger to democracy. Clearly, everywhere in the world it partici-pates by shaping the social consciousness and creating the social reality. One can sometimes get the impression that the Communist propaganda of success has been replaced by propaganda of failure. TV anchormen with grim faces talk only about errors, delinquencies, nonsense, and tragedies accompanying Polish everyday life. Our party is against destruction of the church's stature, is for Christian values, and is for a very responsible press.[13]

A small underground party born independently of Solidarity in the late 1970s, the radical Confederation of Independent Poland (KPN) remains the most vocal, politically violent, and anti-Communist party. It apparently supports a democratic political system, calling for the separation of Church and state, but in reality it is ultranationalistic and authoritarian. For the KPN freedom of speech is only a verbal proclama-tion.

On the left side of the political spectrum is the post-Communist SdRP, the Social Democracy of the Republic of Poland. Since 1993 election, it has been first in number of parliamentary seats. The SdRP, in contrast to its predecessor, the PZPR, has a few media outlets, of which the major one is the daily *Trybuna*. The party lacks a clear formulation of a new communication order. However, since it has been constantly under political attacks, with no opportunity to reply to those in the state-controlled media, the party has become apparently interested in a more objective and pluralistic system. The SdRP filed a suit to the Constitution-al Court opposing the clauses in the new Law on Broadcasting that imposes "respect for Christian values" on all, public and private, broadcasters. The argument was not that the party is against such values, but that these clauses are in contradiction with the constitution, which guarantees equal treatment of different denominations.

Enter the Roman Catholic Church

As an institution seeking to extend the freedom of religious practice and to promote Christian values, the church proved to be the clear winner in the confrontation between the old regime and Solidarity. It gained a dominant position within Polish television and, to a lesser extent, radio. Its position has been based formally on an official agreement between the Communist government and the Episcopate made in May 1989, but it stems more from the moral and political power that the church acquired during its prolonged struggle with communism in Poland.

In fact, the church embodies the most ancient and exalted ideas of traditional Polish life.[14] It has long been a part of the world of Polish politics, culture, and society—sometimes in the forefront, always in the background. Fidelity to the church became synonymous with faithfulness to the spirit of the Polish nation.[15] The convergence of religion and national consciousness nursed both Catholicism and nationalism.

After Vatican II and its resultant document *Inter mirifica* (1963), the Polish church began to stress the need for access to the mass media. But granting access to the church was so contrary to Communist policy that the Episcopate could only develop a distinctive network of communication—Sunday sermons, religious pilgrimages, festivities, and participation in parish life. Of great importance were the Episcopal letters read from the pulpits each Sunday to millions of believers. A phenomenon introduced in the 1970s was the annually organized Days of the Media of Social Communication which were devoted to assessing the Catholic contents of public communications. Special pastoral letters were read in churches on this occasion.

The church's direct mass media influence was limited to a few papers officially regarded as Roman Catholic (that is, those having a "Church assistant" on the editorial board). Beginning in September 1980, these papers were supplemented by religious radio broadcasts, a gain won by the striking Gdańsk workers.

Paradoxically, then, martial law increased the prestige and possibilities of the church in Poland. The generals were more willing to allow the church to operate than they were to tolerate Solidarity. The church was the only legal oppositional institution and remained so to the end of the decade. It equipped thousands of parish centers with VCRs, organized video shows of underground political movies, supported Catholic discussion clubs, and, most important, influenced editors and journalists of many papers to relay the church's position.

The roundtable agreements further increased the church's access to the mass media.[16] Since mid-1989, the church has had its own television programs. The new Law of Telecommunication passed in 1991 gave priority to the Roman Catholic church when new radio frequencies are allocated. The reason given was that the church should be treated preferentially because it had the right (under a separate 1989 Law on State-Church relations) to have access to the airwaves.[17] Therefore, despite the absence of a law breaking the legal monopoly of the state over the airwaves, the Ministry of Telecommunication issued permits to the church for the operation of local radio stations on the FM band.

The church is now more visible on television. The *Evening Prayer* and other religious programs are regularly broadcast. In many other broadcasts, including news bulletins and talk shows, the clergy, especially professors from Catholic University in Lublin, frequently appear.

The church has not been satisfied with the performance of lay journalists. In a communique of the conference of the Polish Episcopate on June 21-22, 1991, criticism of the media was strongly stated:

> Bishops also considered some damaging phenomena in the mass media. For some time, there have been disturbing contents that clearly ridicule the truths of the faith and moral norms. They are also received by many faithful to be blasphemous. These phenomena cannot be in agreement with an elementary culture of common living, with basic rights of humans, and with true tolerance. The faithful have rights, and the duty, to demand respect for their religious beliefs in all social communications.[18]

In September 1991, a thunderbolt struck. From all pulpits in the country a pastoral letter was read that contained a harsh assessment of journalists. It accused them of

> losing elementary sensibility to the basic and the most important problems of the nation and the state. Instead, they expose marginal or secondary issues. They do not teach to a sufficient extent the love of the motherland. The writers do not understand the historical transformations in Poland. They do not undertake attempts to mobilize reliable and scrupulous work for the public good.[19]

The bishops considered the contemporary Polish media as incapable of working for social integration and the rebuilding of community bonds. They claimed that without deep and broad reforms, "the media would inevitably lead us to divisions and quarrels."[20]

Unfortunately, churchmen provided neither good nor bad examples.

Therefore, it was not clear what they meant when they wrote in the communique: "The clear hope for the future is found in certain new periodicals and certain radio and television programs." It was, however, obvious that these did not include the respected Catholic *Tygodnik Powszechny*, whose editor-in-chief had criticized the Episcopate's media stand. This stand has a doctrinal basis in "the theology of nation," introduced by Stefan Wyszyński, primate of Poland during the period 1949-1981. He put forth the idea of a nation as a new ecclesiastical category: the church of the nation.[21] A nation is a product of natural development with God as a primary source. Thus, according to Wyszyński, with God's will there came into existence a true authentic "Church on Vistula," and not just the church in Poland. [22]

Wyszyński's doctrine of theology of the nation and its practical implications should be seen in the context of the political system of the day. He simply demanded respect for religious practices and the position of the church in social life under the Communist system. Although, he considered religion an indispensable element of national life, he did not feel the state should be a "Catholic state." Therefore, Wyszyński accepted the separation of church and state. His successor, Cardinal Glemp, has consistently blurred this division.

With the media, the church has no formal power to control the contents of programming. Its influence is rather weak in the general-interest press. It has the support of a few national dailies but is sometimes challenged by the most influential national paper, *Gazeta Wyborcza*. However, indirect church influence and control, especially in broadcast media, are obvious to all participants in the media system. Furthermore, the church has prepared a communication doctrine for national media. In a draft document of the Commission for the Media of Social Communication, it was clearly stated that "the church in Poland has to embrace, by its pastoral care, the media people. They are in need of spiritual support in order to serve truth and human beings. This refers to all mass media, not only to those under a church patronage."[23]

One of the main issues for the Polish church has been the widespread use of obscenity in the printed media. Without censorship, it is possible only to control the media through Press Law and Penal Code provisions against pornography. The church's position apparently influenced the attorney general when, in the spring of 1991, he issued a memo suggesting the urgent need to prosecute editors who published pornography. The response was a court action against the editor-in-chief of the anti-establishment satirical weekly, *Nie*, on the charge of publishing a pornographic drawing. In July 1991, the district attorney of Warsaw subpoenaed the editor-in-chief, Jerzy Urban (Jaruzelski's former spokesperson), because, as he explained, many citizens complained that materials in the weekly were insulting to their religious feelings. He added that similar trials should be expected, because there were many other such publications. Despite pressures on the court from the attorney general's office, Urban was eventually acquitted. The judge did not consider the illustration to be truly pornographic.

Nevertheless, the church did not give way. During a major religious holiday in Poland in August 1991, Cardinal Glemp repeated warnings that the church cannot tolerate "sweeping pornography and blasphemous periodicals. The law should restrict such phenomena."[24]

To change the allegedly bad situation, the church began to promote special schools and training for journalists in the Catholic press, radio, and television. The periodical *Mass Media* appeared and books on the role of the media in evangelizing were published. Attempts to formalize church influence could be seen within the context of a new journalistic association, the Association of Catholic Journalists, especially in its statutory provision that members can simultaneously be participants in other journalistic associations.

The church has evidently felt the effects of not having a daily. Allusions to the need for one were frequently voiced after the fall of communism. Eventually, the church found a financial sponsor in a new and apparently vigorous insurance company. However, a few days after the Episcopate announced its plan to launch a daily, the company went bankrupt, and the church had to find another patron for a paper. Eventually, it took over the daily of PAX (lay catholic, formerly allied with the Communists association). The daily changed only its title to *Słowo—Dziennik Katolicki* (The World—The Catholic Daily) and appointed a new editor-in-chief.

The biggest church gain in the media was, however, the new law on radio and television, enacted eventually in 1993, which contains a provision concerning "respect for christians values" by both public and private broadcaster. In addition, an indirect church influence over broadcasting media could be seen in the licensing process of new radio and television networks. The Polish episcopate officially endorsed one of the petitioners out of ten applicants, and this person (it was in fact one citizen) was granted the privilege to only one private television national network in the next ten years. When the same strategy seemingly did not work with major radio applicants, at least church network Radio Maryja was allowed to operate on national scale.

Journalists at a Loss

Paradoxically, freedom of the press did not bring more independence for journalists, at least for most of them. Theoretically, anyone can now set up his or her own daily or weekly, but for many reasons, especially because of distribution problems, this it is not a viable option.

Journalists are now free. However, unemployment is a new and serious concern. In 1991 alone, more than two thousand journalists lost their jobs for economic reasons.[25] A smaller number were fired or received early pensions for political reasons. The process continued well into the following year. As one example, I use the case of Jacek Snop-kiewicz, a veteran journalist who was fired several times by the Communist media. After the Solidarity victory, he was nominated to be managing editor of an important and influential television evening bulletin. Yet, despite his efforts to be as independent as possible or perhaps because of them, he was fired one year later by new television management.[26] Then, as editor-in-chief of the popular daily of the Democratic party, *Kurier Polski*, he survived another year, only to be fired by party leadership with the explanation that they could no longer "shiver in fear when taking the paper in hand."[27]

However, it is usually journalists who tremble and not publishers. The fear of losing a job pushes journalists to accept any working conditions and, perhaps worse, to follow orders from their managing editors.

The most serious obstacle to the independence of the Polish media is the lack of a professional code among journalists.[28] Most of those remaining from the days of communism want to relegitimize themselves; they lack the courage to challenge anyone's ideas, whether those of the government, the church, or a pop star. They are afraid to think critically, to probe, or to question.[29] There are some notable exceptions, among the elite newspapers, such as *Rzeczpospolita* and *Życie Warszawy*.

Some, usually the youngest, newcomers to the profession represent the opposite extreme. Instead of tacitly accepting information from official sources, they criticize everyone and everything. They use vulgar language and seek out sensationalized stories at any expense. Having insufficient experience and knowledge of the topics on which they report, they usually blur the line between reporting and opinion. This is evident in some television public affairs programs and in some sensationalist and political dailies, such as *Super Express* or *Gazeta Polska*.

The most visible result of this is the low quality of journalists' editorial work, which is seen in frequent factual mistakes, such as misquoting sources or omitting important data. Usually only one-sided stories are published—either for or against. Those journalists who had worked for the anti-Communist opposition and who presently hold managerial and editorial positions in post-RSW publication have no experience in producing well-balanced perspectives and views: Negation of the system was the principle of their work, and that work was only a negative reflection of official statements. Black was white and white was black.

What was needed was the civic courage to articulate opposing views. The experience from the underground press translated into "normal" press; publications were not to practice critical, independent, factual, objective journalism.

The present psychological stalemate can be explained by both historical and sociological factors, mainly by the traditional shape of the pattern of the role of the journalist in Poland and in Eastern Europe in general. In nineteenth-century Poland, a journalist was a person who received some literary education but was not talented enough to become a novel writer. Polish newspeople were never dedicated professional information providers, but were usually educators, politicians, propagandists, and creative writers. Under Communist rule, the journalist was a living "transmission belt" between the party and society. Thus objectivity, professional values, and professional ethics took different meanings than they held in traditional, liberal journalism. Therefore, these legacies, both old and new, sustained the role of journalists as teachers, preachers, and spiritual leaders of society.

To make things worse, journalists' associations are not standing up to the task of remodeling the profession. In Communist Poland, associations of film directors', writers', and journalists' unions were important actors on the political scene. They promoted professional rights in an adverse political climate and, when the occasion permitted, fought against censorship and in favor of creative autonomy.

Banned after martial law, the Association of Polish Journalists (SDP) was eventually relegalized in 1989. However, then it had a parallel association with which it had to cope and co-exist. The other organization was the Association of Journalists of the Polish People's Republic (SDRPL), which had split off from the SDP in 1982 (when the SDP was banned by martial law). It was expected to fold after the fall of Jaruzelski's regime, but it survived and has continued to operate, while the SDP disintegrated in 1993. The reason was not only that the SDRPL had its own strong financial resource basis, while the SDP depended on the foreign, mainly U.S. financial donations. The main reason for the SDRPL survival was strong loyalty of its membership. The SDP lost its most dedicated members when they were nominated to the highest editorial positions in the newly restructured RSW publication. However, for the first four years after the change of the system, such dualism of professional associations created a deadlock. Because of legal and ethical disputes, both associations did not find time and energy to work on a new professional ethics.

After its congress in 1991 when the SDRPL changed the name to the SDRP (skipping the adjective *People's* in its name), its democratically elected leaders launched a campaign to redress the situation of journalists within the mass media. It continued to focus on the numerous cases of discrimination against its members, the firings without professional reasons, and denials of information by official sources. The SDRP called for a pluralistic, democratic, independent system and self-regulation of the profession through ethical codes of conduct. Most important, the association called for changes in the Polish constitution, including a permanent ban on censorship and support for a strong version of press freedom. Without the political support of the SDP, its campaign was to no avail.

The SDP remained much weaker in membership but was much stronger and more vocal politically. Many of its members were given high editorial or diplomatic positions, then opted out. However, despite its standing, it did little to improve the prestige of the journalism profession, to develop new professional standards, to defend fired colleagues, or to suggest a new state information policy. According to the SDP, the main dangers to the Polish media have been the misunderstanding of the role of the press by political elites, the dependence of many papers upon political parties or foreign newspaper chains, and the decline of the journalistic ethics. However, the 1993 congress of the association disclosed the loss of cohesion and interest among its membership. Legally speaking, being unable, for the reason of inadequate attendance, to elect the new leadership, this organization has ceased to exist.

The role of the two journalism associations in support of freedom of the press has been very small. Struggling with each other for a major share of the material heritage of the initial union, the two were only able to issue occasional lofty statements demanding further democratization of the media and formulation of a new government information policy. They did little to implement new principles, ethical codes, and the like. They should not be blamed entirely for this. Their impotency reflects the low prestige of the profession among the political elite and the public at large.[30]

It is paradoxical that journalists, who had such an important impact on the dismantling of the system, have lost much of their influence on the public. In 1991, the media could not mobilize society to take part in the first free parliamentary election in Poland in fifty years: Turnout was only 40 percent. Perhaps this was a result of the alienation of the media system from Polish society. The language and the views of the media reflect the ideas and opinions of only one social stratum—the Polish intelligentsia. In the past, the media audience was the category that was de facto treated as if it were the least important element in the communication system. This legacy still influences journalists, and audiences reciprocate.

There is also evidence that the new political elites have become alienated from society because of the current situation in the media—the lack of trust and of ties between journalists and audiences. The new elites and officials easily adopted the patterns and attitudes of the old Communist guard. They care little about information or about what the public thinks, even if this costs them an electoral victory. On the other hand, the media is perceived by politicians as being a magic wand regardless of public opinion; they feel the media has the power to mold and reshape public opinion and—if they control the media—they should not worry about what people think. This widespread belief in media power is the main reason the new broadcast law was so long disputed. No politician had wanted the media to be out of his or her reach.[31]

The situation of the journalism profession in Poland is still unclear, as is that of the mass media. The mass media continues to be fundamentally deficient in terms of its comprehensiveness, objectivity, and professionalism. At least, it is so accused by all political actors, although their criticism stems from different perspectives and interests. Nevertheless, it is usually well documented. Even when the media tries to separate news and opinion, it still continues to be advocacy media. The most popular daily, *Gazeta Wyborcza*, cannot resist commenting on all important news reports with signed commentaries in bold font. The media is still far from being truly independent, and many politicians want it to serve as a political trumpet rather than an autonomous information agency. Nowhere can this be more clearly seen than in the debates on the broadcasting act.

The Long Battle over the Airwaves

Since the end of the 1980s the debates on the media have been most intensively concentrated in the area of television. In June 1991, the Sejm decided that until the new broadcasting law was adopted, it would be a moratorium on broadcasting frequencies. When the law did not soon materialize, in February 1992 a group of parliamentarians demanded an amendment to the bill on telecommunications that would allow for the temporary allotment of frequencies to those among the more than eight hundred petitioners that were qualified.

In fall of 1991, Parliament considered two competing broadcasting bills. One was introduced by the Peasant party in response to complaints that the state-owned broadcasting services favored the government and denied the party adequate access to their facilities. The bill provided for direct parliamentary supervision of the country's broadcast service. The second was a government bill; it provided for the establishment of a National Broadcasting Council to assign frequencies, grant licenses, and handle all regulatory functions.[32] Its eleven members would be chosen by Parliament and the government. The state-owned radio and television services would then become a public service corporation. In addition, private citizens would have the right to own broadcasting stations on the FM band. The downside was that new transmitters and a new type of radio sets would be required if the higher spectrum of the FM band were to be employed.

However, the bill was not approved by the Senate because most parliamentarians were not satisfied with one statement: "Programs cannot propagate actions, attitudes, and opinions contradicting the public morals." Several senators demanded the replacement of the weak word "morals" with the stronger term "Christian ethics."[33]

Other themes of debate also took much time and energy. One lengthy discussion concerned foreign investments. In all proposed bills regulating broadcasting, foreign ownership was restricted to a range between 20 percent (which was considered insufficient for the modernization of broadcasting) and 33 to 40 percent.

In an attempt to salvage at least part of its efforts, Parliament hastily prepared a new, shortened, and limited bill. It was referred to as the "little bill," because it only dealt with the setting up of private, commercial stations. In late 1991, the slimmest possible parliamentary majority passed this law.[34] Immediately, the law was to be widely criticized as being too imperfect and narrow. The president was, therefore, advised not to sign it, and he did not.

In 1992, the government finally prepared a new bill that simply repeated the provisions of the 1960 charter about government control over state broadcasting.[35] After three years since the beginning of the media debate, Parliament approved the new radio and television law on December 29, 1992. However, it was obvious that it was far from perfect, and what is more, it introduced a type of airwaves censorship. The law stipulates that radio and television, both public and private, have to "respect the Christian system of values as a basis, while accepting universal ethical principles [and] the Polish vital state interests." The law does not explain, what these requirements mean. For the spokesperson for ZChN, the main party supporting this legislation, "the Christian values are simply there." But no one is clear on specifics. According to a survey of clergy and politicians, for instance, some consider that teaching young people about the use of condoms would be in line with a Christian system of values, while many others do not agree.

The law instituted a National Council of Radio and Television (KRRiT), a body responsible for allocation and supervision of the airwaves. The Council consists of four people appointed by the Sejm, two by the Senate, and four by the President. Their appointments are to last up to four years, but the Council can be dissolved if Parliament and the president fail to approve its annual report. Instead of being an arm of the state, the council is essentially dependent upon the current political setup. It has also become a super-censoring agency, jokingly referred to as the National Council of Airwaves Inquisition, because it has the duty to grant or revoke licenses on the basis of a vague concept of "Christianity." A foretaste of this was seen in the controversy created by a song and a poster.

ZChN induced the district attorney to charge the Piersi (Breasts) rock group for performing a song entitled "Zchn's Coming," which is sung to the tune of the hymn called "Jesus Christ Is Coming." The lyrics describe a priest visiting one of his parishioners. During his visit, the priest consumes a great quantity of vodka, speeds off in his luxury Toyota, and crashes into a fence. The parishioners complain that they will have to put more money into the collection plate. Officially, ZChN explained the suit by stressing the offensiveness of the tune toward religion. Unofficially, a producer at the state radio station was fired for giving the song airplay, and, although she was later reinstated on the intervention of some deputies, the song was no longer played on public radio. However, it instantly became a hit on the cassette market. When Piersi performed publicly, nine thousand young people sang the song with the group.

In another case, a huge poster advertising Benetton, an Italian clothing company, portrayed a priest kissing a nun. The local authorities in many cities, including the capital, Warsaw, immediately banned the ad. ZChN also called for a ban on sales of the Polish translation of Salman Rushdie's *Satanic Verses*. Later, ZChN's leader accused a television cabaret program for being especially dedicated to ridiculing Catholics, which was in his opinion a criminal act. Demanding a banning of the program, he added: "Poland is a country of religious tolerance, because in Muslim countries the producer would have had her throat slit long ago for such acts of blasphemy."

It is little wonder that, in early 1993, a columnist from a fundamentalist Catholic weekly openly called for "setting up sane, humane, and patriotic censorship."[36] This was too much even for some Catholics. Józefa Hennelowa, a commentator from the moderate Catholic weekly *Tygodnik Powszechny*, wrote an open letter to the chairperson of the Association of Catholic Journalists protesting this appeal. However, in his answer, he publicly sustained the idea of amending the press law in a way that would defend "ethical and humane values."

In response, twenty-nine eminent Polish writers and literary critics published an open letter defending the freedom of speech. It was the first act of open, public defiance to the church stand since the fall of communism. The letter was brief and forceful: "As a person highly regarding freedom of speech, I am against any legislation—that is laws and decrees—which could form a basis for by-laws and rules introducing hidden or open censorship."[37]

Communications at the Crossroads

The opposition to Communist control over the media has always stressed faith in an independent, vigorous, pluralistic media. It demanded limiting and eventually abolishing censorship, and creating a free marketplace of ideas; it constantly praised the concept of media independence and autonomy. When some of these conditions materialized and the media began to speak with its own voice, it also began to criticize those in power. Moreover, it began to cater to the needs of less educated people. However, intellectuals and new political elites wanted media loyalty, not censure; thus, in turn, they began to complain and to blame journalists for all social and political evils.

Instead of the expected pluralism in the framework of Solidarity political consensus, a new kind of media polyphony appeared. To the ears of many new politicians, it sounded like cacophony. This has not been a uniquely Polish phenomenon. All over Eastern Europe the media is being accused of irresponsibility and of being post(or crypto)-Communist. New governments and new political parties alike have not been satisfied with the media's performance. The media has many strong critics and only a few, rather weak supporters.

The media debates in contemporary post-Communist countries are fierce and passionate, but the arguments are weak. There are no Eastern European Miltons or Mills to which they can refer; nor is there a tradition of using European political philosophy as a basis for the defense of freedom of speech and of the press. Perhaps this is so for historical reasons: Poles have traditionally been more concerned with the preservation of the nation, national culture, and religion against foreign oppression than with individual civil and citizen's rights.[38] It should be noted, however, that the liberal intelligentsia is once again writing open letters, which were formerly used by the opposition to call for civil rights and freedom of expression. The targets are different—the non-Communist government and the Roman Catholic church—but the wording and arguments are very similar.[39]

The struggle for control over the media—on the part of media elites to sustain their editorial autonomy and on the part of ruling elites for sustaining their power—is based on some false assumptions and some justified concerns. Both sides want to strengthen the democratic system: The conservative-nationalist political parties and the Roman Catholic church perceive themselves as an emanation of the national will and view their main task as preserving national culture and spirit. Both groups believe in enormous media power over the people. They consider media to be not *a* major, but *the* main instrument of politics. Their vision of the media is one-dimensional, overpoliticized, and simplified. They believe in a missionary role for journalists and an idealized media. Ideological discourse in post-Communist media policy debates is marked by a deep feeling of insecurity among the media elites and the ruling political elites. Each is afraid of the other, and politicians are afraid of their constituencies. They believe they are unfairly attacked and respond with attacks of their own. Let me stress again that this is not a typically Polish feature of the media controversy. The same underlying assumptions can be discerned in other Eastern European countries, particularly Hungary.[40]

In summary, I outline some distinctive features of the present-day media in Poland.

- The media system is dynamic, but is also fragmented and contra-dictory.
- The past, both Communist and pre-Communist, influences the present, especially regarding thinking about the media—how its roles, power, functions, and tasks are conceived by political elites, by the Roman Catholic church, by journalists, and by the public at large.
- Publishers and, to a lesser extent, editors and journalists are engaged in reinventing the media system and are redefining their roles within the context of a market economy.
- The media scene is in a state of flux. There are constant changes in top positions. Each prime minister nominates his or her confidants to the government media. Journalists quarrel among themselves, sue each other, despise each other. In the meantime, political "verifica-tion" has been in place since 1989.
- The quality of journalistic output is mixed. There is growing discontent with the results of journalists' work. Conservative politicians accuse the media of being a destructive force in society, mainly because of its social irresponsibility, lack of ethical back-ground, and poor journalistic education. Indeed, the light-hearted coverage of some alleged bank machinations did cause financial losses and customer panics. Left-wing politicians, however, complain that the media is predominantly rightist and that it distributes biased information about the left.
- The media is mainly an advocacy media, still connected to govern-ment (broadcasting) or political parties or factions (the press) rather than being truly independent.

This summary of present-day trends should be seen in a broader context—namely, that of structural changes in the media policies that have shaped the Polish media in postwar Poland. In order to make this review as compact as possible, I specify the changes in Table 15.1.

Some Predictions

We must now ask what does the future hold for the Polish post-Communist media? What will its role be when old-style dissent and critical reports focusing on state etatism and socialism no longer exist? What will be the new target or targets? Gender and women's issues, ecology, nationalism, anti-Semitism, or, perhaps, business and democracy? Will the quality press develop, or will it be replaced by sensationalist tabloids?

What will happen to state broadcasting? Will it find a competitor in sound, private, commercial broadcasting? Or renamed as "public" will it continue as a semimonopoly organization?

These questions are now impossible to answer. Let me, rather, delineate some distinctive dilemmas facing media controllers, owners, and personnel.

- Commercialization or politicization
- Specialized or mass media
- Privatization or monopolization of ownership
- Deregulation or centralization of state control
- Westernization or nationalization of contents
- Modernization or deterioration of the media facilities
- Secularization or christianization of media values
- Globalization or parochialization.

However, more important than guesses is the more definite question, What lessons may be drawn from history, both Communist and the recent post-Communist history? This complex question is addressed in the following chapter.

TABLE 15.1 Structural Changes in Media Policies in Poland

	Semipluralistic media 1944-1948	Monolithic Media 1949-1954	Instrumental Media 1955-1976	Dualistic Media 1977-1989	Chaotic Present 1990-
Media doctrines and values	Leftist control; socialist values	Stalinist; Communist, internationalist	Leninist; Polish, nationalist	In the fore Communist, in the background—dissent	Social responsibility; Christian values
Affiliation	Organs of political parties, organizations, and the government	Planned, monolithic, centralized, uniform party media	Centralized, but not monolithic, regionally organized	Same, however, autonomous media operating	Decentralization in the press; broadcasting still state institution
Economics	Copy price, government and party subsidies	Deficit covered by the state	Copy price, subscriptions, and license fees	The same, plus advertisements (5%)	The same, more advertisements (30%)
Output	Patriotic declarations, official propaganda,	Pure ideological contents, no entertainment	Mixture of news and entertainment, growing criticism	Ever-growing political criticism, specialization	Reemergent politicization, specialization, and competition
Media surges	Print fastest, radio slow	Print declines, radio fastest	Print and radio level off, television grows fastest	Continued television growth, new media; like VCR, appear	Continued television growth, print declines; radio boom; satellite television

Notes

1. "Solidarity and the Media," *European Journal of Communications* 2-3, 1990, pp. 333-354.

2. *Gazeta Wyborcza*, September 6, 1990.

3. *Zeszyty Prasoznawcze* 1-2, 1991, p. 51.

4. James Warren, *Chicago Tribune*, February 4, 1990, p. 2.

5. *Antena* 21, 1990, p. 15.

6. Under martial law repression against nonloyal journalists was more severe and included imprisonment in internment camps. In the political verification following martial law, personnel were asked if they wanted to work in a new situation—that is, to be loyal to the martial law authorities. Those who declared loyalty could usually stay in the profession. After August 1989, it was not loyalty but one's political past that became the major factor in determining whether he or she could retain or obtain a job in the state media.

7. *Gazeta Wyborcza*, March 9, 1992, p. 5.

8. The spokesperson's statement appeared in *Gazeta Wyborcza*, January 12, 1992, p. 3.

9. *Wprost*, April 12, 1992, p. 31.

10. Since 1976 Romaszewski had been an active and a merited dissident; under martial law he was an organizer of a symbolic underground Solidarity radio station. In 1989, he was elected senator. Generally considered as incorruptible, he took the side of Olszewski in an action that amounted to nothing less than a coup against the president and Parliament.

11. *Gazeta Wyborcza*, January 12, 1992, p. 3.

12. *Nowy Dziennik*, January 11, 1992, p. 5.

13. *Gazeta Wyborcza*, January 21, 1991, p. 13.

14. Norman Davies, *God's Playground: A History of Poland* (London: Clarendon, 1981), vol. 1, p. 225.

15. Vincent C. Chrypinski, "Church and Nationality in Postwar Poland," in Pedro Ramet, ed., *Religion and Nationalism in Soviet and East European Politics* (Durham: Duke University Press, 1984), p. 123.

16. An agreement on June 28, 1989, between the Communist government and the Polish Episcopate increased the church's television coverage. See text in *Przekazy i Opinie* 1-2, 1990, pp. 221-225. In September 1989, Catholic radio and television programs began to operate within the framework of state radio and television. Despite all the advantageous changes, the 238th Conference of the Polish Episcopate on December 1, 1989 stated that the needs of the Catholic media were still not being met.

17. The legal basis is the Law on State and Church relations approved by the Communist government and Parliament on May 17, 1989.

18. *Gazeta Wyborcza*, June 21, 1991, p. 17.

19. *Gazeta Wyborcza*, September 14, 1991, p. 14.

20. *The New York Times* concluded that "The Polish Roman Catholic Church lashed out at the press for what it calls distortion and 'blasphemous utterances,'" September 15, 1991, p. 6.

21. Chrypinski, "Church," p. 133.

22. Ibid., p. 137.

23. Prepared in May 1992; unpublished document, p. 9.

24. *Gazeta Wyborcza*, August 20, 1991, p. 1.

25. According to estimates by the Association of Journalists of the Republic of Poland.

26. Snopkiewicz published a book about his editorship, a very revealing depiction of the internal pressures in post-Communist television. *Dziennik Telewizyjny* [Television Evening News] (Warszawa, BWG, 1991).

27. *Gazeta Wyborcza*, February 12, 1992, p. 2.

28. In theory, the Polish journalists' ethics code belongs to the oldest in Europe. It was approved as early as 1916; however, it never had a chance to be implemented.

29. A similar, probably even worse situation exists in other post-Communist countries. As Jim Podesta, an American who opened a short-lived school of journalism for twenty students in Bucharest, remarked bitterly: "In Romania today no one understands the role of an independent, critical press. Essentially there is no journalism here. Opinion is news. Facts are dispensable." Cited in Kevin Devlin, "Postrevolutionary Ferment in the East European Media," *Radio Free Europe Report on Eastern Europe* 28, July 13, 1990, p. 51.

30. Public opinion polls unanimously point out that the journalism profession places near the low end of the prestige scale, well below other intellectual professionals such as professors, teachers, and doctors.

31. The revelations about pressures on the television evening news exercised by Wałęsa's closest advisers were disclosed by the former head of the program, Karol Małcużyński, in "Television Behind the Closed Door," *Gazeta Wyborcza*, August 5-7, 1993, p. 17-18.

32. "The Bill of the Law on Radio and Television, September 13, 1991," *Przekazy i Opinie* 3-4, 1991, pp. 62-73.

33. This stance was obviously influenced by church demands. The bishops asked rhetorically: "Just who are parliamentary deputies representing when, in a country with a decisive majority of Christians, they reject a motion to respect the Christian value system in the mass media?" See *Słowo Powszechne*, October 19, 1992, p. 1.

34. The Law on Broadcasting, October 19, 1991, unpublished.

35. The same stalemate occurred in Hungary, Czechoslovakia, and Romania.

36. Danuta Mastalska, "Polska wieża Babel" [The Polish Babel Tower], *Niedziela*, January 21, 1993, p. 7.

37. *Gazeta Wyborcza*, January 29, 1993, p. 1.

38. This thesis was suggested by Rudolf Tökes, *Opposition in Eastern Europe* (London: Macmillan, 1979), pp. 7-8.

39. See one such letter from the Association for Humanism and Independent Ethics, *Gazeta Wyborcza*, March 12, 1992, p. 17.

40. Tomas Pal, *"Nationalism and Liberalism in the New Media Elites,"* Budapest, unpublished paper, 1992.

16

Some Lessons from the Communist Past: A Case for Prosecution?

We will have so much freedom, as we can wrench with our nails and fingers.
    —Olga Lipińska, a popular television political cabaret director

My purpose in this book has been to show the zigzags in Communist media policy within the broader context of the relationship among media, politics, and society in Poland. I now draw more general conclusions about the role of the mass media in political change, thereby, perhaps, enlarging our understanding of mass communications in general.[1] Any conclusions drawn should not be simplified to the point of becoming exhibits placed before the court of history in the prosecution of an evil empire. Rather, they should serve as multifaceted, complex phenomena subject to scholarly analysis for many years.

Unanticipated Repercussions of Total Control

What can we learn from Polish postwar media history? Should the case be used to frighten schoolchildren and to help educate them to develop contempt for censorship and political media control? The answer is that we do not need to frighten them, but we do need to educate them. We can teach them about those courageous individuals who, despite both open and hidden terror, managed to safeguard their integrity and even to create independent channels of communication. But the story should not be simplified to that of good guys who won and bad guys who lost. The reality of the situation was not so simple.[2] Everything was not perfect with the anti-Communist opposition, and not all criticism of the party was true; but this counterstatement deserves detailed analysis of the contents of the Communist media.[3] The case of Polish media history should not be used to glorify Western-style media as the antithesis of a now defunct and more defective system.[4] Rather, the aim should be to support John Milton's famous argument for freedom of the press: "Whoever knew Truth put to the worse, in a free and open encounter?"[5] Under communism, it was neither a free nor an open encounter, but a Falsehood lost.

The Gdańsk workers discovered this truth in the summer of 1980, when Solidarity was born. Initially, they demanded a relaxation of censorship and wanted honest reporting in the mass media. But they soon became aware that censorship was relatively easy to surpass, which they did by simply ignoring it and printing their own bulletins—publishing "beyond censorship." However, they needed mass media in order to obtain and sustain popular support and also to counter hostile attacks by party propaganda. For these purposes they wanted their own media as well as free access to the mass media. These avenues were controlled by the state and ultimately by the party through the control of newsprint, printing facilities, and the state monopoly on telecommunications. In fact Communist censorship effectively controlled the contents not just of the mass media but of all public communications. This includes printing presses, radio and television stations, photocopiers, telecommunication, and office equipment.[6] Therefore, the workers' subsequent demand was to break that monopoly. Here, characteristically, the Communist government stubbornly resisted. It took the opposition ten years to wrench the right to mass media access from the party. In the meantime, it had to experience and endure Jaruzelski's paralyzing total communication blackout.

This situation draws attention to another key element in the powerbase of dictatorship—the physical control of communications. A regime that controls radio, television, and the press and that has the power to intercept telephone calls and letters and, therefore, keep its citizens under constant surveillance, has an overwhelming advantage in neutralizing any opposition. Such a regime can prevent its potential opponents from organizing.

This was not a uniquely Communist method, although it can best be analyzed and understood within the context of the Soviet and East European experience. It is no coincidence that contemporary revolts, when and wherever they occur, usually begin with the seizure of the national broadcasting station, as epitomized by the Rumanian revolt in December 1989. This example illustrates the close link that exists between control over physical facilities, especially the monopolistic control of the media, and the exercise of power. But I must emphasize that the control of communications has no necessary connection with opinion control or indoctrination. Indoctrination played no part in the consolidation of the Jaruzelski regime. Similarly, Stalin's total power over the Soviet armed forces and secret police rested neither on mere persuasion nor on sheer physical force. It relied upon a system of sophisticated and all-encompassing surveillance that prevented potential conspirators from organizing. An army without communications is only a giant group of soldiers, easy to disperse. The same holds true for citizens who, without their right to communicate and to use communication facilities without fear of being punished, cannot organize, and, therefore, cannot form an effective opposition, let alone a civil society. No individual would be able to make the first move against the dictator. To do so would be far too risky. A Stalinist-type system, which effectively prevents individual citizens from communicating openly with one another, can inhibit the crystallization of public opinion.

In such society, where everybody has to live a lie, that is to hide their true preferences, the citizens are deprived of "voice" of two types: vertical voice, that is channels to express their opinions to the rulers, and horizontal voice, that is channels to communicate with their fellow citizens.[7]

In times of crisis, effective regimes can impose a full-scale communication blackout. If they are not determined enough nor have no means for doing this, they end like the coupsters in the Moscow putsch of August 1991 who were nominated by *Time* magazine as "Blunders of the Year."[8] They knew how to control the media, but Yeltsin's supporters knew how to manipulate them.

The orthodox Communists were indisputably master controllers of the media. They took great pains to orchestrate them in unparalleled ways, diversified their roles, and influenced their structure, ownership, behavior, and output. On the other hand, the reformist Communists, in the prolonged departure from paradigmatic totalitarianism, tried to manipulate media. Khrushchev by his thaw, Gorbachev by his glasnost, and Gierek by his propaganda of success used the media and not only controlled it. They had short-lived triumph; they were popular but eventually all of them lost power. The system was not flexible enough and it could not adapt itself to radical changes.

The history of Communist media also evidences that in any society there is a natural demand for uncontrolled and uncensored information. If the media is state-party controlled, it becomes so unreliable as an information provider that it may intimidate people but fail to mobilize them. This process, known in democratic societies as the "spiral of silence,"[9] is a permanent feature of totalitarian societies. Only when the level of fear is broken does the silent majority become vocal. The human need to be creative drives people to dissent when the official ideology is too strict and monopolistic. The boomerang effect of information might be seen clearly in cases in which the regime was already weakened but still tried to manage the crises through distorted propaganda. This infuriates the masses, and the protests spread.

But what else can be drawn from this complicated and rather repulsive history that could be of value for communication and society scholars?

The natural demand for information, based on its utility and human curiosity, cannot be satisfied when there is censorship and provides fertile ground for foreign influences. This need explains the credibility and popularity of such stations as Radio Free Europe, the BBC, and Voice of America. They are not objective in providing balanced reporting; rather, they are sought as providers of alternative information and commentaries.

It is always dangerous, even for an apparently omnipresent and omnipotent regime, to attack old values and institutions, even if they seem venerable. Gomułka earned this lesson in his antichurch campaign. It is safer and more effective for unpopular regimes to gain support by referring to old prejudices, as the Partisan faction did with the Jewish issue in 1968. An unreliable media does not acquire credibility by using such topics, although doing so did the media in Poland little harm in the eyes of the public. Nationalism always makes good copy and may be used on a mass scale in the post-Communist societies. Many years of physical isolation, combined with the lack of a true market economy and democratic institutions, created a spiritual vacuum pure dissidence cannot fill. The new nationalism might try to find its ecological niche in that sphere.

It is also dangerous for the state to use the media to raise expectations, because generally they cannot be fulfilled and a high level of frustration might result. Moreover, the propaganda of national successes usually fools the leaders, not the masses. But when there is no strong sentiment for such values as personal freedom, nonconformism, and tolerance, a form of informal—that is, social and religious— censorship could rapidly appear. The final, but not the least, important lesson is that technology, especially information technology, does not know borders. Even absolute dictators like Stalin cannot suppress all sources of external information. In addition, meticulous control of communications through censorship of any type is disastrous to the development of the national economy, science, culture, and even defense. Censorship is very costly, because it hinders the free flow of innovation and the development of an information-based economy.

How the Dictatorial Democracy Can Be Built

Another important lesson from the Communist past in Eastern Europe comes from the passage from weak authoritarianism to dictatorial semidemocracy. When considering the sources of stability, there is a more general factor to be remembered, which is the difficulties of actually carrying out a revolution in any country and political system. John Galbraight once pointed out that successful revolution requires determined leaders and disciplined followers (neither of which are usually found in practice). His cutting barb was that "all successful revolutions are the kicking in of a rotten door."[10] The weak authoritarian system, to refer to Galbraight, is a regime that has no supporters, only enemies. Such a regime is easy to abolish when a group of determined leaders associate with masses of frustrated people. Phase one of the new system is, thus, founded on popular outrage and uprising. If the revolution is successful, this means (1) the old regime was weak, (2) new leaders emerged, and (3) they found enough faithful followers.

However, a postrevolutionary situation can easily lead to an apparent democracy but with a totalitarian inclination. Yet, because the old regime was authoritarian, the new one would be democratic by implication. Moreover, the masses that revolted were made up of people. Therefore, their rule completes the definition of democracy—the rule of people, for people, and by people.

The end of communism does not mean temptations to control the media have also ended. The former anti-Communist oppositionists and journalists, often proclaiming freedom of the press, who have become editors and politicians treat the media as if it were theirs, or at least demand a friendly attitude. Those media that are not favorable to the ruling elites are treated as depraved, or deviant, or crypto-Communist. The new politicians rarely support the minority media. They simply do not understand that a truly democratic system demands not only mass media but also alternative media—vehicles that place themselves beyond the mainstream and beyond the recognized spectrum of public opinion.[11]

In postrevolutionary society, at first almost everybody expresses contempt for the old (weak, corrupt, inefficient) regime. Therefore, there is broad consensus to impose dominant views on the followers of the old regime (enemies, counterrevolutionaries). The voice of the people is treated as the voice of God, or the truth itself. There are also occasional counterattacks by deposed rulers or their loyal supporters. In response, the new ruler demands more political control, because enemies are waiting (which could be true). Therefore, censorship should be reintroduced, although only in regard to hostile propaganda. But who is to judge what is hostile? To satisfy liberals, the provision is usually made that these measures are temporary and that as soon as possible, they will be revoked. Moreover, there is little understanding of the rights of minorities, which are viewed as being contrary to cooperation and national unity. Therefore, their rights are often not observed. Soon a new phase of democracy appears, which might be called a tyranny of the majority. The victorious party imposes its views on society at large. However, differences regarding the course of action to be taken quickly appear among the new leaders. From the resulting quarrel, a victorious faction emerges and assumes a dominant position. As only one faction, the views it presents are perceived as being those of the majority, or an actual embodiment of the people's will. The system enters into a democratic-totalitarian phase. Its character is dependent only on the ideology and organization of the victorious faction.

The loss of power by new rulers usually is a long and painful process. It might be called a weakening of the political elite. This group's rule is increasingly supported not by persuasion or ideology, but by bribing citizens with certain benefits and by taking advantage of control over the physical facilities for communication (media). This process makes crystallization of the opposition difficult and risky; therefore, it hinders dissident organization.

At the same time, the official mass media provides a coherent, although not fully accurate, picture of the world. This proves that the mass media can operate without having and offering a realistic picture. This has also occurred in the West. The Western critics of mass media stress its entertainment and advertisement function rather than its role in public decisionmaking. The mass media can offer news and current affairs programs as entertainment rather than serious knowledge.

Free at Last or Fettered Again?

In conclusion, I point out that post-Communist media history provides an excellent example of how historical precedents color even the most determined attempts at conceptualizing and organizing a new kind of liberal communication system. In the summer of 1990, when leading U.S. journalists, including Ben Bradley of the *Washington Post*, toured Eastern Europe, to see with their own eyes the destruction of the old media system, they found that the new system would not be necessarily entirely free. Vaclav Havel, a dissident playwright-turned-president, in an address to U.S. editors, scolded the Czech journalists for "searching for sensations" and forgetting from time to time that "freedom is only one side of the coin, where the other side is represented by responsibility."[12] Trying to soften his criticism of media performers, Havel added, "This is an understandable lapse after forty years of bondage."[13] The same might be said about the Havel lapse—he also has become a victim of forty years of bondage, unable to integrate the principle of unlimited freedom of the press into the legal and social fabric of society. He did not realize that his remark had to infuriate the visitors, because for U.S. journalists the word responsibility—in the mouth of a politician—is simply a euphemism for censorship. Immediately, the Americans published unpleasant commentaries about the freedom-fighter-turned-freedom-jailer. Although this incident was based on a misunderstanding, it also reflected the basic difference in press philosophy. In their perceptive analysis of the incident, Janos Horvat and Jay Roskin, rightly stressed that responsibility cannot be imposed by governments or by presidents. In the U.S., it is build into the media system through mechanisms such as the marketplace of ideas (that is, competition), the rule of law, the pressure of public opinion.[14] Such mechanisms cannot be created in a stroke or overnight. However, I must stress that the basic philosophy, which is not fully understood by political elites in Eastern Europe should be based on the concept of freedom of the press. Freedom comes first, then responsibility, not the other way round. Press responsibility does not equal freedom, as Havel seemed to stress.

This indeed is a major lesson for Eastern European countries, for their societies and political elites, and—above all—for their journalists, editors, and publishers.[15] Freedom should belong not only to the rulers or the majorities, but also to the nation in all its diversity and to mankind. This means the majority may rule, but minorities must also have rights, among them a right to access to various media.

Therefore, the ideal of the free expression, which was so well-expressed in the Solidarity program of a communicative democracy or participative communication, still waits for its implementation. What is worse, there are numerous roadblocks for such development. Among them, most important is a weakness of the civil society due to economic hardships imposed by a pursued model of financial transformation. Young people and intellectuals who yet a few years before were engaged in illegal printing, at present either are apathetic or are occupied with commercial media. Privatization is considered a panacea for all of Communist ills, including the rebuilding the public sphere.[16]

The fight for freedom or, rather, for more freedom of expression has not ended, nor is it ever likely to end in East Europe. Various arguments have been and will continue to be raised against such freedoms: They might jeopardize public security, morals, religious feelings, protection of the youth, national culture, and so on. All of these positions amount to a defense of censorship, although not necessarily governmental and surely not party censorship. These attempts should be countered in the

East, the dangers of censorship be it by government, party or church, be it open or latent, still lurks. Such attempts should be countered in the spirit of the following words of a young, idealistic reporter: "I've been around a lot of places. People do awful things to each other. But it's worse in places where everybody is kept in the dark. It really is. Information is light."[17] However, the nations which were kept for so long in darkness do not adapt themselves easily to the light. Even less, do their new leaders which for so many years fought underground. Thus, they should be reminded of the words of Albert Camus, "The press, when it is free, can be good or bad, but assuredly, without freedom, it can only be bad."[18]

Notes

1. Everette E. Dennis ends a report on post-Communist media (*Media in Transition* [New York: Gannett Center for Media Studies, 1990], p. 88) with an attempt to analyze "what Americans can learn from Eastern Europe," sensing, quite correctly, that the media there should not merely be scorned but that something valuable can be learned. But what? Dennis's answer is filled with much goodwill but is short, general, and unconvincing. In this chapter I try to redress the situation.

2. An interesting essay on the changing roles of professional communicators in Poland was written by Karol Jakubowicz under the meaningful title "Musical Chairs: The Three Public Spheres in Poland." He referred to journalists and writers who worked simultaneously for official media, for so-called alternative media (for instance, legal church publications), and—under pen names—for oppositional (illegal, underground) media (*Media, Culture, and Society* 12, 1990, pp. 195-212).

3. This may be a shocking statement; however, as a wise Roman philosopher once said, *Amicus Plato, sad amicus veritas* [I am a friend of Plato, but also a friend of the truth]. Even during the times under Communism, especially in the early 1950s, intensive party propaganda needed a literate audience; therefore, it organized special crash courses in reading and writing. It is difficult to negate this program, because hundreds of thousands of persons benefitted from it. There are, naturally, better roads to literacy than those taken by totalitarian regimes, but this effort should be counted as an asset, not a liability, for the regime. The same can be said about support of the performing arts, literature, and high-brow culture in the mass media. The Communist media tolerated and sometimes sponsored talented movie and television directors, playwrights, and, although very rarely, journalists. To give but one example of the latter, I mention Polish reporter Ryszard Kapuściński, author of the well-known essay *The Emperor* (New York: Vintage, 1984). He was a veteran journalist of the state press agency.

4. Western-style media is coming under increasing friendly fire, mainly over so-called info-tainment, the growing popularity of low-brow media, and the decline of the elite press.

5. John Milton, *Aeropagitica* (1644); the citation is from A. Herbert Altschull, *From Milton to McLuhan: The Ideas Behind American Journalism* (New York: Longman, 1990), p. 41.

6. In David W. Benn's words of caution: "In Soviet political literature there was a picture of the `propaganda state' although implicit. Or a `terror state'—reign by terror and force alone, or both. It would naturally be wrong to dismiss these assumptions as totally groundless. Yet at the same time they need to be analyzed more closely—both for academic and for practical reasons. Just how important, then, were propaganda and secrecy to the stability of the Communist system? One cannot be absolutely sure." *Persuasion & Soviet Politics* (Oxford: Blackwell, 1989), p. 227.

7. Guillermo O'Donnell, "On the Fruitful Convergences of Hirschman's Exit, Voice and Loyalty: Reflections from the Recent Argentine Experience" in Alejandro Foxley et al., eds., *Development, Democracy and the Art of Trespassing* (Notre Dame, Ind.: University of Notre Dame Press, 1986), p. 256.

8. *Time*, December 31, 1991.

9. The concept was invented by Elizabeth Noelle-Neumann, a German pollster and communications professor, to describe the majority silenced by the outspoken minority (*The Spiral of Silence: Public Opinion, Our Social Skin* [Chicago: University of Chicago Press, 1993]).

10. John K. Galbraight, *The Age of Uncertainty* (London: Deutsch, 1977), p. 96. Quote in Benn, *Persuasion*, p. 219.

11. I have discussed this topic in the book *In the Shadow of Giants: Beyond the Mainstream Media in America* [in Polish] (Wrocław: Ossolineum, 1989).

12. See the description and analysis of the event in Janos Horvat and Jay Roskin, "Singlethink: Thoughts on the Havel Episode," *Gannet Center Journal*, Fall 1990, pp. 31-52.

13. Ibid., p. 32.

14. Ibid., p. 39.

15. The consequences of outspoken journalism are best described by Jane L. Curry in her insightful article "Pluralism in East Central Europe: Not Will It Last But What is it?": "People were accustomed to censored press that kept individual battles between elites and elite failings concealed. . . . With the new freedoms, the media has taken this further. . . . The governments have countered by holding tight to the `government media' and pressing for `loyal reporting.` At the same time, in the struggle for readers, journalists have come from not reporting anything about leaders as people or their conflicts with each other to reporting all of this. For the populace the shift was discomforting" (*Communist and Post-Communist Studies* 4, December 1993), p. 450-451.

16. The public sphere, a term introduced by Jurgen Habermas in "Strukturwandel der Offentlichkeit" (English translation *The Structural Transformation of the Public Sphere* [Cambridge: Polity Press, 1989]), is an excellent concept to describe the major element of contemporary society—fora where the ruled can develop and express their political will. It is an excellent indicator of

society's democratic or undemocratic character. See Peter Dahlgreen and Colin Sparks, eds., *Communication and Citizenship: Journalism and the Public Sphere in the New Media Age* (London: Routledge, 1991).

17. Tom Stoppart's play *Night and Day* (New York: Grove Press, 1979), p. 32, quoted in Altschull, *From Milton*, p. 9.

18. Quoted by Mustapha Masmoudi in *Media, Crisis, and Democracy*, edited by Marc Raboy and Bernard Dagenais (London: Sage, 1992), p. 39.

List of Acronyms

AAN	Archives of New Records
AK	Home army
AR	Workers' Agency
BBC	British Broadcasting Corporation
ChSS	Christian Social Association
CPSU	Communist Party of the Soviet Union
GUKPPiW	Main Office of Control of the Press, Publication, and Performances
KOR	Committee for Defence of Workers
KOS	Committee for Social Defence
KPN	Confederation of Independent Poland
KRRiT	National Council of Radio and Television
MSW	Ministry of Internal Affairs
PAP	Polish Press Agency
PKWN	Polish Committee of National Liberation
PPR	Polish Workers' Party (Communist)
PPS	Polish Socialist Party
PRL	Polish People's Republic
PSL	Polish Peasant Alliance
PZKS	Polish Union of Social Catholics
PZPR	Polish United Workers' Party
RFE	Radio Free Europe
RMF	Radio-Music-Facts
RSW	Workers' Publishing Cooperative
SD	Democratic Alliance
SDP	Association of Polish Journalists
SDPRL	Association of Journalists of the Polish People's Republic
SDRP	Association of Journalists of the Republic of Poland
SdRP	Social Democracy of the Republic of Poland
TASS	News Agency of the Soviet Union
ZMP	Union of the Polish Youth (Communist)
ZMS	Union of Socialist Youth
ZSL	United Peasant Alliance
ZChN	Christian Democratic Union

Archival Sources
and Newspapers Consulted

Archive Files

1. *Archiwum Akt Nowych* (Archive of New Records), Warsaw

   Ministerstwo Informacji i Propagandy (the Ministry of Information and Propaganda): AAN MiIP 1-5, 22-29, 70, 135, 595-96

2. *Archiwum Akt Nowych, VI Oddział* (Archive of New Records, Department 6), Warsaw

   (1) *Polska Zjednoczona Partia Robotnicza, Wydział Propagandy* (Polish United Workers' Party, Department of Propaganda): PZPR WP 295/X/3-6, 20-33

   (2) *Polska Zjednoczona Partia Robotnicza, Wydział Prasy i Wydawnictw, Wydział Prasy, Radia i Telewizji* (Polish United Workers' Party, Department of the Press, Radio, and Television): PZPR WPRT 237/XIX/1-10, 25-27, 50-68, 118-121, 142-143

3. *Ośrodek Badań Prasoznawczych* (Press Research Center), Cracow

   (1) *Archiwum badań: 1956-1991* (Archive of Research: 1956-1991). OBP AB 1-312

   (2) *Kronika prasy polskiej: 1944-1991* (Chronicle of the Polish Media: 1944-1991). OBP. Published in installments in the quarterly *Zeszyty Prasoznawcze*, 1984-1992

4. *Radio Free Europe*, Munich
   Poland: A Chronology of Events, four background reports
   July 1980-November 1980: RAD/91, March 31, 1981
   November 1980-February 1981: RAD/263, September 11, 1981
   February 1981-July 1991: RAD Chron/3, Poland, March 5, 1982

August 1981 - December 1981: RAD Chron/4, July 16, 1982

Newspapers

Dailies: *Gazeta Wyborcza, Rzeczpospolita, Trybuna Ludu, Życie Warszawy.*
Weeklies: *Polityka, Tygodnik Powszechny, Wprost.*

Selected Bibliography

Only foreign-language books and articles are included. Polish publications are referred to in the notes.

Abramski, Chimen, Maciej Jachimczyk, and Antony Polonsky, eds. *The Jews in Poland*. Oxford: Blackwell, 1986.

Albright, Madeleine Korbel. *Poland: The Role of the Press in Political Change*. Washington Papers, 102. New York: Praeger, 1983.

Altschull, A. Herbert. *From Milton to McLuhan: The Ideas Behind American Journalism*. New York: Longman, 1990.

Andrews, Nicolas G. *Poland 1980-1981: Solidarity Versus the Party*. Washington, D.C.: National Defense University Press, 1985.

Anonymous. "I, the Censor, Interview with the Polish Censor." In Abraham Bromberg, ed., *Poland: Genesis of Revolution*. New York: Vintage Point, 1983, pp. 252-259.

Ascherson, Neal. *The Polish August: The Self-Limiting Revolution*. London: Allen Lane, 1981.

————. *The Struggles for Poland*. London: Michael Joseph, 1989.

Benn, David Wedgwood. "Glasnost and the Soviet Media: Liberalization or Public Relation?" *Journal of Communist Studies* 3 (1987), pp. 267-276.

————. *Persuasion & Soviet Politics*. Oxford: Blackwell, 1989.

Bermeo, Nancy. *Liberalization and Democratization: Change in the Soviet Union and Eastern Europe*. Baltimore: The Johns Hopkins University Press, 1991.

Bielasiak, Jack, and Maurice D. Simon, eds. *Polish Politics: Edge of the Abyss*. New York: Praeger, 1984.

Blit, Lucjan. *The Anti-Jewish Campaign in Present-Day Poland. Facts, Documents, Reports*. London: Institute of Jewish Affairs, 1968.

Boyle, Maryellen. "The Revolt of the Communist Journalist: East Germany," *Media, Culture, and Society* 14 (1992), pp. 133-139.

Brodsky, Joseph. *Less Than One: Selected Essays*. London: Penguin Books, 1987.

Brogan, Patric. *Eastern Europe: 1939-1989. The Fifty Years War*. London: Bloomsbury, 1990.

Bromke, Adam, and John W. Strong, eds. *Gierek's Poland*. New York: Praeger, 1973.

————. "The Opposition in Poland." *Problems of Communism* (September-October 1978), pp. 39-44.

Brown, J.F. *Surge to Freedom. The End of Communist Rule in Eastern Europe*. Durham: Duke University Press, 1991.

Browne, Donald R. *International Radio Broadcasting: The Limits of the Limitless Medium*. New York: Praeger, 1982.

Brumberg, Abe. *Solidarity*. New York: Random House, 1984.

Brzeziński, Zbigniew. *The Grand Failure: The Birth and Death of Communism in the Twentieth Century.* New York: Scribner, 1989.

Bullock, Alan. *Hitler and Stalin: Parallel Lives.* New York: Knopf, 1991.

Buzek, Antony. *How the Communist Press Works.* New York: Praeger, 1964.

Carrere d'Encausse, Helene. *Stalin: Order Through Terror.* Translated by Valence Ionescu. London: Longman, 1981.

Celt, Ewa. "Poland Adapts its First Press Law." *Radio Free Europe Report* 11, Part 1 (March 12, 1984), pp. 10-15.

"Censorship and I. Do's: The Task of the Press. Don'ts." In Abraham Brumberg, ed. *Poland: Genesis of Revolution.* New York: Vintage, 1983, pp. 241-249.

Chęciński, Marek. *Poland. Communism, Nationalism, Antisemitism.* New York: Karz-Cohl Publishing, 1982.

Choldin, Marianna Tax, and Maurice Friedberg, eds. *The Red Pencil: Artists, Scholars, and Censors in the USSR.* Boston: Unwin Hyman, 1989.

Chrypinski, Vincent C. "Church and Nationality in Postwar Poland." In Pedro Ramet, ed. *Religion and Nationalism in Soviet and East European Politics.* Durham: Duke University Press, 1984.

Ciolkosz, Lidia. "The Uncensored Press." *Survey* 4, no 109 (Autumn 1979), pp. 9-67.

Colton, Thomas J. *The Dilemma of Reform in the Soviet Union.* Washington, D.C.: Council on Foreign Relations, 1986.

Connor, Walter, and Zvi Gitelman, eds. *Public Opinion in European Socialist Countries.* New York: Praeger, 1977.

Conquest, Robert. *Harvest of Sorrow: Soviet Collectivization and the Terror-famine.* New York: Oxford University Press, 1986.

————, ed. *The Politics of Ideas in the USSR.* New York: Praeger, 1967.

Curry, Jane Leftwich. *The Media and Intra-Elite Communication in Poland.* Vol. 2: *The System of Censorship.* Santa Monica: Rand Corporation, 1980.

————. *Poland's Journalists: Professionalism and Politics.* Cambridge: Cambridge University Press, 1990.

————, ed. *Dissent in Eastern Europe.* New York: Praeger, 1983.

————, translator and editor. *The Black Book on Polish Censorship.* New York: Vintage Books, 1984.

Curry, Jane Leftwich, and J. Dassin, eds. *All the News Not Fit to Print: Press Control Around the World.* New York: Praeger, 1982.

Davies, Norman. *Heart of Europe: A Short History of Poland.* London: Oxford University Press, 1986.

————. *God's Playground: A History of Poland.* Oxford: Clarendon Press, 1981.

Dawisha, Karen. *Eastern Europe, Gorbachev, and Reform: The Great Challenge.* New York: Cambridge University Press, 1990.

Dennis, Everette E., and Jon Vanden Heuvel. *Emerging Voices: East European Media in Transition.* New York: Gannett Foundation Media Center, 1990.

Devlin, Kevin. "Postrevolutionary Ferment in the East European Media." *Radio Free Europe Report on Eastern Europe* 28 (July 13, 1990), pp. 47-53.

Deutscher, Isaac. *Stalin.* London: Pelican, 1966.

Dewhirst, Martin, and Robert Farell, eds. *The Soviet Censorship.* Metuchen, N.J.: The Scarecrow Press, 1973.

Dissent in Poland 1976-77: Reports and Documents in Translation. London: Association of Polish Students and Graduates in Exile, 1977.

Dizard, Wilson, and S. Blake Swensrud. "USSR: Glasnost and the Information Revolution." *Intermedia* 16 (1988), pp. 10-19.

East, R., and Martin Wright. *Revolutions in Eastern Europe.* London: Pinter Publishers, 1991.

Easton, Paul. "The Rock Music Community." In Jim Riordan, ed., *Soviet Youth Culture.* London: Macmillan, 1989, pp. 45-81.

Eberle, James. "A British Perspective and Prospective." In Gwyn Prins, ed., *Spring in Winter: The 1989 Revolutions.* Manchester: Manchester University Press, 1990, pp. 193-204.

Echikson, William. *Lighting the Night: Revolutions in Eastern Europe.* London: Sidgwick and Jackson, 1990.

Eyal, Jonathan. "Why Romania Could Not Avoid Bloodshed." In Gwyn Prins, ed., *Spring in Winter. The 1989 Revolutions.* Manchester: Manchester University Press, 1990, pp. 141-160.

Faisol, Merle. "Censorship in the USSR—A Documented Record." *Problems of Communism* 5 (March-April 1956), pp. 12-19.

Falin, Valentin M. "Glasnost: Getting at the Roots." In Abel Agnabegyan, ed., *Perestroika.* New York: Charles Scribner's Sons, 1989, pp. 281-305.

Fedrigo, Claudio, and Jacek Sygnarski, eds. *Underground Publishing in Communist Poland.* Fribourg (Suisse): Bibliotheque Cantonal et Universitaire, 1990.

Feher, Ferenc, Gyorgy Marcus, and Agnes Heller. *Dictatorship over Needs.* London: Blackwell, 1983.

Feldbrugge, F.J.M. *Samizdat and Political Dissent in the Soviet Union.* Leyden: A.W. Sijthoff, 1975.

Forgacs, D., ed. *A Gramsci Reader: Selected Writings, 1916-1935.* London: Lawrence and Wishard, 1988.

Frank, Roger, and B.C. Kirkham. "Revival of *Pravda* in 1917." *Soviet Studies* 3 (1968/1969), pp. 366-368.

Galbraigth, John Kenneth. *The Age of Uncertainty.* Boston: G.K. Hall, 1977.

Garton Ash, Timothy. *The Polish Revolution: Solidarity.* New York: Scribner, 1984.

―――. *The Magic Lantern: The Revolution of '89 Witnessed in Warsaw, Budapest, Berlin, and Prague.* New York: Random House, 1990.

―――. *We the People: Making the Revolution of 1989.* Cambridge: Granta Books, 1990.

Gati, Charles. *The Bloc That Failed: Soviet-East European Relations in Transition.* Bloomington: Indiana University Press, 1990.

Geller, Mikhail, and Alexandr Nekrich. *Utopia in Power: The History of the Soviet Union from 1917 to the Present.* Translated from Russian by Phillis B. Carlos. London: Hutchinson, 1986.

Gerbner, George. "Instant History: The Case of the Moscow Coup," *Political Communication* 10 (1993), pp. 193-203.

Geremek, Bronisław. "Between Hope and Despair." *Daedalus* 119 (Winter 1990), pp. 91-109.

Gibney, Frank. *The Frozen Revolution. Poland: A Study in Communist Decay.* New York: Farrar, Straus and Cudahy, 1959.

Goban-Klas, Tomasz. "Information at the Time of Sociopolitical Crisis: Poland in the Summer of 1980." In Ellen Wartella and D. Charles Whitney, eds., *Mass Communication Review Yearbook*. Beverly Hills: Sage Publications, 1983, pp. 489-501.

———. "Gorbachev Glasnost': A Concept in Need of Theory and Research." *European Journal of Communication* 4 (1989), pp. 247-254.

———. "Making Media Policy in Poland." *Journal of Communication* 40 (Winter 1990), pp. 50-54.

———, "Politics and the Media in Poland." In Patric Clancy et al., eds., *Ireland and Poland: Comparative Perspective*. Dublin: Dublin University Press, 1992, pp. 61-73.

Goban-Klas, Tomasz, and Władysław Kwaśniewicz. "Art in Time of Transition: On the Relations Between Artists and a Market Economy in Post-Communist Poland." In Robert H. Reichardt and George Muskens, eds., *Post-communism, the Market and the Arts*. Frankfurt am Main: Peter Lang, 1992, pp. 25-40.

Goban-Klas, Tomasz, and Teresa Sasińska-Klas. "From Closed to Open Communication Systems: New Information and Communication Technologies and the Rebirth of Civil Society in Communist Eastern Europe." In Paul G. Lewis, ed., *Democracy and Civil Society in Eastern Europe*. London: Macmillan, 1992, pp. 76-90.

Goban-Klas, Tomasz, and Pal Kölsto. "Eastern European Mass Media: The Soviet Role." In Odd Arne Westad, Sven Holtsmark, and Iver B. Neumann, ed., *The Soviet Union and Eastern Europe: 1945-1989*. New York: St. Martin Press, 1994, pp. 110-136.

Goodwyn, Lawrence. *Breaking the Barrier: A Political History of Poland's Working Class Democratization*. Princeton: Princeton University Press, 1991.

Gorbachev, Mikhail. *Perestroika: New Thinking for Our Country and the World*. New York: Harper & Row, 1987.

Graffy, J., and G.A. Hoskings, eds. *Culture and Media in the USSR Today*. London: Macmillan, 1989.

Graham, Lawrence S., ed. *The Polish Dilemma: Views from Within*. Boulder: Westview, 1987.

Griffith, William, ed. *Central and Western Europe: The Opening Curtain*. Boulder: Westview, 1989.

Gross, Natalie. "*Glasnost*: Roots and Practice." *Problems of Communism* (November-December 1987), pp. 69-80.

Gruliov, Leo. "How the Socialist Newspaper Operates." *Problems of Communism* (March-April 1956), pp. 3-12.

———. "All the News That's Fit to Print?" *Problems of Communism* (March-April 1960), pp. 62-64.

———. "The Role of the Press." *Problems of Communism* (January-February 1963), pp. 34-40.

Hahn, W.G. *Democracy in a Communist Party: Poland's Experience Since 1980*. New York: Columbia University Press, 1987.

Halecki, Oscar, ed. *Poland*. New York and London: Praeger and Stevens & Sons, 1957.

Hankiss, Elemer. "The `Second Society': Is There a Second Society Special

Paradigm Working in Contemporary Hungary?" Typescript, Budapest, 1986.
———. "What the Hungarians Saw First." In Gwyn Prins, ed., *Spring in Winter: The 1989 Revolutions*. Manchester: Manchester University Press, 1990, pp. 14-36.

Harasymiw, Bohdan, ed. *Education and Mass Media in the Soviet Union and Eastern Europe*. New York: Praeger, 1976.

Haraszti, Miklos. *The Velvet Prison*. New York: Universe Books, 1987.

Hart, Henry. *Emergent Collective Opinion and Upheaval in East Europe and the Role of Radio Communication*. Munich: Radio Free Europe/Radio Liberty, 1980.

Hauser, Ewa. "Censorship and Law." *Poland Watch* (Washington, D.C.) 4 (1984), pp. 43-62.

Havel, Vaclav. *Living in Truth*. Edited and translated by Jan Vladislav. London: Faber and Faber, 1987.

Hawkes, Nigel, ed. *Tearing Down the Curtain: The People's Revolution in Eastern Europe*. London: Hodder and Stoughton, 1990.

Heinrich, Hans-Georg, and Sławomir Wiatr. *Political Culture in Vienna and Warsaw*. Boulder: Westview, 1991.

Heller, Agnes, and Ferenc Feher. *From Yalta to Glasnost: The Dismantling of Stalin's Empire*. London: Blackwell, 1990.

Henehgan, T.E., and Eva Celt. "*Polityka* and Polish Politics." *Radio Free Europe Background Report* 151 (Poland), July 26, 1977, pp. 5-11.

Herzog, Dietrich, August Pradetto, and Helmut Wagner, eds. *Revolution und Reconstruction*. Berlin: Freie Universität Berlin, 1991.

Hester, Al, and L. Earle, Reybold, eds., *Revolutions for Freedom: The Mass Media in Eastern and Central Europe*. Athens, Georgia: The James M. Cox Jr. Center for International Mass Communication Training and Research, 1991.

Hiscocks, Richard. *Poland: Bridge for the Abyss? An Interpretation of Developments in Post-War Poland*. London: Oxford University Press, 1963.

Hollander, Gayle Durnham. *Soviet Political Indoctrination: Developments in Mass Media and Propaganda Since Stalin*. New York: Praeger, 1972.

———. "Political Communication and Dissent in the Soviet Union." In Rudolf Tökes *Dissent in the USSR: Politics, Ideology and People*. Baltimore: Johns Hopkins University, 1979, pp. 263-264.

Hollander, Paul. "Ideological Noise." *Encounter* (December 1989), pp. 67-70.

Holt, Robert T. *Radio Free Europe*. Minneapolis: University of Minnesota Press, 1958.

Hopkins, Mark. "Lenin, Stalin, Khrushchev." *Journalism Quarterly* 42 (1965), pp. 523-531.

———. *Mass Media in the Soviet Union*. New York: Pegasus, 1970.

———. "Media Economics in the Communist World." In Anju G. Chaudhary and John Martin, eds., *Comparative Mass Media Systems*. London: Longman, 1983, pp. 281-289.

Hughes, G., and Simon Welfare. *Red Empire: The Forbidden History of the USSR*. London: Weidenfeld and Nicolson, 1990.

Inkeles, Alex. *Public Opinion in Soviet Russia: A Study in Mass Persuasion*. Cambridge, Mass.: Oxford University Press, 1950.

Jakubowicz, Karol. "Musical Chairs? The Three Public Spheres in Poland." In Dahlgren, Peter, and Colin Sparks. *Communication and Citizenship: Journalism and the Public Sphere in the New Media Age.* London: Routledge, 1991, pp 155-175.

Jerz, Tomasz, "The Telephone Booth Strike," *Studium Papers* 4 (1988), pp. 114-115.

Jones, Ellen, and B. Woodbury. "Chernobyl and Glasnost." *Problems of Communism* (November-December 1986), pp. 28-39.

Jonge, Alex de. *Stalin and the Shaping of the Soviet Union.* New York: Morrow, 1986.

Karpiński, Jakub. *Countdown: The Polish Upheavals of 1956, 1968, 1970, 1976, 1980.* New York: Karz-Cohl Publishers, 1982.

Kaplan, Frank. *Winter into Spring: The Czechoslovak Press and the Reform Movement: 1963-1968.* New York: Columbia University Press, 1977.

Kaufman, Michael. *Mad Dreams, Saving Graces: Poland, a Nation in Conspiracy.* New York: Random House, 1989.

Keane, John H., ed., *Civil Society and the State: New European Perspectives.* London: Verso, 1988.

Keenan, Edward, "Muscovite Political Folkways." *Russian Review* 45 (1986), pp. 115-181.

Kenez, Peter. *The Birth of the Propaganda State: Soviet Methods of Mass Mobilization, 1917-1929.* Cambridge: Cambridge University Press, 1985.

————. "Lenin and the Freedom of the Press." In Peter Kenez, Abbott Gleaso, and Richard Stites, eds., *Bolshevik Culture: Experiment and Order in the Russian Revolution.* Bloomington: Indiana University Press, 1985, pp. 274-296.

Kirkpatrick, Jeanne. *The Withering Away of the Totalitarian State . . . And Other Surprises.* Washington, D.C.: AEI Press, 1990.

Kołodziej, M. "Underground Press in Poland." *Radio Free Europe Report* 42, part 1 (1986), pp. 1-5.

————. "A Survey of the Underground Press: December 1981-June 1985." *Radio Free Europe Report* 33, part 4 (August 23, 1985), pp. 1-29.

Kölsto, Pal. *An Appeal to the People: Glasnost'—Aims and Means.* Oslo: Institutt for Forvarsstudier, 1988.

Konrad, Gyogry. "Censorship in Retreat." In *Index on Censorship* 10 (April 1983), pp. 10-15.

Kowalski, Tadeusz. "Evolution after Revolution." *Media, Culture, and Society* 2 (1988) pp. 183-196.

Kraus, Sidney. *The Great Debates: Background-Perspectives-Effects.* Bloomington: Indiana University Press, 1962.

Kremish, Joseph. "On the Underground Press in the Warsaw Ghetto." In *Gazette* 1 (1962), pp. 1-21.

Kuran, Timur. "Now out of Never: The Element of Surprise in the East European Revolution of 1989." In Bermeo, Nancy. *Liberalization and Democratization: Change in the Soviet Union and Eastern Europe.* Baltimore: The Johns Hopkins University Press, 1991.

Kuroń, Jacek, and Karol Modzelewski, "Open Letter to the Polish United Workers' Party." In Jacek Kuroń et al., *Revolutionary Marxist Students in Poland Speak Out, 1964-1968.* New York: Merit Publishers, 1968.

Kurski, Jacek. *Lech Walesa: Democrat or Dictator?* Translated by Peter Obst.

Boulder: Westview, 1993.

Laba, Roman. *The Roots of Solidarity: A Political History of Poland's Working Class Democratization*. Princeton: Princeton University Press, 1991.

Labedz, L., ed. *Poland Under Jaruzelski*. New York: Scribners, 1984.

Laqueur, Walter. *The Long Road to Freedom: Russia and Glasnost*. London: Hyman, 1989.

————. *Stalin: The Glasnost' Revelations*. London: Hyman, 1990.

Lendvai, Paul. *The Bureaucracy of Truth: How Communist Governments Manage the News*. Boulder: Westview, 1981.

————. *Hungary: The Art of Survival*. London: I.B. Tauris, 1988.

Lenin, Vladimir. "Where to Begin (1901)." In *Lenin About the Press*. Prague: International Organization of Journalists, 1972, pp. 67-71.

————. "What Is to Be Done? (1902)." In *Lenin About the Press*. Prague: International Organization of Journalists, 1972, pp. 72-105.

————. "Decree on the Press (1917)." In *Lenin About the Press*. Prague: International Organization of Journalists, 1972, p. 205.

————. "Letter to G. Myasnikov (1921)." In *Lenin About the Press*. Prague: International Organization of Journalists, 1972, pp. 198-201.

Lepak, Keith John. *Prelude to Solidarity*. New York: Columbia University Press, 1988.

Lewis, Flora. *A Case History of Hope: The Story of Poland's Peaceful Revolutions*. New York: Doubleday, 1958.

Lincoln, W. Bruce. *In the Vanguard of Reform*. DeKalb: Northern Illinois University Press, 1983.

Lipski, Jan Józef. *KOR: A History of the Workers' Defence Committee in Poland, 1976-1981*. Berkeley: University of California Press, 1985.

Lisann, Maury. *Broadcasting to the Soviet Union*. New York: Praeger, 1976.

Łopiński, Maciej, et al. *Konspira: Solidarity Underground*. Translated by Jane Cave. Berkeley: University of California Press, 1990.

Mandelstam, Nadezhda. *Hope Against Hope*. Translated by Max Hayward. London: Penguin Books, 1975.

Marx, Karl, and Friederick Engels. *Selected Works*. Moscow: Progress, 1960.

Mason, David S. *Public Opinion and Political Change in Poland: 1980-1982*. Cambridge: Cambridge University Press, 1985.

Medish, Vadim. *The Soviet Union*. Englewood Cliffs: Prentice-Hall, 1984.

Medvedev, Roy. *Let History Judge: The Origins and Consequences of Stalinism*. Translated by Georges Shriver. Oxford: Oxford University Press, 1989.

Mianowicz, Tomasz. "Unofficial Publishing Lives On." *Index on Censorship* 12 (April 1983), pp. 24-25.

Michnik, Adam. *Letters from Prison and Other Essays*. Translated by M. Latynski. Berkeley: University of California Press, 1985.

Mickiewicz, Ellen. *Split Signals: Television and Politics in the Soviet Union*. Oxford: Oxford University Press, 1989.

Mikołajczyk, Stanisław. *The Pattern of Soviet Domination*. London: Sampson Low, Marston and Co., 1948.

Miłosz, Czesław. *The Captive Mind*. New York: Alfred A. Knopf, 1953.

Mink, George. "Polls in Poland in the late 1970s'" In *Telos* 46 (1981), pp. 125-132.

Mond, George, and R. Richter. "Writers and Journalists: A Pressure Group in East European Politics." Journalism Quarterly 43 (Spring 1966), p. 93-102.

Neumann, Johanna. The Media: Partners in the Revolution of 1989. Washington, D.C.: Atlantic Council, 1991.

Noelle-Neumann, Elisabeth. The Spiral of Silence: Public Opinion, Our Social Skin. Chicago: University of Chicago Press, 1993.

Nove, Alex. Glasnost' in Action: Cultural Renaissance in Russia. Boston: Unwin Hyman, 1989.

Nowak, Leszek. Power and Civil Society: Toward a Dynamic Theory of Real Socialism. Westport: Greenwood Press, 1991.

Nugent, Margaret Latus. From Leninism to Freedom: The Challenge of Democratisation. Boulder: Westview, 1992.

Pater, Alan, and Jason Pater, eds. What They Said. Palm Springs: Monitor Books, 1990.

Paulu, Burton. Radio and Television Broadcasting in Eastern Europe. Minneapolis: University of Minnesota Press, 1985.

Pelczynski, Zbigniew. "Solidarity and the `Re-Birth of Civil Society.'" In John H. Keane, ed., Poland. Civil Society and the State: New European Perspectives. London: Verso, 1988.

Peleg, Ilan, ed. Patterns of Censorship Around the World. Boulder: Westview, 1993.

Pethybridge, Roger W. "The Significance of Communications in 1917." Soviet Studies 1 (1967), pp. 109-114.

————. "Railways and Press Communication in Soviet Russia in the Early NEP Period." Soviet Studies 2 (1986), pp. 194-206.

Piekalevicz, Jaroslaw. Public Opinion Polling in Czechoslovakia: 1968-9. New York: Praeger, 1972.

Piontkowsky, Andriei. "The Russian Sphinx: Hope and Despair." In Gwyn Prins, ed., Spring in Winter: The 1989 Revolutions. Manchester: Manchester University Press, 1990, pp. 164-190.

Pipes, Richard. The Russian Revolution. New York: Alfred Knopf, 1990.

Podemski, Krzysztof. "The Nature of Society and Social Conflict as Depicted in the Polish Press in 1981." In Zbigniew Rau, ed., The Reemergence of Civil Society in Eastern Europe and the Soviet Union. Boulder: Westview, 1991, pp. 51-75.

"Poland's Uncensored Publications." Radio Free Europe Report (February 9-15, 1978 and continuing in 1979, 1980).

Pomian, Anna. "Financing the Underground Publications." Radio Free Europe Report (March 19, 1986) Part 3, pp. 11-12.

————. "Village Prints an Underground Paper." Radio Free Europe Report (June 13, 1986) Part 1, pp. 23-24.

Popper, Karl. The Open Society and Its Enemies. London: Routledge, 1980.

Pospielovsky, D. "From Gosizdat to Samizdat and Tamizdat." Canadian Slavonic Papers 20 (March 1978), pp. 26-45.

Preibisz, Joanna M., ed. Polish Dissident Publications: An Annotated Bibliography. New York: Praeger, 1982.

"Press Council." Radio Free Europe Report (August 15, 1985) Part 1, pp. 17-20.

Prins, Gwyn, ed. Spring in Winter: The 1989 Revolutions. Manchester: Manchester University Press, 1990.

Przeworski, Adam. "The `East´ Becomes the `South.´ The `Autumn of the People´." *PS Political Science and Politics* 24 (March 1991), pp. 20-25.

Pszenicki, Chris. "Polish Publishing, 1980-81." *Index on Censorship 1* (1982), pp. 8-11.

Puddington, Arch. *Failed Utopias: Methods of Coercion in Communist Regimes.* San Francisco: ICS Press, 1988.

Raina, Peter. *Political Opposition in Poland: 1954-1977.* London: Poets and Painters Press, 1978.

———. *Independent Social Movement in Poland.* London: London School of Economics and Political Science, 1981.

———. *Poland 1981: Towards Social Renewal.* London: George Allen & Unwin, 1985.

Rau, Zbigniew, ed. *The Re-Emergence of Civil Society in Eastern Europe and the Soviet Union.* Boulder: Westview, 1991.

Reinventing Civil Society: Poland's Quiet Revolution. New York: U.S. Helsinki Watch Committee, 1986.

Remington, Thomas. *The Truth of Authority: Ideology and Communication in the Soviet Union.* Pittsburgh: University of Pittsburgh, 1988.

Remmer, Alexander. "A Note on Post-publication Censorship in Poland." In *Soviet Studies* 41 (July 1989), pp. 415-425.

Robinson, Gertrude. *Tito's Maverick Media.* Urbana: University of Illinois Press, 1977.

Rotschild, Joseph. *Return to Diversity.* Oxford: Oxford University Press, 1989.

Roxburgh, Angus. *Pravda: Inside the Soviet News Machine.* London: Victor Gollanch, 1987.

Rozenbaum, W. "The Background of the Anti-Zionist Campaign." *Essays in History* (University of Virginia) 1972-1973, pp. 17-32.

R.S. "Foreign Press on Sale in Poland." *Radio Free Europe Report* (December 12, 1986) Part 1, pp. 50-51.

———. "*Polityka* and Its Influence on Polish Politics." *Radio Free Europe Report* (August 21, 1987), Part 1, pp. 13-15.

Rupnik, Jacques. *The Other Europe.* London: Weidenfeld and Nicolson, 1988.

Ruud, Charles A. *Fighting Words: Imperial Censorship and the Russian Press, 1804-1906.* Toronto: University of Toronto Press, 1982.

Sabbat-Swidlicka, Anna. "Poland's Provincial Press Under Martial Law." *Radio Free Europe Report* (February 12, 1982), Part 1, pp. 1-17.

———. "Poland's Underground Press." *Radio Free Europe Report* (July 29, 1983), pp. 1-27.

———. "The Poles Get Soviet Television." *Radio Free Europe Report* (April 10, 1987), Part 2, pp. 27-29.

Saunders, George, ed. *Samizdat: Voices of the Soviet Opposition.* New York: Monad Press, 1974.

Sanford, George. *Polish Communism in Crisis.* New York: St. Martin's Press, 1983.

———. *Military Rule in Poland: The Rebuilding of Communist Power, 1981-1983.* London: Croom Helm, 1986.

Sanford, George, ed. and translator. *The Solidarity Congress, 1981: The Great Debate.* Houndmills: Macmillan, 1990.

————. *Democratization in Poland, 1988-90: Polish Voices*. New York: St. Martin's Press, 1992.

Sawisz, Anna, "Back from Monopoly to Normal: Changes in Mass Media in Poland." *Innovation* (Vienna) 2 (1990), pp. 385-401.

Schapiro, Leonard. *The Origin of the Communist Autocracy. First Phase: 1917-1922*. Cambridge: Harvard University Press, 1955.

Schatz, Jaff. *The Generation: The Rise and Fall of the Jewish Communists in Poland*. Berkeley: University of California Press, 1991.

Schmidt, Dana A. *The Anatomy of a Satellite*. London: Secker & Wartburg, 1953.

Schopflin, George, ed. *Censorship and Political Communication in Eastern Europe*. New York: St. Martin's Press, 1983.

Selbourne, David. *Death of the Dark Hero: Eastern Europe: 1987-1989*. London: Jonathan Cape, 1990.

Serge, Victor. *Year One of the Russian Revolution*. Translated by P. Sedgwick. London: Allen Lane of Penguin Press, 1972.

Seton-Watson, Hugh. *The East European Revolution*. Encore Reprint. Boulder: Westview, 1985.

Shlapentokh, Vladimir. *Soviet Public Opinion and Ideology: Mythology and Pragmatism in Interaction*. New York: Praeger, 1986.

Shostakovitch, Dimitri. *Testimony*: the Memoirs of Dimitri Shostakovitch as related to and edited by Solomon Volkov. New York: Harper & Row, 1979.

Siebert, Frederick S., Theodore Peterson, and Wilbur Schramm. *Four Theories of the Press*. Urbana: University of Illinois Press, 1956.

Skilling, H. Gordon. *Samizdat and an Independent Society in Central and Eastern Europe*. London: Macmillan, 1989.

Smith, Gordon B., translator. *Soviet Politics. Struggling with Change*. London: Macmillan, 1992.

Smolar, Aleksander. "The Polish Opposition." In Ferenc Fehler and Andrew Arato, eds., *Crisis and Reform in Eastern Europe*. New Brunswick: Transaction Publishers, 1991, pp. 175-237.

"Solidarity Goes on the Air." *Radio Free Europe Report* (June 6, 1982), Part 2, pp. 1-7.

Splichal, Slavko, and Ildiko Kovats, eds. *Media in Transition: An East-West Dialogue*. Typescript, Budapest-Ljubjana, 1993.

Stalin, Joseph. *Leninism*. London: G. Allen and Unwin, 1940.

Staniszkis, Jadwiga. *Poland's Self-Limiting Revolution*. Edited by Jan T. Gross. Princeton: Princeton University Press, 1984.

"Statistics on the Underground Press." *Radio Free Europe Report* (1986), Part 3, pp. 13-14.

Stefanowski, R. "Catholic Press in Poland." *Radio Free Europe Report* (November 1, 1984), Part 1, pp. 1-11.

Stilman, Leon. "Freedom and Repression in Prerevolutionary Russian Literature." In Ernest J. Simmons, ed., *Continuity and Change in Russian and Soviet Thought*. Cambridge: Harvard University Press, 1955, pp. 417-432.

Stokes, Gale, ed. *From Stalinism to Pluralism: A Documentary History*. Oxford: Oxford University Press, 1991.

Szajowski, Adam. *Next to God . . . Poland*. New York: St. Martin's Press, 1983.

Szczypiorski, Andrzej. *The Polish Ordeal: The View from Within*. Translated by C. Wieniewska. London: Croom Helm, 1982.

Taras, Ray. *Poland: Socialist State, Rebellious Nation*. Berkeley: University of California Press, 1984.

Tarrow, Sidney. "Aiming at the Moving Target." *PS Political Science and Politics* 24 (March 1991), pp. 12-18.

Terestyeni, Tamas. "Changing Media Policy in Hungary." *Innovation* (Vienna) 2 (1990), pp. 403-416.

"The Media in Eastern Europe." *Radio Free Europe/Radio Liberty Research Report* (October 2, 1992).

Toch, Marta. *Reinventing Civil Society: Poland's Quiet Revolution, 1981-1986*. New York: U.S. Helsinki Watch Committee, 1986.

Torańska, Teresa. *Them: Stalin's Polish Puppets*. Translated by A. Kolakowska. New York: Harper & Row, 1987.

Ulam, Adam B. *Stalin: The Man and His Era*. London: I.B. Tauris, 1983.

Vachnadze, George. *Secrets of Journalism in Russia*. Commack, New York: Nova Science Publishers, 1992.

Vale, Michael, ed. *Poland, the State of the Republic: Reports of the Experience and Future Discussion Group*. London: Pluto Press, 1981.

Vinton, Louisa. "Sejm Approves New Law on Radio and Television," *Radio Free Europe/Radio Liberty Research Report* 43 (1992), pp. 32-34.

Wałęsa, Lech. *The Path of Hope*. London: Collins Harvil, 1987.

"Wałęsa-Miodowicz Debate." *Radio Free Europe Report* (December 16, 1988), Part 3, pp. 1-12.

Wandycz, Piotr. *The Land of Partitioned Poland: 1795-1918*. Seattle: University of Washington Press, 1974.

Wankel, Charles. *Anti-Communist Student Organizations and the Polish Renewal*. New York: St. Martin's Press, 1992.

Wasilewski, Jacek. "Dilemmas and Controversies Concerning Leadership Recruitment in Eastern Europe." In Paul G. Lewis, ed., *Democracy and Civil Society in Eastern Europe*. London: Macmillan, 1992, pp. 113-114.

Welsh, A. *Survey Research and Public Attitudes in Eastern Europe and the Soviet Union*. New York: Pergamon Press, 1981.

Weschler, Lawrence. *The Passions of Poland: From Solidarity Through the State of War*. New York: Pantheon Books, 1984.

Westoby, A. *The Evolution of Communism*. Cambridge: Polity Press, 1989.

Wettig, Gerhard. *Broadcasting and Détente: Eastern Policies and Their Implication for East-West Relations*. London: C. Hurst, 1977.

Weydenthal, Jan B de. *The Communists of Poland*. Stanford: Hoover Institution, 1978.

Weydenthal, Jan B. de, Bruce D. Porter, and Kevin Devlin. *The Polish Drama, 1980-1982*. Lexington, Mass.: Lexington Books, 1983.

Wiatr, Jerzy J. "The Hegemonic Party System in Poland." In Eric Allard and Stein Rokkan, eds., *Mass Politics: Studies in Political Sociology*. New York: Free Press, 1970.

Wiio, Osmo A. "The Mass Media Role in the Western World." In Anju G.

Chaudhary, and L. John Martin, eds., *Comparative Mass Media Systems*. New York: Longman, 1983, pp. 85-94.

Wintrop, Norman. "Marx." In David Close and Carl Bridge, eds., *Revolution: A History of Idea*. London: Croom Helm, 1985, pp. 90-95.

Yasman, Victor. "Glasnost' Versus Freedom of Information: Political and Ideological Aspects." *Radio Liberty: Report on the USSR* 29 (1989), pp. 1-6.

Zeman, Z.A.B. *Pursued by a Bear: The Making of Eastern Europe*. London: Chatto and Windus, 1987.

——— . *The Making and Breaking of Communist Europe*. Cambridge: Blackwell, 1991.

Ziółkowski, Janusz. "The Roots, Branches and Blossoms of Solidarnosc." In Gwyn Prins, ed., *Spring in Winter: The 1989 Revolutions*. Manchester: Manchester University Press, 1990, pp. 40-62.

Zubek, Voytek. "Walesa's Leadership and Poland's Transition." *Problems of Communism* (January-April 1981), pp. 69-83.

Zuzowski, Robert. *Political Dissent and Opposition in Poland: The Workers' Defense Committee "KOR."* Westport: Praeger, 1992.

About the Book and Author

By virtue of his position as the research director of the main Polish mass media center—Ośrodek Badań Prasoznawczych—in Cracow, Tomasz Goban-Klas was assured access to documents of various type and orientation and was permitted to attend Party caucuses on the tasks of the press and informal caucuses of journalists. Above all, he was allowed on behalf of the state to organize empirical research on the mass media and journalism. He was also an expert on the mass media during the 1989 roundtable talks that broke the monopoly of the Communist media. The result is *The Orchestration of the Media*, an insider's study of the history of Polish media emphasizing its incarnation after the fall of communism and the democratization of the state.

In sixteen brief chapters the author provides a coherent and comprehensive description of the creation and then the erosion of the monolithic media system in Poland and investigates the professions, institutions, and individuals supporting, opposing, or reforming the existing media system at various times. He also identifies the dilemmas involved in shaping the new communications system in Poland today; the dilemmas shared by all former Soviet bloc countries and Russia itself.

Combining Polish reference sources in the notes with a popular writing style, *The Orchestration of the Media* will appeal to both the scholar and the educated general reader. It will prove interesting to students in journalism, mass communication, political science, history, and Eastern European and Russian studies and perhaps to the growing number of Western-based consultants involved in various forms of assistance or joint ventures in media, education, banking, and business. For the general reader, the last chapters with updated reviews of the present media landscape and analysis of the post-Communist media policy, should be of special interest.

Tomasz Goban-Klas is Professor and Chair of Sociology of Culture and Communications at Jagiellonian University; he is also the head of the Committee for a Free and Responsible Press.

Name Index